D0082770

Homophobia

Homophobia

The State of Sexual Bigotry Today

Second Edition

MARTIN KANTOR, M.D.

Westport, Connecticut
London

Library of Congress Cataloging-in-Publication Data

Kantor, Martin.
Homophobia : the state of sexual bigotry today / Martin Kantor. — 2nd ed.
p. cm.
Includes bibliographical references and index.
ISBN 978–0–313–35925–5 (alk. paper)
1. Homophobia—Psychological aspects. 2. Heterosexism—Psychological aspects. 3. Homosexuality—History. 4. Gays—Violence against. 5. Paranoia. 6. Toleration. I. Title.
HQ76.25.K35 2009
306.76'6—dc22 2008045546

British Library Cataloguing in Publication Data is available.

Library of Congress Catalog Card Number: 2008045546
ISBN: 978–0–313–35925–5

First published in 2009

Praeger Publishers, 88 Post Road West, Westport, CT 06881
An imprint of Greenwood Publishing Group, Inc.
www.praeger.com

Printed in the United States of America

The paper used in this book complies with the Permanent Paper Standard issued by the National Information Standards Organization (Z39.48–1984).

10 9 8 7 6 5 4 3 2 1

To M.E.C.

Contents

Introduction

In the past decade the civil rights and gay pride movements, antidiscrimination laws, and the liberalization of large segments of society have changed the character of homophobia, possibly forever. But while gays and lesbians have made great strides in calming the homophobic waters, they have not been able to fully drain the swamp. For many homophobic attitudes and practices of yesterday have persisted more or less unchanged today. As a result, although the homophobic weather may have improved, the climate has continued much the same, and in some ways has even gotten considerably worse.

Although actual violence toward gays and lesbians still exists, it is less common than it used to be. I well remember the times when, on a regular basis, gays and lesbians were hunted down and beaten up or killed. A gay man I know, after buying a house in a straight neighborhood in a blue-collar town, was attacked by a gang of thugs who beat him up and threatened to set him on fire—but stopped after merely trying to burn down his house.

Threats of violence are still common today. Just recently an intoxicated man staggered past me and, entirely unprovoked, started yelling that he hated faggots and was going to kill me. As an article in the *New York Times* pointed out, in 2007 in Newark, New Jersey, gays and lesbians "might as well live on another planet," for when the tenants of a gay couple's building discovered that their landlords were gay they "called them 'faggots' and threatened to blow up their house."[1] Hip-hop songs still have openly homophobic lyrics containing threats to kill gay men, which are excused as merely a reflection of their underlying culture—one (as if this makes it better) in which all the singer's buddies share the same sentiments!

A new art gallery just opened up in the town where I live. One day the proprietor was receiving boxes of merchandise but not disposing of the excelsior properly, upsetting a gay restaurateur a few doors down, who felt that the mess was discouraging customers from entering his premises. So the restaurateur asked the store owner to please clean up after himself, whereupon the store owner held his temper until the restaurateur left, only to blow up afterwards—rushing into the store next door and loudly saying to that store owner (whom he did not know was himself a gay man) that he "hated, and wanted to kill, all the world's fucking faggots."

Hate speech and actions are still very much with us. Just the other day, as I was walking past a restaurant in town, a man, whom I surmised was the restaurant owner, who was likely either somewhat drunk, hypomanic, or both, was loudly expostulating either to no one in particular, or to me in specific, as I was passing by: "I hate all, and I do mean all, c**ksuckers." Even today the leader of Zimbabwe would not surprise many people with his driven, stinging attack on homosexuals, in which he did not advocate violence, but just called "homosexuality a repugnant offense against nature by sodomists and sexual perverts," adding that "if the nation accepts homosexuality as a right...what moral fiber shall our society ever have to deny organized drug addicts or even those given to bestiality the rights they might claim under the rubrics of individual freedom and human rights?...I don't believe they have any rights at all. I hope the time never comes when we want to reverse nature and men bear children."[2]

In addition, recently, a gay man in a blue-collar town called the police to complain about the neighbor's dog's constant barking, only to have the police, who did not hear the dog barking when they arrived, threaten to arrest and book him for filing a false report.

Even today not a few medical people would agree with the statement that "homosexuals who contract AIDS should be persecuted." This month I discovered that a pediatrician at a large, respected suburban hospital in a famous college town refused to be assisted by a technician he knew to be gay because he did not like to work with "someone of that sort." While I was working on this book, a (generally favorable) review of my book *Distancing* by "reader 2008" appeared, which, however, included a homophobic rant about how "most of the examples are about gay patients [or] gay lifestyles," and as such produced material that was "elitist" and not relevant to the reviewer or even to the topic at hand, leading the reviewer (who seems not to have known of my work with military veterans) to conclude that "all concerned should skip the examples...and just read the text of the book."[3]

Not long ago, a colleague of mine called her publisher and asked about having one of her books placed in gift shops in New York City. The spokesperson of the publisher, an organization that actually publishes books by and about gay men, told the author who the distributor's representative was, the person who needed to be contacted to get her books into gift shops in New York. Then the spokesperson added, "He's gay, but he's such a great person." No doubt, my colleague thought, "Just like some of her best friends." This colleague also recently went to a bookstore with a very accomplished gay friend who had authored several popular self-help books for gay men, looking to arrange for a book signing. After the woman behind the counter, who originally was polite, took one look at one of the covers of his books (two gay men embracing), suddenly her whole demeanor changed—from professional courtesy to rudely rushing the couple out of the store.

Bill Bowman, writing for the *Asbury Park Press*, noted that two lesbian couples charged that the Ocean Grove, N.J. Camp Meeting Association (CMA) "broke the state Law Against Discrimination when it refused to rent them [their open-air] boardwalk pavilion for use in their civil-union ceremonies." The state agreed that discrimination was involved and ordered the discrimination to stop, whereupon the CMA "sued the state Division on Civil Rights, alleging the division violated the association's free speech and religious freedom rights [simply] by investigating two complaints against it."[4]

Ocean Grove is a little Victorian enclave by the sea that is home to many gays and lesbians, who in fact rescued the tiny town from oblivion by buying houses and fixing them up at a time when the town had been seriously deteriorating for years, both physically and economically. But the town is also home to a rather conservative branch of the Methodist Church, one so strict that it only recently allowed driving in town on Sundays and still sees to it that the whole town be kept dry. This church owns the open-air boardwalk pavilion by the beach, which it uses for church functions and also keeps open to the public. The church, as well as a reverend representing the Methodists, insists that the "pavilion is a religious structure [and] argues that the Methodist Book of Discipline, which it follows, prohibits the use of religious structures for ceremonies such as same-sex civil unions."[5] The gays and lesbians insist that since the pavilion, though church owned and operated, is rented out to the public and even receives favorable state tax treatment as a religious organization, it is "a public accommodation"[6] and therefore should abide not by church teachings but by state laws against discrimination. As a result, when two lesbians wanted to get married in the pavilion but were not allowed to proceed, they sued. The CMA refused to budge. Publicly the CMA says this was a matter of principle. Privately, the CMA told the girls, one of whom is, perhaps not incidentally, Jewish, that that particular principle was so strong that they would sooner take a match and burn the pavilion down than let two lesbians marry there.

Fortunately, some things have actually gotten a bit better. People still drop the "faggot bomb" with abandon. According to the *New York Times* just recently, "when [the just-mentioned Newark couple] called 911 . . . the responding police officer...appeared unconcerned and only reluctantly agreed to take their complaint. [Then] back at the station house [they found the officer who took their complaint] snigger[ing] with coworkers as he typed up the paperwork, once [even] blurting out, 'How do you spell "faggot"?'"[7] Today, however, homophobes often justify the use of that word with aplomb: by redefining it as a general term meaning "someone I have a beef with," as distinct from a more specific term meaning "someone whom I dislike for being gay." Yesterday's talk radio host who came right out and said that gays and lesbians are an abomination and ought to be wiped off the face of the earth has mostly been replaced by today's purveyor of innuendo and euphemism. Today's talk show host merely speaks in the same breath of reporting illegal aliens to the Feds and lobbying against gay marriage. The president of the United States, seemingly in at least partial agreement with the president of Zimbabwe, only *suggests,* in effect, that gays and lesbians should have their individual freedoms and civil rights curtailed, as he reminds us that marriage is, and must remain, an institution between a man and a woman. Many in a powerful political position only *question* gay adoption, claiming there is considerable evidence that children of same-sex couples do not do as well as children brought up in households where there is a mother and a father; they merely *suggest* that gay marriage is inherently unacceptable because it is contrary to nature and the natural order of things—as they *wonder* whether, if you let gays and lesbians marry, will it, going down the Zimbabwean slippery slope, end in social chaos, for you will have to allow polygamists to wed multiple partners, permit nuptials for child brides, condone necrophilia for those so inclined, and even let a man truly in love with his dog go ahead and tie that beastly knot.

A while ago Pat Robertson, in his book *The New World Order,* wrote that lasting peace will come only when "drunkards, drug dealers, communists, atheists, New Age worshippers of Satan, secular humanists, oppressive dictators, greedy moneychangers, revolutionary assassins, adulterers, and homosexuals are [no longer] on top."[8] Yet, more recently, Robertson came out in support of an overall conservative Republican presidential candidate who, at least at one point in his career, was manifestly gay-friendly and on several occasions had even appeared in public in drag. And today gays and lesbians, no longer having to fear exactly the same amount of discrimination as they used to, are openly involved in civil unions; regularly have, adopt, and raise children; are more and more successfully pushing to be officially married; and are appearing side by side with straights on television house and garden shows as couples with unexceptional domestic lives that are deemed just as worthy of portrayal on television as are the lives and homesteads of their straight counterparts.

Currently, antihomosexual sentiments have mostly gone underground and been taken private. People are still full of homohatred, only, if they own up to it at all, they are more circumspect about how they express it. The game now seems to be, "How can I express my homophobic sentiments publicly while sugarcoating them so that they are superficially inoffensive enough to skirt the antidiscrimination laws and avoid getting me into trouble?" The answer, in so many cases, is that aggressivity yields to passive-aggressivity, so that homophobes can express their homophobia in a more socially acceptable way—specifically forged to protect them from the consequences of being homophobic.

Although this passive-aggressive homophobia of today may be less focused, it is still very pervasive. It may be less acute, but it is still chronic, and it may be less appalling, but it remains considerably more harmful. Although it may not take as many lives as it once did, it ruins even more than ever.

As a result, today's gays and lesbians need to go on general alert to identify homophobia and then discover new and better ways to contain, cope with, and manage its subtler forms. To more effectively thwart bigots' attempts to put obstacles in their way and keep them from succeeding in life personally and professionally, and to be able to maintain their self-esteem as high as it can be in the face of all bigots' attempts to lower it, today's gays and lesbians must, first, identify discrete homophobia and, second, understand it through and through. Ignoring discrete homophobia and just going about the business of living can temporarily spare feelings, but it will not heal the scars and solve the serious and often permanent emotional and practical problems that homophobic prejudice and discrimination create for victims. Certainly, gays and lesbians should not think that they are paranoid when in fact they are actually being persecuted. Or, if they are in fact paranoid, they need to recognize that in this instance at least, even though paranoid, they actually do have some very real enemies.

As I see it, understanding discrete homophobia through and through involves getting beyond viewing it as a strictly conscious phenomenon originating entirely in and fully explainable by sociocultural factors. It involves uncovering the roots of homophobia, and that means seeing it for what it is: a phenomenon closely related to, or in some instances exactly like, emotional disorder or mental illness. It means getting past the widespread belief that straights hate gays and lesbians because they do not know them and will likely come to like them better after gays and lesbians introduce themselves, for, as Michael Carter counters, such introductions only work to the extent that now gays and lesbians have gone from being an "abomination" to being an "exception."[9] It means embracing a scientific approach to the problem that recognizes that the so-called culture of homophobia is as much a product of the individual as individual homophobia is the product of its culture. Because prejudice serves an adaptive, psychological function, it will not just go away because we educate people not to be prejudiced, vigorously proselytize against homohatred, or change the laws to protect the innocent. Such things alone will not stem the homophobic sea. We also have to uncover and treat the raging psychoneurotic tide. We can applaud the changes in homophobia over the past years, but we must never forget that, as Byrne Fone's brilliant history of homophobia amply illustrates over and over again throughout the text, the neuroses of the human beings who create that homophobia in the first place remain depressingly the same over the ages.[10] If we really want to make significant inroads into this widespread problem, if we truly desire to soften homophobia's impact on society as a whole and on gay and lesbian individuals in specific, we have to get beyond scratching homophobia's surface and start exposing, and attacking, its not-so-tender underbelly.

By calling homophobia an emotional disorder or mental illness, I am not overlooking all social explanations for homophobia in favor of explaining it strictly in terms of personal deviation and trying to brand haters of gays and lesbians as mentally ill so that they can all be sent off to psychotherapy or shipped to a mental hospital, then at a later trial gotten off on grounds of being insane. I am not trying to emphasize psychic determinism over individual choice and free will in a way that should trouble those who proclaim the sanctity of the freethinking, homohating, independently operative self. I am also not demanding individual change, which is the true province of psychotherapy, while forgetting all about social change, which is the legitimate province of activism. There are many causes of homophobia, social as well as individual. I am just trying to remedy the current imbalanced state of affairs in which, to date, the study of homophobia has thoroughly documented its social, while relatively neglecting its individual, causes.

Of course, most homophobia is not exactly the same thing as full mental illness. For here, as always, a symptom is not a syndrome (a full disorder) unless certain criteria—involving the level of severity, exclusivity, and degree of persistence—have been attained. Consideration must also be given to the homophobe's current reality, such as where he lives and where and with whom she works. Homophobia is a complex, varied phenomenon, with not all homophobes created equal. Many homophobic attitudes, expressions, preoccupations, and behaviors represent full mental illness, but others reflect the operation of mental mechanisms that are also, when operative at a lower level, found in normals, although they have a great deal in common with the mental mechanisms of true emotional disorder. Whether or not even severe homophobia is a full mental disorder is at bottom a semantic issue. As always, it is necessary to use one's clinical judgment, although that is a complex and unreliable yardstick that requires drawing a firm line on a shifting bed of sand, yet avoiding creating artificial cutoff points that represent nothing more than temporary demarcations on a gradually and continuously changing and evolving continuum. What is obvious to me is that the defense of *projection* ("It's not I who is remiss for being queer, it's you who is bad for seducing me") plays as much a part in the development of some homophobia (and other bigotry) as it does in the development of much paranoia; and that a certain politician's *dissociation* from his own gayness ("I am not gay"—then what exactly were you doing in that men's room?) probably plays a significant part in his need to introduce and support antigay legislation. These laws are external commands to others that are issued to affirm an inner prohibition within oneself. I believe that the scrupulous religious right's overly resolute focus first on gay sin and then on straight redemption, figuratively demanding that gays do penance for homosexual acts by genuflecting a hundred times a day, is highly reminiscent of the obsessive-compulsive person's guilty need to wash constantly to get that damned spot out. Furthermore, homophobes who ceremonially avoid gays and lesbians because they think being gay is catching and fear that gays and lesbians might make them or their children gay by contiguity or osmosis remind me in some respects of the obsessive-compulsive's ritualistic avoidance of anything literally (or figuratively) dirty based on an irrational fear of being soiled and contaminated. I see the demands homophobes make that homosexuals conform to their moral views, or else, as akin to the controlling behavior of the obsessive-compulsive patient who, when it is time for the family to leave for a special occasion, starts washing her hands and cannot get moving until all the grime is gone for certain. I believe that the hysterical excesses of some homophobes, for example, those who believe that two lesbians getting married is the spark that will light a conflagration and cause the downfall of our civilization as we know it, are not so different from the histrionic excesses of the patient who blows up minor events, views them as major life-threatening occurrences, then has an *attaqué*—figuratively and, in the case of old-time hysterical epilepsy, even literally foaming at the mouth. For me, the cognitive errors that homophobes make in reasoning toward, then rationalizing their homophobia are very close to the neurotic's false cognitions that lead to failing to distinguish something from all things, and similar things from the same thing, so that some homophobes who feel that homosexuals are responsible for the world going under remind me of many depressives who conclude that life is not worth living *at all* because there are *a few* bad things happening out there and that *all* the people in the world are evil because a *select few* admittedly are.

I certainly do not buy into two arguments that homophobes themselves use to rationalize their homophobia as perfectly acceptable. I do not agree that just because homophobia is widespread, that makes it normal, for such things as dental cavities are both widespread and abnormal. I also do not agree with those who say that they should not be accused of being homophobic simply because, as Barron Laycock "Labradorman" says in his review of Fone's *Homophobia,* "An Interesting, Absorbing, but Seriously Flawed Study," they are "not in agreement with the currently chic politically correct notion of what the contemporary social attitudes towards gays and lesbians should be."[11] I do not buy the argument that you are not a bigot because you express shock and dismay about homosexual life and homosexuality itself, just because you are not politically liberal when it comes to antigay legislation, do not advocate social acceptance of gays and lesbians in all areas, and do not approve of accommodating gays and lesbians in every way. Choice and free speech are only two of the issues here, for it is also a matter of avoiding confounding individual preference with neurotic compulsion as the individual cites *preferences* that are supposedly freely determined *by* the individual when what he or she is actually expressing are *compulsions* neurotically determined *for* the individual. That is not to say that all gays and lesbians are perfect and do not provoke some of the antagonisms felt toward and expressed about them. But it is one thing to get annoyed with and dislike individual gays and lesbians whose behavior is questionable and quite another to despise and devalue a whole class of individuals without making exceptions for many of its members.

As for the remedy for homophobia, understanding the deep psychopathology of homophobia paves the way to using time-tested psychological methods for dealing with this as with any other variety of emotional illness. Dealing adequately with the politician who, although himself gay, puts time and energy into passing antigay laws involves knowing exactly where he is coming from, so that one can expose and deal with the real basis of his hypocrisy: denial and projection of his own not-so-latent forbidden desires outward as this homophobe goes from "I am gay" to "I am guilty about being gay" to "I deal with my guilt by condemning not myself but gays and lesbians as an abomination" to "I will introduce antigay legislation to keep those abominable gays and lesbians in check." Only with such understanding in place can we develop the most effective antidotes, such as insightful ad hominem (in a good sense) defenses along the lines of "Don't rail at me; instead rail at yourself, in full awareness that it takes one to condemn one."

Many years ago Matthew Shepard was killed—some, looking at the way he was strung up to die on that fence, say crucified—possibly because he may have made a pass at some men he met in a bar. One possibility is that, whether or not (or actually because) drugs were involved, he aroused their guilty homosexual wishes, leading them to feel compelled to disavow those internal messages by killing the so-called messenger. Dealing fully and efficiently with the likes of his murderers means knowing how to deal most effectively with dangerous paranoids. In a parallel way, dealing with homophobic talk show hosts involves being able to have an intelligent debate with them, and one can best do that after understanding the cognitive errors they make in coming to their essentially homophobic conclusions. Thus, one homophobe says, "Gays and lesbians shouldn't actually marry" as if "nontraditional" marriage means not "different" or "better" but instead "bad," "worse," and "dangerous"; another says, "If you let gays marry, then you have to allow polygamy," as if dissimilar things are exactly the same thing, even though, in the case at least of monogamous gay marriage, unlike polygamy, no partners get hurt.

Although my book emphasizes homophobia, mine is in fact a generic method that applies to understanding and managing all forms of bigotry, not only about sexual orientation, but also about race, ethnicity, gender, body size, and disability, for the underlying details remain pretty much the same no matter who the targets of the bigotry happen to be. For example, all bigots use the same irrational cognitions, especially false equivalencies (some = all), to create stereotypes as they tar all members of a class with the same brush, paradoxically discriminating against all members of a class by entirely failing to discriminate among them. And, perhaps most importantly, to some extent all bigotry can be managed, and all bigots can be subdued, with the same counterstrikes, particularly those based on the recognition that because the bigot is really self-referential, his or her bigotry is not to be taken personally since it arises not from the bigot's carefully made external observations but from his or her carelessly made (or carefully crafted) internal distortions.

This book starts with a *description* of homophobia. I discuss some general characteristics of homophobia, such as the widespread erotophobia (a fear and disgust of sex, a kind of malignant Puritanism) that regularly forms its basis, for this fear of, distaste for, and dislike of all sexuality so often finds its ultimate expression in a displacement onto just one of its manifestations, that is, homosexuality. Then I discuss the different models of homophobia (the medical model, that is, gays and lesbians are supposedly sick; the religious model, that is, gays and lesbians are supposedly sinners; the criminal model, that is, the things gays and lesbians do are illegal; the political model, that is, gays and lesbians are convenient common enemies put on earth to help politicians get elected; the sociocultural model, that is, gays and lesbians are supposedly pariahs and lepers properly dispatched to Siberia or, if not to Siberia itself, then to some local version of the Siberian ghetto; and the biological model, that is, gays and lesbians are genetic deviates). The distinctions I make between the models are important, for clearly the religious homophobia model of the pope, who categorizes gays and lesbians as sinners, is different and so requires different countermeasures from the political and sociocultural homophobia of the talk show host who, Nazi-like, categorizes gays and lesbians as *Untermenschen* and straights as *Übermenschen,* that is, inferior and superior men and women, respectively. That distinction is, of course, politely expressed not as "Summer camp is for me, and concentration camp is for you" but as "Marriage is for me, and civil unions are for you"—with the addition that it is unbelievable that gays and lesbians expect parity with straights, for that would be like atheists expecting parity with believers.

All the hot topics of homophobia today—gay marriage; gay civil rights; gay adoption; gays and lesbians being accepted into the military and ministry; gays and lesbians having equality of employment in the civilian sector; gay pedophilia (gays as Boy Scout leaders, gays and lesbians as teachers); and being gay as an individual choice as distinct from being gay as an inborn biological trait or defect—are ultimately little more than manifestations or spin-offs of these different models of homophobia. These topics are hotter today than they were yesterday, not because they were not on the table at all yesterday, but because today everything gets channeled into them as the safest ones to discuss in the current, more permissive, more progay social climate, with practical restraints on openly hating gays and lesbians (such as "Yesterday we had the draft, but today we need soldiers, so maybe we shouldn't be throwing good men and women out of the service because we didn't ask and they didn't tell, but someone found out about it anyway").

I next go on to discuss the other side of the story of homophobia: gay self-homophobia, which can look exactly like straight homophobia, only it occurs in, by, and about gays and lesbians themselves, and gay hypersensitivity to possible homophobia, where gays and lesbians improperly accuse straights who are in fact sympathetic to them of being homophobic. I then ask whether it is sometimes rational to be homophobic and whether there are any extreme instances in which this may be the case. Next, I discuss the specific negative effects that homophobia can have on gays and lesbians.

In my section on *causation,* I then detail the illness model not of homosexuality but of homophobia. In this, the body of my book, I start with a general discussion of the developmental and psychodynamic considerations of the homophobic condition and the psychodynamics of the myths homophobes perpetuate about gays and lesbians, along with the bad names they call them. I demonstrate how much homophobia originates in familiar psychopathology. We all use mental mechanisms associated with psychopathology, for they are part of normal psychology as well as of psychopathology. But those who use these mechanisms *excessively* (for our purposes, "serious homophobes") appear to presently have or be well on their way to developing an emotional problem, if not a full disorder. Based on the primary mental mechanisms in play (and the related symptoms and syndromes these spin off), I differentiate between categories of homophobes, so that projection of latent homosexual desire leads to predominantly paranoid homophobia; displacement from the inherently meaningful to the inherently trivial prompt (with gays and lesbians the psychic equivalent of a feared dog or a feared plane trip) leads to predominantly phobic homophobia; and the like. In particular, I relate homophobia as it is practiced today to paranoia in its substance and to passive-aggression in its expression—that is, much homophobia today is paranoid in origin but in the current climate, with its paradoxical juxtaposition of free speech and "watch what you say or else," paranoid homophobic ideation has to be expressed indirectly, in a refined or passive-aggressive manner, so that the homophobe can find a way to be freely homophobic without being accused of depriving gays and lesbians of their civil rights and in the process being fingered for committing a hate crime.

I then describe some other aspects of homophobia including its experiential/behavioral, biological, symbolic, and sociocultural faces. Finally, I conclude with a section on *interventions.* I first suggest ways to help homophobes themselves and then, the payoff of this text, ways to help gays and lesbians lessen the occurrence of, cope with, and mollify the effects of homohatred on them. I offer gays and lesbians specific antitheses to the different homophobias, which are derived from depth understanding that allows precise retaliative counterstrikes geared to resisting specific homophobic strikes. Now gays and lesbians can hit their targets more precisely and taste, now and perhaps forever, some of the rewards of the battle—without having to settle for triumph on the battlefield, only to discover that they have won a highly unsatisfactory Pyrrhic victory.

In this book I have chosen to use the term *gays and lesbians* to refer to all homosexuals, including, when applicable, bisexuals and transsexuals. In addition, since, at least in my clinical experience, men are more homophobic than women, I have generally abandoned the "he or she" format and, with a few exceptions, simply refer to "he" when speaking of homophobes. I have generally retained the term *homophobia* instead of using the newer term *sexual prejudice* because the former but not the latter terminology emphasizes the connection between homohatred and familiar emotional disorder that I stress.

PART I

Description

CHAPTER 1

General Characteristics of Homophobes (and Other Bigots)

HOW HOMOPHOBES ARE ALIKE

Unoriginality

To consider themselves brilliant and effective thinkers, homophobes have to overlook the historical view—that through the ages everything they think today has been thought before, and everything they say today has been said before, repeatedly, from ancient times to the present, making their present bigotry little more than an unoriginal recycling of old ideas amounting to a plagiarized history. As Fone's book *Homophobia*[1] amply illustrates in examples scattered throughout, ancient homophobic pundits already claimed, among other things, that homosexuality goes hand in hand with child abuse; that because some gays have feminine traits and some lesbians have masculine traits, all gay men are like women and all lesbians are like men; and that all gays and lesbians are infantile, immature, and irresponsible men and women who function personally under par and so can never be as successful professionally as the vast majority of heterosexuals. Nor has anyone to date been able to formulate a new and cogent reason why gays and lesbians should not marry. Rather, all homophobes recycle the same three mantras, the first of which is correct but meaningless (that gay marriage is nontraditional) and the other two of which are ideological postulates presented as nonnegotiable incontestable reality (that gay marriage is immoral and that gay marriage goes against religious teachings). Less creative and generative, and more derivative and unoriginal, their philosophy, and with that their so-called rationality, is more like banality, making their homophobic ideation stale, though presented as fresh, and impoverished, though presented as rich, consisting as it does of saws that amount to very old wine in highly overused bottles. Although homophobes are unoriginal and derivative thinkers merely echoing recycled homophobic ideas and opinions of yore that are now currently in circulation and in vogue, they regularly see themselves as having clever, original minds and making observations about gays and lesbians that are so unique and perceptive that others simply must sit up, take notice, and take what they say seriously and to heart. Not surprisingly, then, they feel justified in airing their ideas widely on talk show radio or disseminating them in the columns of letters to the editor or on passionate Internet blogs, all of which clogs the media without contributing anything new, or anything at all, to their content.

Subjective Thinking (Feelthink)

Homophobes live in a world of their own where they find what they seek and see what they believe. In this, the bigot's world, reality is made up entirely of myths about and stereotypes of gays and lesbians. These are typically derived from limited samplings drawn from only the most easily identifiable gays and lesbians, such as the gay buffoons displayed in television comedies and gays and lesbians in open non-monogamous relationships. Next, homophobes use a series of partial denials and clever sophistic rationalizations to justify and maintain their new, subjective reality in the face of serious evidence to the contrary. As a result, their homophobia flourishes in a climate of ignorance bred by the homophobia itself—since their homohatred keeps them from meeting enough gays and lesbians to discover truths that might conceivably lead to their liking those people whom they have unrealistically come to despise. (I discuss homophobic myths in greater detail in chapter 7 and stereotyping in chapter 11.)

Faulty Logic

Homophobes are obsessive hairsplitters who favor seemingly weighty ideological differences without true distinctions, such as "love the sinner, but hate the sin." They also use gross or subtle cognitive errors to develop homohating stereotypes as they create singularly homogeneous groups out of heterogeneity, leading them to wax monothematic in an age of diversity, as when they equate "some" with "all" ("some gays and lesbians are pedophiles; therefore, all gays and lesbians want to rape kids") and make similar into dissimilar things, so that the name they give to a sexual activity depends on who is doing it ("when straights do it, it's 'foreplay,' but when gays and lesbians do it, it's 'sodomy.'")

Theirs is emotional reasoning involving cognition originating in feeling, presented as feeling originating in cognition. In a vicious cycle of swirling delusional elaboration, their hatred of gays and lesbians influences how they see gays and lesbians; then, in turn, they hate gays and lesbians because of how they see them. Thus they might conclude that since all the world's ills are caused by homosexuals, suppression of gays and lesbians will cure our sick society, whereas, conversely, our healthy society will become sick unless all gays and lesbians are controlled, treated, or quarantined. Homophobes' logic is not much different from the logic of the patient who felt that Picasso's *Guernica* was staring and jeering at him, then (in his view correctly and logically) concluded that he should stick a knife in it and proceeded to do so. What he did made perfect sense in light of his initial feelthink, but his initial, hate-filled premise was entirely off the mark right from the start.

Convictions of Absolute Certainty

The more entrenched and vocal homophobes are grandiose sophomoric narcissists who think and act as if they know it all and have all the answers even in areas where the experts disagree. Their supposedly expert opinions belie their status as rank amateurs who have developed their so-called expertise without actual experience, having formed their conclusions by reasoning implicitly about such key issues as gay marriage, gay adoptions, civil rights for gays and lesbians, and freedom from discrimination in employment for gays and lesbians. No matter what truly knowledgeable clinicians say about how well children do who are brought up by two dads or two moms, these homophobes, after thinking things through and without ever having met or examined such a child or such parents, know better and become certain that adoption by gays is not good for children and demand that only straight couples be allowed to adopt, based on their so-called scientific conclusions, which are little more than the product of a personal loss of perspective in which the reality they create has nothing to do with the truth that exists, for their reality has been derived from cogitation without observation, created in a state of almost total self-absorption.

Not surprisingly, thinking they know more about gays and lesbians than does the American Psychiatric Association, these homophobes comfortably assert that homosexuality is an illness that can and needs to be treated and cured, without ever having actually examined a homosexual or attempted to treat one. As one gay psychiatrist noted in a personal communication, "No one would argue with astrophysicists; but in my experience there are two fields that people think they can practice without any formal training whatsoever: interior decorating, and psychiatry, and not necessarily in that order."

Hypersensitivity

Many, if not most, homophobes have a sore spot for input of a homosexual nature. They tend to be surprisingly rational people until the subject of homosexuality comes up, at which point they become overwrought, panicky, and defensive. These are often histrionic individuals for whom everything gay hits an exposed nerve, creating a response out of all proportion to the nature and intensity of the stimulus. Their anxious response then feeds on itself and spreads until panic supervenes, so that gays and lesbians become frightening creatures—monstrous adversaries who are not merely sharing this earth but trying to take over the entire planet.

Self-Referential Attitudes

Homophobes regularly take homosexuality in a personal light, so that they feel themselves individually and deeply affected by what gays and lesbians do in bed, as if gays' and lesbians' bedtime behavior somehow has a direct connection to their own. They become so irrationally preoccupied with homosexuality and so caught up in it that they come to resemble paranoids caught up in the problem of being persecuted even by people who have no interest in them or phobics caught up in the problem of Friday the 13th, however much it is just another date on the calendar.

Nowhere else than with homophobia is the truism so valid that it takes one to know (and condemn) one. These days virtually everything anyone says can be interpreted at least in part as a self-statement. Therefore, it is not surprising that when homophobes speak about gays and lesbians, they are actually speaking about themselves; their self-referential (and so self-indulgent) ideation is in turn based on a projection, along the lines of "I condemn you to avoid condemning myself." Particularly rife are narcissistic, self-aggrandizing, self-serving, defensive attempts to contrast "me" with "you." Thus, "you are a despicable sissy" means "and I am not, for I am, unlike you, extremely masculine," while "I am ashamed of what you are and stand for" means that "since I am the exact opposite of you, I have nothing to be ashamed of myself for."

For one homophobe, virtually every one of his criticisms of gays and lesbians was a self-criticism implying a hoped-for self-improvement. This homophobe, when claiming to dislike gay men because they acted like women, was really downplaying and disavowing his own feminine side by criticizing and condemning the supposed femininity of others. Furthermore, his every criticism of gays and lesbians was self-puffery, making it hard to tell whether he was criticizing gays and lesbians or complimenting himself. For example, his accusations that to be homosexual is to be a sinner was his way of disclaiming guilt about how he himself had considered sinning in just that way and thus of convincing himself and others that his was a surfeit, admirable in the extreme, of personal innocence.

Dynamically speaking, homophobes' fears about and criticisms of gays and lesbians almost always reflect hidden forbidden wishes and needs buried deep within the self, so that "Don't do that" means "that is what

I would like to do, or not do, but I can't or won't." Attempting to keep gays and lesbians from getting out of control and making significant inroads into (and so eroding) straight society is the homophobe's way to convince himself that "I am in the process of exerting control over myself." At a deeper level, in many homophobes an erotophobia exists that is characterized by an inordinate amount of sexual guilt and shame, which leads to degrading all varieties of sex, as if sex is entirely a personal desire and not at all a biological function and, besides, as if it is a bad thing to have a body. Erotophobes view much about sex as immoral and virtually criminal, making sex unacceptable unless it is between one man and woman, in the dark, in the missionary position, and for the purpose of making babies. In addition, erotophobic homophobes single out homosexuality as a major example of what they mean by "sex is dirty," so that, in cleansing the world of homosexual evil, they are making a good start at cleansing it of all dirty sexuality—and ultimately cleansing their own fantasies by lysing the evil they discover within. Unless a minister has actually consulted with God, his saying that God is wreaking havoc on the world for its homosexual sins is likely to be conjecture, and this conjecture about the macrocosm in turn based on a microcosmic self-statement, such as "God will get me for what I am thinking" and "God will do to the world what I ought to do, or am actually doing, to myself, for wanting to do it."

Not generally recognized is how often homophobes are speaking about the person they are actually speaking to, with the content politely displaced onto gays and lesbians. They displace personal criticism away from the person they are with onto a distant, remote gay stranger who is a stand-in for their immediate audience. When they say "I hate queers" or the like to someone they are with, the person listening should always think, "He suspects me of being queer or evil, and it is not some gay or lesbian out there but me that she hates."

Socially Oriented Behavior

The lone homophobe has as his or her counterpart the groupie homophobe, that socially minded individual who routinely hangs out with like-minded homophobes, banding together to form political and religious cadres that, like coral reefs, are effectively monoliths consisting of multiple individual units who associate because they are alike and become alike because they associate.

Tendency toward Universal Bigotry

Few homophobes are bigoted only about certain targets. Almost all are racist, ageist, anti-Semitic, and xenophobic as well, if only because all these things additively enhance the bigots' self-image; they seem out to elevate their own self-esteem by deflating the self-esteem of others.

Tendency toward Being Emotionally Disordered

Homophobia, as is emphasized throughout this book, resembles a symptom of an emotional disorder in significant ways. To anticipate, homophobic individuals are like neurotic individuals of all ilks, although not in all ways. One significant way they are neurotic is that they are in conflict about their hidden wishes, and, as with other neurotics, these conflicts, more than reality, are the source of their manifest fearful and defensive criticisms of others. Conflicts about sexual wishes are discussed throughout. For example, in speaking about a gay man, a homophobic patient said, "I was afraid he would blow me a kiss." This patient was in fact expressing three forbidden wishes in the form of a fear. He was expressing two erotic wishes: to be more physically attractive than he actually was and to be more attractive to homosexuals than he could ever allow himself to actually be. He was also expressing a wish to condemn his own fantasized guilty transgressions by noting, and condemning, similar transgressions in others. As William McGurn puts it, in him we recognize how often behind "traditional fire and brimstone [we find] pinched eroticism."[2]

Additionally, many homophobes, like many neurotics, are in conflict between their wish to be and their fear of being passive. Homophobes' blatant expectations that all gay men must be effeminate—and subsequent demands that they act in a more masculine manner—are their way to distinguish themselves from passive, yielding, penetrable, girly men, a distinction that they carefully make in order to feel less like the penetrated and more like the penetrator—as they see it, more like the macho man and less like the wimpy woman.

Like obsessive neurotics these individuals constantly brood about intellectual matters, especially those relating to issues of morality. Here they cast aside all their humanity for transcendent principle, too readily throwing out the baby in order to improve the quality of the bathwater—that is, all too willingly offering up actual humans in sacrifice for the strictly theoretical purpose of appeasing an angry God whose existence they cannot prove, thereby saving us all from a wrath of a Him they can generally only imagine.

Many homophobes are depressives who reject gays and lesbians as their way of handling their own angry feelings about having themselves been rejected and who cast gays and lesbians out as their way of handling feeling similarly cast out in their own lives.

Many homophobes resemble aggressive sadistic individuals—mean and nasty people who use gays and lesbians as an outlet for their hostility and as a scapegoat for an anger that they themselves generally feel. An aspect of their sadism involves always having to be in control, that is, wanting to impose their view of how things ought to be on others. Their heterosexism is another form of control, in which their own heterosexuality becomes the standard by which they judge all others: "conform to me, be like I am, and do what I expect you to do, or else."

Ultimately, these are also masochistic individuals who maintain their homophobia even though (or because) it proves to be counterproductive and self-destructive. As masochistic businessmen they put antigay ideology over profit, and as masochistic politicians they would rather lose the gay vote than change their homophobic stance, even consenting to bring their own political parties down as long as they can keep their moral purism up.

Many are histrionics—highly envious individuals living in an uneasy equilibrium with gays and lesbians of whom they are jealous. Typically they envy their gay victims what they have—ranging from their high status in life resulting from the disposable income they have as so-called "DINKS" (double income, no kids) to their supposed unfettered sexual freedom. Since these homophobes' hatred arises out of jealousy over thwarted desire, we not surprisingly also see the worst gay bashers acting like hypocrites, as they themselves sneakily strive to do, or actually do, exactly the things they condemn gays and lesbians for having done, for example, when they take their fashion cues from gays and lesbians (rarely acknowledging the source) or move into the neighborhoods gays and lesbians have gentrified (rarely acknowledging their debt).

HOW HOMOPHOBES DIFFER

There are, however, some differences among homophobes. Some are relatively more tolerant than others, making exceptions, especially for gays and lesbians who are in the closet, in conflict about being homosexual, and/or sexually inactive. Some feel that homosexuality is fixed, whereas others believe in the possibility of spontaneous change or cure through therapy or by the church. Some are prejudiced but try not to discriminate. Others believe in segregation of gays and lesbians or in excluding them absolutely. Some are insightful about being homophobic, whereas others do not know or care that they are homophobic or, knowing they are, choose to present a tolerant façade that can actually be a passive-aggressive cover-up, for example, by expressing their homophobia in the form of complaints without teeth, I might say by praising with faint damnation, vocally leading boycotts of companies they do not deal with anyway, and demonstratively refusing to buy goods they can easily do without or never had any intention of purchasing in the first place. Some struggle with their homophobia whereas others accept it as it is, and their views differ as to whether or not gays and lesbians are more an annoyance than a social danger as gays and lesbians amass with the goal of taking over the world.

It would seem as if there are mild and severe homophobes. But this does not mean that there are good and bad homophobes. I do not buy into the theory that homophobes can minimize the extent and seriousness of their homophobia by claiming that they are not as homophobic as they could be, either because their homophobia does not cross the line from prejudice to discrimination (and so has no practical implications) or because they have second thoughts or even guilty conflicts about being homophobic. Almost all bigotry tends to start small and grow exponentially, and therefore any degree of homophobia that is not countermanded immediately, effectively, and by the homophobes themselves tends to spread rapidly and too soon becomes as entirely unacceptable as it is thoroughly inexcusable.

CHAPTER 2

Models of Homophobia

Homophobia falls into six focused categories, each of which constitutes a distinct homophobic model or paradigm. These models are:

1. The medical model: gays and lesbians are sick, that is, too unhealthy to be permitted to raise children or even to be allowed to move freely through society, and they may even need to be quarantined or, better still, exiled.
2. The religious model: gays and lesbians are sinners and ought to do penance for their sins.
3. The criminal model: gays and lesbians do things that are illegal; for example, they are pedophiles and ought to be jailed.
4. The political model: gays and lesbians make good common-cause enemies for those who want to get ahead personally and professionally, for example, to get out the conservative vote.
5. The sociocultural model: gays and lesbians and their homosexual lives are dangerously subversive and poised to disrupt the world order and keep us all from ever having lasting peace.
6. The biological model: gays and lesbians, like gypsies, Jews, or aborigines, are inherently genetically inferior and so ought to be put into a symbolic version of a concentration camp, confined to a real ghetto, sterilized, or even exterminated for the greater good and well-being of society as a whole.

This chapter describes the private thoughts and public thinking and pronouncements of homophobes categorized according to these different models and how each model in turn leads to specific wastages: trying to cure gays and lesbians of a nonexistent gay disease; condemning gays and lesbians as morally bereft sinners, then trying to get them to reform and repent; criminalizing homosexual acts and attempting to enforce laws against them; riding into political office on the backs of the suppressed; letting children without parents rot in orphanages just to avoid adopting them out to a gay couple who would rear them with love; and invalidating gays and lesbians as mental defectives, then treating them as inferior, second-class citizens or exiling them, if only symbolically, to a latter-day Devil's Island.

Distinguishing among the models is of practical use because a somewhat different corrective exists for each. Thus, the antithesis of the religious model of homophobia may involve joining a new church or moving to a town predominantly populated by a different religious group; the antithesis for political-model homophobia may require social activism, such as disseminating information about what minority groups are really like and getting out the simpatico vote; and the antithesis for medical-model homophobia starts with understanding that it is the homophobe, not the gay man or lesbian, who is emotionally troubled and that people who are emotionally troubled need to be cured, not taken seriously.

The following discussion focuses on homophobia both for itself and as a paradigm of other bigotry—that is, it applies to all forms of prejudice and discrimination ranging from xenophobia to anti-Semitism.

THE HOMOPHOBIC MEDICAL MODEL OF HOMOSEXUALITY

In the homophobic *medical model* of homosexuality, the homosexual is viewed as sick and in need of being treated and cured. Two broad groups of individuals see homosexuality as a sickness and call gays and lesbians sick. The first consists of *laypersons,* and they tend to use the term sick pejoratively, that is, to mean pathetic and disgusting. Their fantasies about what it means to be sick include the beliefs that

- Homosexuality is self-created, just like an addiction where addicts refuse to stop being addicted although they could, if they would only "just say no." Thus, homosexuality is a choice, and gays and lesbians could, if they only would, modify their behavior. They could either go straight or, if not, be celibate, and if they did that, their disease would at a minimum be under control to the point that they could lead lives of a little happiness and joy and even be accepted into mainstream society, although with important reservations.
- Homosexuality is abhorrent, reprehensible, dirty, and disgusting, just like leprosy.
- Homosexuality is a defect, just like an undescended testicle.
- Homosexuality is metatastic, just like cancer, that is, it invariably spreads to affect all areas of functioning, not only gays' and lesbians' sexual but also their

professional and personal lives. Gays and lesbians are infectious in one of two ways. First, being homosexual is almost literally catching. For gays and lesbians both passively present as (bad) role models and actively encourage others to be homosexual, recruiting them not only into having gay sex now and then but also into becoming gay permanently. Second, gays and lesbians not only catch but pass on physical illnesses venereally, spreading them to innocent others, gays and straights alike. Therefore, gays and lesbians should be quarantined not only so that they do not recruit but also so that they do not physically contaminate innocents around them.

- Homosexuality is treatable and needs to be treated, just like schizophrenia, with drugs, shock, ablation of parts of the brain, or, in the case of homosexuality, chemical or physical castration.

Recently, when I was doing a radio interview, the interviewer asked me whether I thought that homosexuality was an illness or was normal. I told him that homosexuality is not an illness but rather simply one healthy variant, with heterosexuality and homosexuality each traveling the legendary different road, with homosexuality no more abnormal, that is, no more an illness, than is having red hair or being left-handed. Instead, homosexuality is (very roughly) comparable to being a lone gorilla or a specialized ant in the ant colony.

The second group consists of *professionals* and would-be professionals, who view homosexuality as a destructive psychic disability. Thus, referring to the presumably pathological psychological factors operative in the development of homosexuality, a psychoanalyst says that heterosexuality occurs when psychic development has progressed without incident or complication from the most primitive, or oral, to the most mature, or phallic/oedipal, stage. In contrast, homosexuality is supposedly the product of a developmental lag or reversal that subverts normal sexual development; that is, it occurs when this normal progression is thwarted or reversed, so that the patient's sexuality remains undeveloped, becomes somehow derailed, or backslides from the mature phallic/oedipal stage to the immature pregenital phase of anality or orality. So, as Otto Fenichel claims, gay object choices "represent . . . a state between the love of oneself and the love of a heterosexual object."[1]

In such a view, homosexuality is comparable to a neurosis and, like a neurosis, is the product of abnormality that interferes with normal functionality. For example, in this view, gay sex is a substitute gratification, more like foreplay than intercourse, and as such a lesser form of sexuality. Naturally, the developmental lag and regression found in homosexuals predictably go hand in hand with personality problems, dooming gays and lesbians to a lifetime of compromised interpersonal relationships and those around them to victimization by gays' and lesbians' poor object relations. In particular, gays and lesbians are seen as inveterate narcissists who in their daily lives preen and pose, swish and swagger, and have a superficial value system that downplays the importance of long-term affectional human relationships in exchange for the thrill of the new sexual encounter; this leads gays and lesbians to have sex only with a mirror image of themselves because they are not mature enough to have a truly adult relationship with anyone else.

Some therapists—calling themselves *reparative therapists*—try to cure gays and lesbians of their homosexuality. With this in mind they present case examples of what they call successful cures using psychoanalytic methods to reverse fixations and regressions. If they do actually bring about some so-called cures, it is because they treat a very select group—mostly those about to convert anyway, such as uncommitted homosexuals who are actually straights just going through a gay phase, bisexuals of the moment, who might easily have become heterosexual spontaneously, without treatment.

In evaluating the mental state of homosexuals, reparative therapists regularly fail to distinguish a patient's homosexuality from coincidental psychopathology, such as histrionic personality disorder, as well as from nonpathology, so that they call camping pathological as if it is a sign that gays cannot take anything seriously when it is, in fact, more like a normative antidote to the loneliness that arises out of being excluded. Simultaneously, in evaluating the consequences of homosexuality, reparative therapists overlook gay strengths, especially the benefits that can accrue from being homosexual, such as homosexuality's ability to cut across class distinctions and open up interpersonal opportunities not otherwise available and homosexuality's ability to heal. In the realm of the latter I have seen some schizophrenic, asthmatic, and psoriatic teenagers get better both emotionally and physically when they became openly homosexual. It seemed that the healing process began when the individual came out of the closet and stopped rankling inside its confines.

In short, in my experience, when some reparative mental health practitioners say that gays and lesbians are sick, they really do not mean "I am so sorry and I will do what I can to help you reverse your chemical imbalance and feel better." They really mean "I think of you as a leper, and the sooner you get over that, and out of my sight, the better."

Affirmative therapists, in contrast, strongly believe that many theories proposed to explain the development of homosexual orientation—even learning theories that postulate pathological reinforcement of run-of-the-mill homosexual fantasies—are homophobic simply because they suggest that something went wrong somewhere along the line to create an abnormality, disorder, or disease. For affirmative theorists, theories that homosexuality is not one of two equally constituted variations but a deviation from the norm are flawed for any number of reasons but chiefly because they are based on observations selected to fit preconceived notions that in turn arise out of emotionally driven negative mindsets; these mindsets create hypotheses, then look for and, not surprisingly, find supposedly rational proof through the simple expedient of cherry-picking the evidence.

Physicians are paradoxically among those who discriminate the most using the homophobic medical model of homosexuality. Doctors, the very people who should be the most compassionate, call gays and lesbians sick, then discriminate against them either by giving them inferior medical care suitable for incurables or by completely denying them any care at all, for, after all, "Why bother?" Nonpsychiatric physicians conclude that gays and lesbians are not worth wasting their time on. Psychiatrists are happy to give gays and lesbians time but tend to overdiagnose them, calling them paranoid when they in fact have real enemies or depressed when they are just demoralized (then pushing antidepressant drugs on gays and lesbians who simply want someone to talk to).

Of course, homosexuals do have mental health concerns like anybody else, and some homosexuals do need psychotherapy, as do many people. But generally these are the same mental health concerns and problems that everybody else has. A possible difference does, however, exist: some gays and lesbians have to contend with negative social attitudes regarding their homosexuality, putting up with more of what Joe Kort calls "covert cultural sexual abuse"[2] than do heterosexuals, so that they feel detached from an accepting mainstream society, which creates stress due to feeling isolated and unworthy. Generally, then, as I mention throughout my 1999 book *Treating Emotional Disorder in Gay Men,* any psychotherapy needed should not be directed to the homosexuality itself but to any coincidental or consequential manifestations of emotional disorder that might be present in a person who simply happens to be homosexual.[3]

In conclusion, today much discrimination against gays and lesbians is based on the homophobic medical model of homosexuality. This results, among other things, in limitations on gays' and lesbians' professional opportunities. For example, they are unwelcome in some medical subspecialties because they are supposedly sick and cannot heal themselves and therefore predictably cannot heal others or because they are supposedly too brittle to tolerate stress, too corrupt to be fair and neutral, too sexually preoccupied to resist seducing patients, or, as gay men, too passive to make good authority figures and give a guiding hand or, as lesbians, too aggressive and authoritarian to do anything but overcontrol others, always trying to rule them imperiously.

Patients as well as therapists use the homophobic medical model of homosexuality to discriminate against gays and lesbians. For many patients, gays and lesbians are supposedly too sick to be *their* health practitioners. One patient, himself with a number of gay experiences in his past, fired his psychiatrist because he ran across him in the street wearing a leather jacket and walking next to a much younger, similarly dressed man. For this man the psychiatrist's professional qualifications did not count nearly as much as his so-called personal misbehavior. (He fired his psychiatrist after equating the doctor's presumed unacceptable gay behavior with the behavior of a children's entertainer whom he said was properly banned from television for being caught masturbating in a gay movie house.)

Clearly, all concerned need to recognize that when it comes to homosexuality, which is innate, there is nothing to fix since nothing is broken. It does not need to be cured since it is not an illness. The homophobic medical model of homosexuality must not serve as a rationale for discriminating against gays and lesbians personally or professionally, as if homosexuality interferes with competency or effectiveness, and it certainly should not be a reason to treat gays and lesbians as if they were sick lepers to be avoided and so denied the opportunity to receive needed medical and psychiatric care that is up to standards and equal for all.

Gay and lesbian targets of the medical model need to recognize that they are not sick as the homophobic doctor says they are. Except for those homosexuals in serious conflict about their homosexuality and those who are really bisexual and not liking that, the best idea is for gays and lesbians to accept themselves as they are and not get involved in *any* form of therapy geared to turning them into something completely different.

THE HOMOPHOBIC RELIGIOUS MODEL OF HOMOSEXUALITY

While the homophobic medical model of homosexuality has changed a great deal over the past decade, in contrast the homophobic religious model of homosexuality has hardly changed at all. This model is especially dangerous because it is ingrained in much of society and because many gays and lesbians, internally self-homophobic for some of the same reasons that others are homophobic toward them, already imagine themselves to be sinners and take the thinly disguised or open accusations that stem from this model very personally and seriously and act on them in self-destructive ways. Of course, not all gays and lesbians buy into the homophobic accusation that they are sinners. Those who do internalize the homophobe's words and are unable to shake them off often, but not always, have an underlying emotional problem, such as depression, that makes them prone to brood and obsess about what others say and take it too much to heart. Often that does not mean that they should beat up on themselves but instead that they need to seriously consider seeking help, possibly from a personal therapist.

Those who espouse the religious model view gays and lesbians as sinners and their sins as threatening the straight's own internal emotional homeostasis. Gays and lesbians fire them up, and their negative inner homophobic response extinguishes the dangerous searing flames to keep them from being burned inwardly by uncivilized thoughts and feelings that they can neither integrate nor suppress. For such precariously adjusted homophobes, homosexuals are the dirty pictures they long to see but fear visualizing—the forbidden porn that, if they viewed it, would result in God's smiting them, along the lines of turning them into a pillar of salt.

They typically rely on biblical passages that they cite in self-justification, such as

Leviticus 18:22: "Thou shalt not lie with mankind, as with womankind; it is abomination."

Leviticus 18:29: "For whosoever shall do any of these abominations . . . shall be cut off from among their people."

Genesis 19:4–5: "The men of Sodom . . . compassed the house round . . . And they called unto Lot, and said unto him: 'Where are the men that came in to thee this night? bring them out unto us, that we may know them.'"

Genesis 19:24: "Then the Lord caused to rain upon Sodom and upon Gomorrah brimstone and fire from the Lord out of heaven."

1 Kings 14:24: "And there were also sodomites in the land; they did according to all the abominations of the nations which the Lord drove out before the children of Israel."[4]

Because on some level many ordinary people believe that sodomy is a sin, many individuals buy into some aspects of the homophobic religious model of homosexuality, and so most people should be adjudged to be homophobic only if they go beyond being religious to becoming *scrupulously* religious. Scrupulously religious individuals say, "My church hates homosexuals, and it is right to do so." Becoming preoccupied with homosexual sin, they seek to rid not only themselves but everyone else of its taint. They grandiosely believe that they are the only ones who know right from wrong, and they know that because they know it, almost as if they have consulted with God and are now acting as His emissary to spread His word.

While some religious-model homophobes are laypersons, others are men and women of the cloth. In my view, the latter are wrongheaded individuals with the right credentials. The man who was Cardinal Joseph Ratzinger and is now Pope Benedict XVI is, according to Peter Tatchell, one such person, for, as Tatchell says, "he represents the hardline, fundamentalist strand of Catholicism [that] has always put church dogma before the Christian values of love and compassion. [He supported] Vatican efforts in March 2005 that successfully blocked recognition of gay human rights by the United Nations, effectively endorsing continued homophobic persecution in two-thirds of the world [thus] condemning millions of lesbians and gay people to be rejected by their families, sacked from their jobs, evicted from their homes, and to be subjected to homophobic abuse, threats, arrest, imprisonment, rape, assault and murder—either by vigilantes or by state agents such as the police and military."[5]

In 1986 Ratzinger wrote the "Letter to the Bishops of the Catholic Church on the Pastoral Care of Homosexual Persons." He wrote that "a person engaging in homosexual behaviors...acts immorally. To choos[e] someone of the same sex for one's sexual activity is self-indulgent," and he notes that "when civil legislation is introduced to protect behavior to which no one has any conceivable right, neither the Church nor society at large should be surprised when...irrational and violent reactions increase."[6]

In 1992, the Vatican sent the following letter from Ratzinger to all the U.S. bishops. The letter was titled "Some Considerations Concerning the Catholic Response to Legislative Proposals on the Non-Discrimination of Homosexual Persons." This letter calls a homosexual orientation "a strong tendency ordered toward an intrinsic moral evil," says "there are areas in which it is not unjust discrimination to take sexual orientation into account," and expresses concern about how proposed progay legislation might affect "adoption or foster care...public housing [and] 'family' participation in the health benefits given to employees."[7]

Ratzinger recently became pope in spite of, or because of, his proclamations, which, stripped of their religious context, could readily be called, at best, controlling and sadistic and, at worst, paranoid in the sense of having a "get them before they get you" mentality. Clearly, one function of Ratzinger's religious homophobia is to be a theoretical shining beacon—regardless of how many real individuals' lives he darkens in the process.

Ratzinger represents the extreme view. Generally, there are some more and some less extreme thinkers in the ranks of religious-model homophobes. As Margaret O. Hyde suggests in her book, *Know about Gays and Lesbians,* "Not all religious people are morbidly prejudiced against gays and lesbians" or use the religious model of homosexuality to express their homophobia. For "the subject of homosexuality causes tremendous controversy in many religious groups. These feelings run deep, and many faiths are in turmoil about whether or not homosexuals are sinners, may be ordained as leaders in the church, or be accepted only if they refrain from sex."[8] Similarly, according to Alan Cooperman, "Like many Protestant denominations, Conservative Jews are divided over homosexuality: torn between the Hebrew scriptures' condemnation of it as an 'abomination' and a desire to encourage same-sex couples to form long-lasting, monogamous relationships."[9]

Religious homophobes often read the scriptures as if they were inkblots on a Rorschach test, taking out what they put into them, so that while they claim their homophobia is based on their religion, in fact their religion is based on their homophobia. That is, they use the Bible to justify an already-existing homophobia—to make their homophobia both doctrinaire and official, so that their amateur gay bashing can look professional and so that, instead of suffering from severe pangs of guilt, they can, with the blessings of all concerned, continue to bash gays with abandon, with few or no qualms, and, they can at least hope, with a maximum effect and a minimum of negative personal consequences.

When parents tell their children that unless they repent of their homosexuality they are bound for hell, they should be counted among the morbidly religious homophobes espousing the homophobic religious model of homosexuality. Congregations are also to be counted as such when they ban other congregations for accepting homosexuals because homosexuality is not only contrary to biblical teachings and the sanctity of the family but is also personally offensive to all the good individual church members. Likewise, in my opinion, are religious groups who forbid ordaining practicing homosexuals, arrange boycotts of progay and gay-owned businesses, and officially discourage the use of condoms to prevent the transmission of illness.

In my view, there is a considerable overlap between morbidly scrupulous religious homophobia and familiar psychopathology, and in this arena we find some of the clearest examples of that widespread confluence between psychopathology and homophobia that I emphasize throughout this book. With scrupulously religious homophobes their religion is less theology than psychopathology, less a reflection or representation of sanctioned official religious dogma than a reflection and expression of personal emotional conflict. If we strip religious homophobes of their higher calling and theological trappings and take their thoughts and actions out of a religious context and put them into a psychological one, we clearly see how morbidly religious homophobes share certain important mindsets with emotionally disordered individuals.

For one thing, many are simply mean, punitive *sadists.* In my view, equating homosexuality with sin serves a pathological aggressive need that, like all serious aggressivity, departs from considerations of basic humanity. These are, after all, biting, mean-spirited, critical people full of hate and a desire for hate-filled vengeance. They may not beat gays and lesbians up physically (although sometimes they do, and often they encourage others to do that for them), but they certainly beat them up emotionally via exclusion, banishment, excommunication, and thinking of them as dead and so treating them as deceased when they are in fact still very much alive. They cruelly put, and relish putting, gays and lesbians in an impossible position—as when they assert that abstinence is the only morally acceptable path if you are homosexual, knowing that for most people abstinence is a difficult and even an impossible goal. They are also *controllers* who demand that they be the ones to determine what gays and lesbians do, especially what they do in bed, then try to forcibly convert gays and lesbians to their views in much the same way they try to force everyone else to become just like them; they respond with even more anger when gays and lesbians resentfully refuse to succumb, to the point that they escalate—bashing gays and lesbians for being gay when they are also, or mainly, bashing them for challenging their authority.

Dynamically speaking, many of these sadists, themselves feeling too passive and overly submissive to church authority, become active by turning on gays and lesbians and attempting to run their lives for them, imposing their own standards on gays and lesbians through the use of the loving carrot of salvation, backed up by the big stick of damnation.

Others are *depressives* whose homophobia is reactive, sounding uncomfortably like the pain of a lover scorned. For these homophobes, the true homosexual sin involves gays and lesbians ignoring them and loving someone else. They rage at gays and lesbians not only because they want control but also because gays and lesbians, by rejecting their strictures, are rejecting not only their ideas but them personally as well.

They are often *narcissistic* individuals whose complaints that gays and lesbians do not produce children are complaints that gays and lesbians do not breed the children they want and need to create the new parishioners that they have to have to fill their churches. They also narcissistically believe that they alone know it all and so infallibly know right from wrong. This belief goes along with a self-anointed elevated status that implies that they not only worship their God but have also identified with Him, and may even be on the way to becoming one of His personal assistants, or even launching a takeover.

They are also often *obsessive* hairsplitters who make clear distinctions without actual differences—famously, the distinction between the sin and the sinner—as if what one does and who one is are absolutely two entirely different things. Also, like obsessives, they see the world in terms of black or white, with the so-called homosexual imperfection rendering gays and lesbians entirely defective, and like obsessives they alternate between condemning gays and lesbians ("hate the sin"), then, believing themselves too harsh, atone by forgiving them ("love the sinner"), then, believing themselves too soft on sin, condemning gays and lesbians once more—behavior that reminds me of some of my patients with a cleaning compulsion who always manage to soil what they are scrubbing, so that they have to start the cleaning ritual once more from the top, ad infinitum. In their wavering they also remind me of my patient who took more than 10 minutes to get out of the men's room because after he washed his hands, he had to touch the doorknob to open the door, contaminating his hands, which he had to decontaminate by washing them again, and so on. Their turnarounds make them hypocrites who disregard not the letter but the spirit of the Bible, feeling entirely free to cast the first stone, even though they themselves are sinners, as they proclaim the Judeo-Christian ideal of love while overlooking how their cruelty to gays and lesbians is incompatible with that ideal. In the most severe cases of hypocrisy, they bash gays and lesbians today yet tomorrow do forbidden gay and lesbian things themselves. (The relationship between homophobia, religious-model homophobia, and familiar psychopathology is discussed in detail in chapters 8–10 on homophobia as a manifestation of psychopathology.)

Gays and lesbians, like all targets of religious bigotry, can feel less oppressed by telling themselves over and over again that they are hearing only from the minority of religious people—scrupulously religious people who are, in reality, not so much religious people as fanatics and extremists with a religious bent (who, additionally, like the public eye and know how to get it focused on them). Many observers would agree that *truly* religious people either have few thoughts on homophobic matters or view gays and lesbians as they view everyone else: as people with flaws (to be overlooked) and virtues (to be counted) in the usual proportions. Truly religious people are out to discover God's intent and to spread his word. Bigoted fanatic religious people are out not to mouth God's word but to put words into God's mouth.

Gay and lesbian targets of religious-model homophobes who regularly quote the Bible should consider reading the Bible to see what it actually says and how it, too, contradicts itself internally, meaning that one can quote it to prove almost any point one chooses to make. They should also remember that there are problems of translation that might warp the original biblical messages as they come down to us. No one really knows how to translate the Bible exactly to capture its true original spirit and intent. For example, in the Sodom and Gomorrah story what exactly does the word *know* mean? And who is to say that the translation we are reading is not the work of an original homophobe who has taken words with multiple meanings and bent them to his or her will? Is the original word really to be translated as *abomination* (with a mainly sexual connotation) or instead as *heretic* (with a mainly religious connotation)?

THE HOMOPHOBIC CRIMINAL MODEL OF HOMOSEXUALITY

In the homophobic criminal model of homosexuality, gays and lesbians are not sinners but antisocials. This view of homosexuals as criminals extends to the Supreme Court where, as Eric Berndt forcefully reminded us in 2005, Justice Scalia "has no pity for the millions of gay Americans on whom sodomy laws and official homophobia have such an effect" when he "sarcastically rants about the 'beauty of homosexual relationships'...and believes that gay school teachers will try to convert children to a homosexual lifestyle" and "dissent[s] in Lawrence vs. Texas, the 2003 Supreme Court case that overturned Bowers vs. Hardwick and struck down the nation's sodomy laws."[10]

The criminal model of homosexuality is to some extent based on circular reasoning: being homosexual is a crime because it is against the law, and being homosexual is against the law because it is a crime. It also originates in a blurring of the different meanings of the word *crime,* a word that refers not only to the breaking of a specific law but also to a moral offense or even just to something offensive. Is Scalia, therefore, acting the part of a judge or of an activist, claiming the neutrality of jurisprudence as a cover for personally condemning what he believes to be imprudence? Of course, the view of homosexuality as criminal contains another basically fatal logical flaw: those who see gays and lesbians as sick are often the same individuals who see gays and lesbians as criminals. As such, if they thought about it at all, they would recognize that they are putting themselves in the untenable position of recommending that we punish people for being ill.

THE HOMOPHOBIC POLITICAL MODEL OF HOMOSEXUALITY

In the political model, gays and lesbians are not sick, sinful, or criminal but are useful polarizing social elements for politicians hoping to win elections. Such politicians play the gay card, telling their constituents, "Gays and lesbians are a threat to the legitimate family, so vote for me and I'll make certain that the family unit survives the onslaught." Politicians who embrace this schema attempt to win over members of the electorate first by creating and enhancing their fears of homosexuality and then by offering protection against the newly feared homosexual. They are also soft-soaping the electorate by pandering to it, enhancing its collective narcissism by speaking unfavorably of gays and lesbians as outsiders, in order to make straights feel more comfortably and proudly like insiders.

Not uncommonly, such politicians, hypocrites at the core, either court gay groups in private but deride them publicly, or vice versa. Too often we are surprised, considering their private personal gay behavior, to find gay politicians publicly condemning homosexuality.

THE HOMOPHOBIC SOCIOCULTURAL MODEL OF HOMOSEXUALITY

In this model gays and lesbians are not sick, sinners, criminals, or convenient political tools or subjects for political manipulation and assassination but are at best eccentrics and at worst deviants who do not belong in polite society and should therefore be banished entirely. These homophobes give as their reason for gay bashing that gays and lesbians will undermine the fabric of society, adding that unless we stick to the traditional definition of marriage as a holy sacred institution between a man and a woman, the institution of marriage will itself be permanently destroyed. They also note that if we let gays and lesbians adopt children, they will predictably bring them up badly and in the process seriously damage them, if not physically, then at least emotionally. According to this model, gays and lesbians, predictably undermining the natural order of things by infiltrating the herd, will ultimately decimate society. Taking things one step further, these homophobes accuse gays and lesbians of doing such things deliberately—being antisocial on purpose after having made a conscious decision to become separatists who thumb their noses at mainstream society by living outside of its admirable boundaries and yet planning to destroy society as we know it from within.

This sociocultural model is often found in small towns that are traditionally family oriented and as such view gays and lesbians as nontraditional interlopers and therefore pariahs to be isolated from the acceptable small-town family herd. The citizens there enforce traditional roles by actually isolating gays and lesbians through shunning. They do so less for their actual behavior (which is in any case usually ultraconservative, considering that only ultratraditional gays and lesbians tend to move to small towns in the first place and then act in a way that is often as or more traditional than the behavior of straights) or for any lack of accomplishment (many gays and lesbians are highly accomplished individuals who have a great deal of potential and actual value to the town), but more out of personal and shared moralistic views that they then go on to spread in the closed small-town culture until all concerned become infected and proclaim in concert that gays and lesbians should be relegated to the category of the black sheep of the family. One result is that in some of the blue-collar small towns I know, the least accomplished citizens wind up in the position of condemning the most accomplished, ignoring or even banishing some of their best-qualified and highest-level people—precisely those who are most able, and therefore most likely, to do the town and its individual inhabitants a great deal of good and give them reason for pride.

Small-town homophobes are particularly adept at throwing out the baby in order to improve the quality of the bathwater. For they allow the satisfaction of real needs and the attainment of real accomplishments to take second place to shining a holy beacon on the proceedings, even though that particular beacon sheds only theoretical light on the so-called darkness of what is in fact a nonexistent evil.

THE HOMOPHOBIC BIOLOGICAL MODEL OF HOMOSEXUALITY

In this form, homophobes view gays and lesbians not as sick, sinners, criminals, objects of political convenience, or social deviates but as strangers in their midst, much like stranger baboons interloping on their territory and threatening to decimate their herd. The resultant gay bashing is perceived to be justified by a reasonable need to protect philosophical, moral, and even genetic purity from contamination by outsider minorities who are distinctly not of a feather, who threaten insiders—majorities—and the defined, structured, sanctified entity to which they belong, that famous nuclear family. Collectively, these homophobes figuratively set out to protect the purity of the race and the quality of life of its individual members by culling the breed, that is, by killing off what they view as the runts of the litter so that there is no chance that these so-called defectives will grow up and in turn reproduce their own kind. They are also of a more practical bent, hoping to preserve limited resources for the younger, reproductively active members of the tribe, among which persons they, quite naturally and invariably, number themselves.

In addition to a primary self-protective response meant to destroy outsiders, figuratively to keep them from contaminating the gene pool and eating all the food, a secondary longing exists to idealize oneself as thoroughly belonging to the mainstream (more so than others) and a tertiary longing to be idolized and rewarded in this world in turn—by the citizenry and by the lower and higher powers that be—for protecting the tribe from all those barbaric invaders and so to be rewarded in the next world by the highest Power of them all. An innate goal-directed competitiveness rules as well, as these homophobes band together to grow tall by dwarfing the gay competition in order to maximize the light available for themselves. They are in effect casting gays and lesbians in the shadows or making certain they will not see the light of day at all, so that they themselves can photosynthesize more and so better survive, prosper, move to the first rung of the pecking order, and alone remain at the top of the food chain, where they can then, from their powerful perch, pillory those they have consigned to the perches way below.

CHAPTER 3

Rationalizations of Homophobia

Most bigots claim that their bigotry is justified and rational, and they base their claims on considerations of human nature, culture, religion, matters of preference, freedom of speech and thought, unimpeachable logic, and reality, as described in more detail in the following.

HUMAN NATURE

In the realm of justifications like "it's only human nature," some homophobes, overdoing the claim that homophobia is ingrained in all of us, say that all straights dislike all gays and lesbians because we are all normally somewhat suspicious of others who are different, especially of others one might call outsiders. Then they cite the following paradigms in self-justification: children playing only with other children of the same age while excluding all others; adults grouping according to a given ideology while savaging those of contrasting ideologies, for example, forming voting blocs along racial and ethnic lines; birds of a feather flocking together while avoiding all others not similarly endowed; ducks condemning baby swans as ugly; baboons fighting with baboons from other tribes to keep them out of their territory; and gardeners damning a flower for being a weed just because they do not happen to want it in their garden.

The more theoretically inclined suggest that there is a primary taboo against homosexuality that is "only human." In particular, they postulate a taboo against anal penetration and claim it is just as powerful and basic as the incest taboo and for some of the same reasons—that is, it encourages or assures reproduction of the species while preventing diseases such as genetic and psychological disorders in the case of incest, venereal disease and physical trauma in the case of anal penetration.

CULTURE: EVERYONE IS HOMOPHOBIC, AFTER ALL

In this realm, homophobes pass off their intolerance as natural and expected because no moral person can, should, or would want to tolerate a deviancy like homosexuality; they also view homophobia as desirable, because homophobes are simply good citizens in their home towns, and their homophobia is a sign that they are socially attuned to the locals and their mores. Hence if they sing homophobic rap lyrics, these do not come from within, for these just reflect what the people they live with are thinking, saying, and doing and so what their audiences want to hear.

It is true that homophobia is very common and that to some extent it is in the bones of all societies to discriminate against gays and lesbians. Also, to the extent that a given bigot's personal negative attitudes originate with generalized social opprobrium directed toward gays and lesbians throughout his culture and condoned by the particular society in which he lives, it is true that that bigot becomes less neurotic simply by virtue of being socially attuned, thus socially well adjusted. In addition, it is a fact that many people, scientists included, with reason define emotional health in terms of commonality ("everyone is that way") and in contrast define emotional sickness in terms of individual deviation, so that there is some validity to the bold-faced suggestion that homophobes would be emotionally ill if they *did not* go along with their homophobic society. But in my view, those who are in fact socially well adjusted are those who ignore the bigoted elements in their society and, detaching themselves from them, become their own nonbigoted person.

RELIGION

Some homophobes claim that if their homophobia has a religious content, it is only because they believe what their minister says and do the things he or she urges them to do. They use the Bible to excuse their homophobia, citing its undoubtedly homonegative passages. However, they pick and choose their citations to align with a personal negativity already in place. Loving men and women with positive feelings toward all, gays and lesbians included, avoid focusing on these passages exclusively. Instead of overlooking the book's internal inconsistencies and treating the Bible as the sum of a few of its parts, they find a way to work and think around the Bible's homophobic passages so that, as moderates, they can avoid, on the one hand, being overly scrupulous, fixating on homophobic biblical passages and quoting them incessantly as if they were not an occasional aberration but the whole thing, and, on the other hand, being excessively heretical, condemning the entire Bible as essentially fallacious because of individual inconsistencies that mean that as a whole it does not add up. They also avoid claiming the Bible as their incontrovertible authority while themselves following only some but not all of its tenets, disregarding those they need to ignore to make their homophobic case already in place. In short, they do not say that the Bible proves their point, when what is truer is that they make their point first, then find something in the Bible to justify it.

Religious homophobes often cite the true gratification to be derived from the renunciation involved in religious asceticism. They say that they hate homosexuals simply because, reasonably preferring Spartans to Athenians, moralists to immoralists, and saints to sinners, they dislike homosexuals' extreme pleasure orientation. But analysis reveals that their so-called preferential asceticism is so often in fact more like a compulsive erotophobia, so that for these homophobes gays and lesbians are the worst sort of sinners because to them they represent the epitome of sexual reprobates—dangerous pleasure seekers poised to get out of control and take others, "me and mine," along, and down, with them.

PREFERENCE

In this realm, homophobes, saying "I just happen to like straights better than I like gays and lesbians," feel, wrongly, that they can reliably distinguish preference from prejudice, that is, that they can distinguish free will from determinism, making their homophobia not a matter of prejudice but one of individual taste or discernment. What they overlook is that preference is a very complex matter, including, to cite the synonyms listed in Microsoft Word's thesaurus: "first-choice, partiality, penchant, predilection, fondness, liking, inclination, and favoritism." They particularly overlook the unconscious determinants of prejudice: their heterosexist preference originates less in a true favoring of heterosexism than in an abject fear of its opposite, making this particular preference a reverse prejudice. Analogously, a patient's masculine protest took the form of a rabid preference for dissonant music (of the modern sort) because he felt that it was a welcome manly refuge from music that was effeminate because it adhered to the classic principles of harmony and consonance. As I see it, there is no real difference between heterosexism and homophobia, for heterosexism is little more than a preference for one thing (straights) that develops as the flip side of a fear of the other (gays and lesbians).

In short, homophobes' dislike of gays and lesbians is usually not as voluntary and consciously considered as they claim it to be. So often it does not arise out of a homophobe's free will but represents the unconscious resolution of personal conflict. Those who insist that their dislike of gays and lesbians is a fully conscious, purposeful, conflict-free decision to hate them (as they say, "what is there to like, for they are all bad characters ranging from unladylike women who cut their hair short to unseemly men who pad daintily about wearing tight jeans and codpieces or, worse, are actual criminals who flout the sodomy laws") just provide us with yet another example of how homophobes regularly fail to understand their own motivation and so of how "I hate gays and lesbians preferentially" really means "I am in conflict about, and fearful of, liking them," ultimately proving the basic Freudian principle that behind every fear is a hidden, forbidden wish.

One homophobe's so-called preference for masculine men and clearly enunciated hatred of sissies originated in his dislike of his passive wuss of a father. Underneath he did like feminine men, finding them pleasantly soft and seductive. He liked them because they reminded him of his father's loving aspects and because their passive ways made him feel comparatively more active and so more manly. As a result, on more than one occasion he had picked up a transsexual prostitute and had sex with her. But his macho male conscience forbade his acknowledging such positive feelings, and he also had to consider his self-image and the image he presented to others. Therefore, he defensively changed his positive feelings into their negative opposites in order to deal with his guilt and the social opprobrium he anticipated and feared if he were caught picking up transsexuals. As a result, he consciously believed and openly proclaimed that he preferred macho men. Once when he was very drunk, he even picked up and beat up a transsexual. He did so in order to hide what he feared the most: how readily all he-men, like macho him, were on the cusp of becoming she-women, like effeminate sissies.

Many homophobes like to claim that their so-called preferences originate entirely in what they believe to be painful experience. For example, a mother said she was appropriately saddened and depressed to find her only son was gay, saying, "I am human too, entitled to grieve for my child's being gay, and to miss the grandchildren I will never have. My feelings are justified—I would have preferred him to be straight. It is cruel for gay men to disparage me for feeling this way by mocking me by saying the likes of 'she hates to see her only son go down.'" But her son was a happy, successful, famous musician with a fine home life, making her pain, as she subsequently herself admitted, somewhat exaggerated. In like manner, a patient said he preferred straights because gays and lesbians regularly behaved in an unpleasant, provocative, and even threatening manner because they deliberately set out to shock, offend, or threaten him in ways ranging from "claiming a superior lifestyle" to "having sex out in the open," for example, on the beach or in the shadows on the streets of his Greenwich Village neighborhood. This man claimed, "I am no more homophobic because I cannot stand the transsexual prostitutes that hang around the street outside my door than I am heterophobic because I dislike the heterosexual prostitutes turning tricks in cars parked in front of my house." It seemed only right to fully empathize with him—until

I learned that the things he was complaining about happened 10 blocks away from where he actually lived, at 3:00 A.M., while every night he went to bed at 10:00 P.M.

FREEDOM OF SPEECH AND THOUGHT

In the realm of freedom of speech and thought (that is, "I can dislike anyone I want to; it's a free country"), it is true that one is free to develop one's preferences and dislikes fully. But one is not necessarily free to express them fully, at all times and under all circumstances. Expressing them openly in a hurtful way is irresponsible since it turns preference into prejudice and prejudice into discrimination. Homophobes' freedom to think and speak limits gays' and lesbians' freedom to be treated well—if not with the full respect that they ultimately desire, then at least with the tolerance that they would find acceptable, if only barely.

UNIMPEACHABLE LOGIC

Some homophobes, while admitting that they are prejudiced, deny that they discriminate, as if prejudice and discrimination are fully separable, conceptually and behaviorally. They say that their prejudice, having few real consequences, is of no significance and, in fact, harmless—just something the guys down at the corner bar spout after a few drinks, then forget about the next morning. But I have yet to observe that singular human being whose prejudice is so well contained and controlled that it does not spill over somewhere and somehow to become at the very least a covert form of discrimination, moreover, often specifically of the passive-aggressive sort I discuss in chapter 9.

REALITY

Homophobes like to claim that gays and lesbians are at the very least very hard to stomach, if not downright disgusting, along the lines of "we all know that there are some undoubtedly unsavory and even dangerous aspects of what supposedly constitutes gay life."

It is true that certain aspects of gay life are the pits, but so are certain aspects of straight life, and it is all too easy to focus on the negative aspects of gay life up close, without humor or tolerance, creating a complete evil out of an overall good and so a negative out of a mixed and often overall relatively benign picture. Certainly gays and lesbians do not constitute a defined class. Some follow Steven Froias's lead: "puttin' on [my] slut clothes and picking up every boy… Saturday night."[1] Others search the many Web sites whose goal is to help gays and lesbians find a lifelong relationship and whose philosophy is that cheating is anathema and that gays and lesbians should develop and stay in lifelong monogamous relationships.

In favoring the familiar slippery-slope arguments ostensibly reflective of an almost physical reality, these homophobes overlook that while these arguments have some basis, gays and lesbians getting legitimate rights is a long way from gays and lesbians taking over the planet and repealing the laws of nature en masse. Also, there are some good things about slippery slopes for all concerned, for example, when gains gays and lesbians make in one area quite naturally provide the groundwork for further gains in another.

Most importantly, these "I am just being realistic" homophobes regularly overlook something very important: that their homophobic provocations anger gays and lesbians who, mere humans like everyone else, feel provoked, then do the negative things homophobes too readily accuse them of having done.

In short, just as paranoids are never 100 percent unjustified in their suspicions, homophobes are never 100 percent wrong in their homophobia. It is generally true, as Fenichel puts it in another context, that paranoid homophobia is not "'hit or miss' but occurs in the field in which reality meets it halfway. The . . . paranoid [homophobe] sees the mote in his neighbor's eye [and uses a] type of defense known as 'displacement to the minute.'"[2] In like manner, gays and lesbians do have problems, and some of these at least appear to encourage homophobic responses. But many people have the same problems, and gays' and lesbians' problems are mostly run of the mill and not on the level of something that should seriously concern many people, few of whom are as directly affected as they imagine themselves to be. Besides, many of the undoubtedly unsavory aspects of what can at times constitute gay life originate not in being gay but in being neurotic—and being gay neither makes one neurotic nor protects one from being neurotic. For example, promiscuity in a gay man can so often be not a gay problem but the product of a fear of commitment that is part of an avoidant personality disorder or a symptom of depression in which gays' and lesbians' need for love is a bottomless pit that can never be filled to capacity, so there is always a degree of unfulfilled yearning that persists no matter how much gays and lesbians try to make it disappear.

When homophobes attribute anything they dislike in a given gay man or lesbian to being homosexual, even when the given problematic behavior originates outside of the homosexual sphere and in the realm of emotional problems that are just like the ones straights have, they forget that, when they espy the equivalent problems in straights, they never, ever attribute them to being heterosexual.

CHAPTER 4

Homophobia in Gays and Lesbians (Internalized or Internal/Self-Homophobia)

Achieving full acceptance is one of the greatest challenges for gays and lesbians today. But to date that ideal remains elusive, partly because there is almost as much homophobia among gays and lesbians and in the gay community as there is among straights and in the straight community.

Although some psychologists favor the term *internalized homophobia* to describe gays' and lesbians' homophobia toward themselves and toward other gays and lesbians, I believe that that term is incomplete because it fails to take into account how so-called internalized homophobia in gays and lesbians can result not from having internalized others' homophobia but from within—in the ego's (or self's) unfavorable attitude toward itself and its own sexual and homosexual desires and behaviors, akin to head banging as the conscience sucks up negative energy from the instincts, or id, analogously to how a hurricane sucks up negative energy from the warm water and turns that negative energy against the water, the self, in the form of a raging storm leading to excessive, brutal, masochistic self-destructiveness.

This self-destructiveness can, in turn, take a number of forms. It can take the form of completed suicide, overt suicidal-like behavior, such as symbolic cutting, or covert suicidal behavior, such as having unprotected, unsafe sex. In a committed relationship, unsafe sex can represent not only an unconscious suicidal but also an unconscious homicidal act, a way to hurt a partner by sharing a newly caught disease or by spitefully and angrily leaving the partner by killing oneself.

In its less obvious forms, it can involve an avoidance of close intimate relationships: gays and lesbians punish themselves for being gay by distancing themselves from potential lovers, either by not developing close relationships in the first place or by abandoning close relationships already formed. They may favor anonymous sex as a way to make a negative statement about being homosexual, in effect saying, "I would not want to have a serious loving relationship with gays or lesbians I know well because once you get to know gays or lesbians well you will predictably find them all despicable." Some gays and lesbians will not have sex with other homosexuals because of what homosexuals do to their bodies during sex, so they seek out straights (rough trade) for sexual encounters. Others turn to hustling, saying that they do it for the money, which they believe to be acceptable, in order to convince themselves that they are not doing it for the sex, which they believe to be unacceptable. One gay hustler denied he was in it for the sex, saying he was only in it for the money. He left a relationship precipitously after he got less than he expected from a man who took him home and supported him for months, broadly hinting just before he left, "We are having a good time, and you are giving me a good life, but I am not any richer these days than I was before I met you." Yet afterwards he kept coming around, inviting himself over for dinner and telling the other man his life problems. So it was not only the money after all—for him the money was, as with so many gay hustlers, just an excuse to have sex guilt free, a way to say, "I am not having gay sex, which I abhor. I am just doing a job, trying to earn a living, which I approve of." In other words, out of self-hatred, this hustler denied that it was in his nature to be gay or even to be a gay hustler by telling himself that he was just a businessperson trying to put food on his table.

Some gays and lesbians become erotophobic, inhibiting their sexuality partially out of shame, so that they accept being gay but seriously limit their activities via a number of ritualistic caveats about which relationships and what sexual activities are and are not permissible. Paradoxically, some become wildly promiscuous as they go to one sexual extreme so as to master its inhibitory opposite—denying that they have sexual conflicts at all or, if they are at all aware of them, that these conflicts have any hold on them.

Others, eschewing sex entirely, become celibate; capitulating to asexuality, they renounce sexual pleasure completely to salve their inner guilt. They often simultaneously develop a compulsive preference for pornography with onanism over actual sexual relationships, their way to have virtual sex in order to avoid interacting with real flesh-and-blood sexual partners. Perhaps most commonly, gays and lesbians hurt themselves by avoiding a degree of self-fulfillment in the nonsexual arena. They might waste time in pursuit of substitute gratifications as they indulge in activities that divert them from fully tapping their personal and professional resources, wasting time and energy in unsatisfactory, unrewarding, or useless activities that do not really benefit them or have any future, such as a preoccupation with the latest clothing style, while avoiding those that could have potentially propelled them into lives of joy and success, such as developing their relationships or job-related skills.

Not a few become sadists who hurt others more than they hurt themselves. They come down on other gays and lesbians as harshly as they come down on themselves. They abuse their lovers physically or mentally by cheating on them or demanding that they participate in threesomes they do not want to have. Or they become shrewish satirists of gay and lesbian life, even condemning other gays and lesbians both for a thing and its opposite, so that with them other gays and lesbians cannot win, no matter what. They condemn gays and lesbians who come out of the closet as indiscreet, and those who stay in the closet as dishonest; they criticize sophisticated gays and lesbians for being too snooty, hoping to burst their bubble, yet criticize less sophisticated blue-collar gays and lesbians for being low-rent people who ought not to even think about bubbles in the first place. They condemn femmes for swishing and leather men for phony butchness. They accuse gays and lesbians who pick companions and lovers younger than themselves of robbing the cradle, those who pick older companions and lovers of being opportunists, and those who prefer companions of the same age of being narcissists (men and women who, if they have sex with someone else at all, can only have it with someone who is a mirror image of them).

They might sadistically out other gay men (or, more rarely, lesbians), justifying their actions by claiming that their means justify their ends. Some sadistic lesbians keep gay men out of their bars and lives, just as vigorously and with finality as some straight men keep gays and lesbians, Jews, or blacks out of their clubs and make certain that no gay man can be found anywhere in the army barracks, which, as they see it, are for straights only. Many disrupt friendships by resorting to backstabbing or by reporting cheating to those cheated on, ostensibly to inform them of what they need to know but actually to rub their noses in all the goings-on, just so that they can sit back and enjoy a good laugh at their expense.

Speaking developmentally, gays and lesbians often become self-homophobic after going along with and identifying with homophobic parents, then internalizing their parents' critical, unaccepting attitudes toward them to the point that they adopt their parents' attitudes as their own and, in turn, treat themselves and other gays and lesbians just as shabbily as their parents treated them. Not a few who succumb to parental admonitions act out by distancing themselves from their lovers at the behest of parents who warn them: "Don't be so obvious about being gay. You will certainly ruin yourself professionally if you continue to foolishly live openly with another man."

Many hold on to their parents' abusive values for the purpose of proclaiming their ongoing love for mom and dad—their way to tell them how sorry they are for having turned out homosexual and how much they deserve to be beaten up for being bad sons and daughters. Such self-directed homophobia can worsen later in life when gays and lesbians lose their parents and identify even further with their lost parents in order to resurrect and maintain the relationship with them, now inside themselves.

Some of these abusive parents hated their sons and daughters specifically for being gay and lesbian. Others were general erotophobes (sexophobes) who felt negatively about all sexuality and criticized the child as much for masturbation and heterosexual leanings as they criticized him or her for homosexuality. Such gays and lesbians might have become self-homophobic as one instance of a global erotophobia (sexophobia) that led them to criticize themselves not only for being homosexual but also for having any sexual and loving feelings at all. Theirs is a rigid punitive conscience composed of harsh, shrill, unloving, intrapsychic self-destructive messages, with no forgiving, softening nuances anywhere.

Here are some cases in which critical fathers and mothers challenged a child's gender identity, criticized a child's budding sexuality, and generally withheld love to the point that the child went through life unable to give himself or herself a vote of confidence and in turn confidently vote for other gays and lesbians.

A mother and father put their son's masculinity down by curling his hair like a girl's and swatting him when he tried to straighten it out. They regularly humiliated him for his loving feelings, once, for example, even beating him up for what turned out to be his last heterosexual venture—playing doctor with the little girl next door, for, as they put it, "Nice little boys don't play such games." They then went on to insist he steer clear of all little girls "so that you don't contaminate them with your germs" and then, when he had finally reached puberty, "so that you don't screw up their lives in an even worse way by making them pregnant."

An overly possessive father repeatedly made the point that he did not want his teenage daughter talking to those dykes on the Internet. Later he forbade her to go online at all. Then he declared that she should not date men until she was 30 years old. Then he forbade her to have any women friends staying overnight at the house because "who knows what you two might do in the way of diddling each other should I leave you alone together."

A father beat his son and threatened to cut off his funds if he did not see a psychiatrist to be cured of his promiscuity, which, according to the father, consisted of his having a platonic relationship with more than one girl at a time. Later in life, when the son became openly gay, the father was so ashamed of him that he regularly spirited him and his lover out of the restaurant where they were having dinner together before any of the father's cronies could arrive and see the son and his lover there together making an obvious couple. He would not let the son bring this partner to a birthday dinner the family wanted to throw for the son; when the son bridled at this, the father simply canceled the party. Another time, with the son and his partner standing right there, someone asked the father,

"What are you going to do today?" "I am going to New York," he replied. "Don't get lost" was the rejoinder. "Don't worry," he said," I have my son who has been there before to show me around," then, referring to the son's partner, in a marginalizing way added, "And a friend of *mine* who had once been to the East End of Long Island." Not surprisingly, the father's message to the son, "I am ashamed of you," soon became the son's very own internal message, "I am ashamed of myself."

A woman's parents punished her for being promiscuous by selling her their house, knowing, but not telling her in advance, that a building project across the way was going to block the ocean view. To rub salt in her wounds, they built a new and better house and gave it to her brother; they also gave him a large business they had built up over the years. Not surprisingly, when their daughter grew up to be a lesbian, she became a self-destructive, self-homophobic, remote woman distant not only from her own family but also from potential and actual gay and straight friends. She felt too undeserving to enjoy the company of good people and too worthless to allow herself to have a great life, especially one that included having a happy gay family.

As a child, a man preferred playing with girls over boys. His father, becoming concerned that he would grow up to be a sissy, abused him personally, calling him "faggot" and the like in order to frighten him into changing. Later in life, when he did become openly gay, the son himself demeaned anything he enjoyed doing that was short of chopping wood and playing ball as "faggots' work." Eventually the son attempted suicide because "I cannot stand being queer."

Although these self-homophobic gay men and women certainly did become self-homophobic through introjecting negative family and social messages, some of their self-homophobia was also innate, however, for historically they had also been bashing themselves long before others bashed them, mistreating themselves before they ever had much chance to be mistreated. To a great extent, such self-gay bashing results from the guilt that all sexuality elicits in everyone, gays, lesbians, and straights alike—a universal negative attitudinal mindset toward having a body and using it that makes all sex into something wicked and sinful, unless the sex is between a man and a woman, in the missionary position, in the dark, and strictly for the purpose of procreating—and sometimes even then.

Not surprisingly, gay bashing by gays and lesbians can be a symptom of an emotional problem. The following examples illustrate this, as well as showing how self- and other-directed homophobia in gays and lesbians tend to go hand in hand.

Homophobic *paranoid* homosexuals are suspicious, jealous individuals who bash other gays and lesbians as a way to condemn them for doing the very things they feel guilty about doing themselves. Guilty about their own sexual wishes, they hold others, including their lovers, to an unreachable standard, for example, defining fidelity as "don't even think about it," then putting their partners down when predictably they cannot meet their expectations, although no one ever could.

Homophobic *depressed* homosexuals, like all depressives, see the world not as a pleasant place in which to live but as an arena for conflict resolution; crime, punishment, and absolution; and perceived or actual trauma occurrence and recurrence. A self-dislike already in place causes, explains, and justifies their treating other gays and lesbians badly, as if they were their own ugly reflections in the mirror, as they attack other gays and lesbians as a way to attack themselves, giving others the black eye they feel that they themselves deserve. They devalue their lovers as they devalue themselves, openly in fights, covertly by cruising with their eyes as a way to say, "That one has what you do not have," or by just not coming home when expected—in one case, for example, not until 3:00 A.M., then excusing the absence by saying, "I was at my mother's, and the time just got away from me and I couldn't call because I left my cell phone in the car." Like all depressives, in their virtually universal interpersonal fault-finding they are cruel and unforgiving. One depressed lesbian devalued every romantic relationship she got involved in because she heard a little voice saying something like, "You can do better, with someone bigger, stronger, richer, and less-queer appearing. After all, this lover of yours smokes constantly and has such a deep voice that you would think you are talking to a man."

Characteristically, depressed homophobic gays and lesbians abuse themselves masochistically by caricaturing themselves by dressing outlandishly. They might indulge in self-deprecating, melancholic, gloomy graveyard humor as their way to say "kick me" to the world. They might seriously mutilate their bodies with various piercings or abusive and dangerous physical sexual practices like inserting a fist anally or drinking urine. Some are masochistic in the way they come out of the closet, which they do not only to be free and open, as they claim, but also to create personal and professional trouble for themselves. Some deliberately engineer their own downfall by baiting others to dislike them. One gay man admitted, "I incite bigotry by acting like a rebellious sadomasochistic adolescent through playing annoying off-putting adolescent games, then claiming that any negative response I get is prejudicial—although I am in fact just acting like the teenagers I know who play loud abrasive music whose main virtue and goal is to distinguish themselves from, and get on the nerves of, their hoi polloi parents." Still others (often those who had a sadistic father or mother whom they tried, unsuccessfully, to convert to become a more ideal, more loving parent) pick and stick with friends and lovers who do not like them much. They say they are doing their best to love someone and to have that someone love them back, but they are really just throwing themselves at the feet of unrepentant, hate-filled people who can never return their love. They pick lovers who are rough so that they can find someone to brutalize them further or lovers who are feminine even if that is not what they actually desire, because, even though they really want a real man, they are deliberately, self-punitively, arranging never to find one.

Homophobic *hypomanic* gays and lesbians self-destruct by cruising frantically for someone new when the old partner they have is good enough or even perfect for them. Their compulsive nonstop barhopping, backrooming, and street cruising are their calculated way to take a harsh toll on their lives by wasting time and passing good, solid relationships by. Professionally, many become restlessly dissatisfied, quietly arranging over time to get themselves fired from their jobs or taking new jobs at the last minute after simply quitting a previous job in a snit, abruptly and without warning, even though the old job was good enough.

Homophobic *dependent* gays and lesbians say they hate other gays and lesbians as part of a plan to pass as straights. They willingly do anything at all to be accepted by heterosexuals.

Homophobic *avoidant* gays and lesbians become remote to hurt themselves and others by keeping to themselves, isolating themselves from others just so that they can remain personally lonely and relationally ungratified. Someone cruises them, and they consciously or unconsciously find themselves thinking about something or someone else in order to deny that the other person is interested. They might retreat after thinking, "He or she is not cruising but staring at me" or "That one must be a hustler to come on so strong to little old me." Or they might subject someone clearly interested in them to ridicule. Many of my gay patients can attest to having had the following experience: when they approach one of two homosexuals who are together but both available, the other one moves in and ridicules the one doing the approaching. Furthermore, these gays and lesbians may self-destruct by abandoning their real family because they do not feel worthy of having such a good thing. If their avoidance is not too severe, they look to make a new family out of one-night stands held over. This can work well, or it can just be unsound practice that leads them to seriously neglect their real family as they fruitlessly try to create a new one from strangers who mean little to them, and vice versa.

Younger avoidant gays and lesbians often miss out when they avoid older gays and lesbians after devaluing them. Instead of relating to them, they make fun of them for being ancient. Instead of developing real friendships with them, they use them. If they have anything at all to do with them, it is for their own selfish purposes, as might happen when a younger, less-established gay man needs the older gay man's apartment to shack up in for the night. They often avoid old people because old people symbolize all the defects they see in themselves now and in the future—with old people conjuring up the loneliness and physical deterioration that younger gays and lesbians fear awaits them just around the corner. Ultimately, for them being old is a wound that lets the first blood that attracts the shark; that is, it inspires the sadistically inclined to move in for the metaphorical kill.

Homophobic gays and lesbians with *dissociative* tendencies have self-defeating fuguelike episodes or attacks of amnesia at moments of interpersonal triumph to assure the iron is struck when cold—their way to condemn the validity of, and so to avoid having, pleasurable relationships.

Homophobic *narcissistic* gays and lesbians miss out when they bash other gays and lesbians for not being just like them. The two messages they send are "I (not you) am the greatest" and "What I know, stand for, and exemplify is the only, best, and one right thing to do and be" (which are familiar from the messages straight homophobes send gays and lesbians). Many such gays and lesbians view other gays and lesbians as much too butch, too femme, too rough, or too elegant compared to themselves, and they talk and act accordingly, as hurtfully toward other gays and lesbians as their straight homophobic counterparts act toward them.

Homophobic narcissistic gays and lesbians often reject other gays and lesbians specifically for the purpose of enhancing their own self-image. One gay man had a friend over regularly except on holidays, when he would invite everyone over but him, just so that he could deliciously contemplate how the friend was alone for Christmas and Easter and how lucky *he* himself was, in comparison, to have a house full of company. Envy, where what you have automatically becomes what I lack, their version of sour grapes, is a reason they put other gays and lesbians down. Selfishness leads them to ask only what other gays and lesbians can do for them and to become resentful of and vengeful toward their own kind, should they feel that these others are not being sufficiently forthcoming. Such gays and lesbians become house guests who do not write thank-you notes or offer return invitations. When the time comes to return a favor, they instead turn their backs. One gay man put up friends every summer but never got a return invitation, even though he asked for one repeatedly. He asked a friend, a travel agent who stayed at his house all summer, for a travel brochure, but his good friend was always too busy to get one for him. Such gays and lesbians send the message to other gays and lesbians that they are not valuable as a whole person. "Yes, you make a good mother when you give on demand, but yes, too, you make an off-putting child when you insist on asking for something in return: to be taken seriously and to be shown the respect and consideration everyone, straights and gays and lesbians alike, wants and deserves."

Homophobic *histrionic* gay men bash lesbians as if lesbians, like all women, are out to emasculate everyone—gays, lesbians, and straights alike. Histrionic lesbians in turn bash gay men because they imagine that they, like all men, possess the masculinity that these lesbians either hate or envy, or both, and would, if they could, passively or actively (forcibly) either avoid or assume. All concerned are highly competitive people who put others down just to be able to see them as have-nots, hence as inferior, at least compared to them, the superior haves of this world.

Homophobic *traumatized* gays and lesbians (those suffering from post-traumatic stress disorder) bash other gays and lesbians as they were once themselves bashed or traumatized. Those who were beaten by their mothers or fathers after being caught in flagrante playing sexual games might symbolically repeat their trauma by tempting fate, say by exposing themselves or masturbating in public places, hoping this time not to be caught and punished, yet at the same time hoping to be caught and punished, just like old times.

Sexual *impotence* is a manifestation of self-homophobia when gays cannot get an erection or lesbians cannot obtain orgasmic pleasure because they brood right through the sexual act about whether or not they are good enough to be entitled to have an orgasm and/or about whether or not sex, and their actual sexual activity, is dirty. They brood until they cannot have that orgasm, which they do not have—just to stay innocent and remain clean.

Many gays and lesbians become self-homophobic after making the same homophobic cognitive errors about themselves that homophobic straights make about them. For example, some gays and lesbians equate homosexuality with a sickness, based on superficial similarities between the two, such as "both are relatively infrequent in the general population." Gays and lesbians in conflict about their homosexuality might do that in order to have a reason to undergo interminable self-punitive reparative psychiatric therapy, based on the belief that since their homosexuality is a sickness and they want to get well, they must take the cure.

CHAPTER 5

Heterophobia (Excessive or False Accusations of Homophobia)

The following discussion applies only to a small proportion of the gay and lesbian population—those gays and lesbians, often ones with an activist bent, who are extremely sensitive to any hint of homophobia or who even look for homophobia because they actually want and need something to feel outraged about.

Just as all homophobes are unnecessarily fearful of and excessively hateful toward gays and lesbians, some gays and lesbians can be unnecessarily fearful of and hateful toward straights. I call this irrational fearfulness of and hatred toward straights by gays and lesbians *heterophobia.* Heterophobic gays and lesbians use many of the same mental mechanisms in developing and expressing their irrational fear and hatred of straights as homophobic straights use in developing and expressing their irrational fear and hatred of gays and lesbians. Like straight homophobes, gay heterophobes range from those who can be corrected through persuasion to those who are virtually delusional about being feared and hated and who go beyond the suspicion that they are disliked to develop a conviction that they are targets of a cabal, on their way to becoming victims of a pogrom.

As is so often the case with straight homophobia, gay heterophobia often originates in personal psychopathology. Irrational, unfair, heterophobic accusations of being homophobic can be *histrionic* in nature when complaints with ounces of truth are so overdramatized that they become pounds of wild new reality. Some heterophobia is the product of *obsessive* perfectionistic thinking originating in the belief that if others are slightly imperfect, that is, not *all* positive toward gays and lesbians, then they are necessarily, by definition, entirely negative toward gays and lesbians, because anything short of accepting gays and lesbians completely means that they at best are siding with the enemy or at worst are the enemy themselves. Still other heterophobia originates in a *hypomanic* across-the-board free-floating irritability; is the product of intense *overanxiousness* with free-floating anxiety lighting on excessive fears about deprivation and loss; or comes from a *sadomasochistic* need to start a good fight even though, or just because, that leads to personal suffering for all concerned—not only me, the victim, but also you, the supposed victimizer.

Not surprisingly, false accusations of homophobia are mainly *paranoid* in nature. Paranoia is operative when gays and lesbians view those who treat them fairly as adversaries and persecutors after projecting their self-hatred so that "I hate me" becomes "You are against me." It also comes about when gays and lesbians create adversarial relationships cognitively, after making whole out of part truths, then creating negative scenarios from neutral or positive situations.

Gays and lesbians who claim homophobia as part of their paranoid worldview think like this:

1. I am under attack/siege.
2. The attack/siege is irrational, for
3. I am being unfairly charged with this and criticized for that, since
4. I have done nothing to deserve this or that, for I am the completely innocent victim who is guilty of and blameworthy for nothing, and it is you who is guilty and to blame for everything. I am not the source of any of my own problems, for all my problems reside outside of me in the doings of others—you. So I am never a problem person; it is the world I live in that is a problematic place.
5. My complaints about and attacks on you are therefore not first but second strikes, so
6. I am justified in defending myself by attacking you, for you attacked me first, and
7. The attacks will not stop until you change your mind about me and alter your negative behavior toward me,
8. And that means saying and doing exactly what I want you to do.

One paranoid gay man was less a manipulative individual than he was a semidelusional person who developed either fragmentary and unelaborated or extensive and elaborate false convictions of system-specific or systemwide persecution. His motivation was not so much external gain as internal (psychological) reasons, which were typically of a defensive nature, that is, his way to deal with his inner anxiety.

One of his delusional beliefs was the pathological fantasy that the world was full of homophobes and that they were all out to provoke, aggravate, hurt, deprive, mistreat, and neglect him. First, he focused on the supposed misdeeds and base actions of only one person, a formerly admired and beloved friend and mentor, who, as he saw it, was formerly a good person "now gone all bad." He responded to this man's mostly imagined provocations with what he believed to be justified rage and the appropriate battle with an enemy who was, to him at least, not merely shadowy or distant but perceptible and close. So he viewed the battles he fought with this man as a justified counterattack against a person (and the system he represented) who was supposedly out to get him for nefarious, malignant reasons of his own. Then, he demanded a degree of protection from this neglect and mistreatment and, by filing a series of complaints to right wrongs, sought vengeance against those who supported his enemy. An always-looming danger was that he would come to feel so strongly and get so angry that he might become violent, with his violence set off by some trivial issues that he readily allowed to become triggers for his subsequent major and full rage reactions.

Eventually his blaming, becoming less focused, spread to become a blaming of the whole world. He began focusing on the misdeeds and base actions of all of society and came to believe that all of society mistreated him. He was not out to obtain some actual gain in the real world. His was an attempt to reduce inner anxiety by defensively relegating that which made him anxious to the category of "not me but the system." He would demand changes be made in the system when what he really needed was to make changes within himself. Thus, "I hate myself for being gay" became "Everyone is prejudiced against me," and the solution became not "I have to treat myself more kindly" but "the world must start treating me better." Clearly, the adversarial relationships this paranoid gay heterophobe developed with the world paralleled and grew out of the adversarial relationship he had with himself, so that his complaints that others were homophobic toward him originated at least in part as self-complaints starting with self-homophobia. He blamed externals to avoid dealing with internals, and instead of taking responsibility for the fearful things inside made society shoulder the full blame for what in fact he himself was mostly responsible for. He would fly into a rage at the world when he should instead have been making the world a better place for himself—by changing how *he* related to the world, which, in turn, ultimately depended on how he related to himself.

He was simultaneously a grandiose individual concerned that a conspiracy consisting of a federation of enemies was dedicated to trying to deprive *him personally* of what he desperately needed, desired, and ought to have right now. His grandiosity was part of his need to claim superiority to others in an attempt at self-healing along the lines of "I am not defective as you see me, but a better person than you believe me to be and than any of you actually are."

Cognitively speaking, this paranoid gay heterophobe developed his persecutory convictions after maximizing the actual but trivial cabals that did in fact exist and were not difficult for him to uncover, as they existed and would be easy to uncover within any system. (It is a fact of life that in almost any given reality some of that reality is going to be imperfect—for example, for impersonal reasons there is always some underfunding in any given system, including in AIDS research.) So his full persecutory beliefs were ultimately created out of mere fragments of what was at bottom a slim reality—by omitting contrary facts that might prove him wrong and rejecting elements of a situation that did not suit his desired interpretation. He would draw specific unflattering conclusions about others without sufficient evidence after cherry-picking one or a few negative details and overvaluing their overall (negative) impact while ignoring other more important and salient positive aspects of an experience, predictably coming to fear and dislike individuals and the whole world completely if and when he found anything about them to dislike at all. Thus, although people treated him well overall, he would only remember, then emphasize, those times when people put him down or did not give him things that he felt he desperately needed, and as rapidly and immediately as he felt he needed to have them.

Ultimately, he got what at first he only feared he might be getting because, allowing his expectations to guide his actions, he would behave in a way that actually created his imperfect reality. Viewing the whole system as guilty until proven innocent, he created true negative situations out of his own self-fulfilling pessimistic guidelines and doomsday prophecies. Once his suspiciousness and pessimism had taken over and come to rule, he could blame the system for being fallen when this very blaming had led him to act in a way that provoked the system's downfall. All told, he made life very difficult even for those who wanted to be kind and helpful to him. He made it hard to be nice to him, for his accusations of being homophobic ultimately became self-fulfilling prophecies in which his paranoid premises that no one cares, that everyone mistreats him, and that everyone is an adversary were seemingly validated by circumstances. But he had just created his own negative facts of life by creating these very adversarial circumstances through antagonizing others. Clearly, if he believed that an individual or group had it in for him, he would have no difficulty whatsoever antagonizing the individual or group until they actually did have it in for him. By changing his perception of reality he ultimately changed his reality itself in a way that seemed to validate the pessimistic and angry primary assumptions about others' homophobia that daily flooded his mind. Now he could claim that his paranoid you-hate-me beliefs were no longer so paranoid but were thoroughly realistic. Although these beliefs were ultimately at least somewhat attuned to reality, it was nonetheless a reality that he, in a vicious cycle, had created in the first place, out of his own flourishing paranoid ideation.

Additionally, he had an angry, mean personality. He was understandably angry *with* the world. But not all of his anger rightfully came *from* the world. Some of it did come from the bad treatment or the neglect that befell him because of his homosexuality. But much of it came from something in his past, in his childhood. He should have been less attuned to where others were coming from and more attuned to where he himself had at one time been. His tendency to color adult events with loaded childhood experiences accounted in great measure for another dynamic: how his paranoid premises remained invalid and untrue because the pessimistic comments he made and the negative things he foretold were of sufficient quantity to be of necessity borne out in impressive numbers by chance alone.

Hard-core gay activists (like all other activists) often fall into the *manipulative* paranoid category; that is, they use such paranoid mechanisms as projection not to relieve their inner anxiety but to influence their outer environment—and they do so in order to create a distortive view of others precisely as part of their plan to get their own way. These individuals create, foster, and thrive on adversarial situations so that they *can* have something to complain about and so have a rationale for making self-serving demands for gratification and reparation on a practical level. They want to hold the world hostage to accusations and threats that they will agree to drop only when the world meets certain demands and comes forth with desired rewards, if then. There is often a litigious quality to their kind of paranoia—they cannot readily sue homophobes in general, but they can do the next best thing and "hold their feet to the fire" to obtain what they consider to be justice, which for them is often an abstract concept meant to obscure a concrete desire—to obtain some practical advantage such as power and control, as well as to get a little emotional satisfaction, vengeance in particular, along the way. These manipulative paranoids know how to make a good case that their complaints of wrongdoing are in fact justified philosophically and morally, so that others should feel guilty, then respond accordingly along predetermined lines. And their thoughts are usually not entirely unjustified. The world actually does contain many irresponsible people who cause innocent gays and lesbians to suffer. That is certainly true. But it is also certainly true that this is one of these manipulative paranoid gay activists' most cherished beliefs and, for them, hopefully most useful social premises.

One typically manipulative paranoid gay activist was an outwardly oriented, publicly demonstrative, vocal, intimidating, haranguing, threatening individual who warned his targets of the potential for doom and disaster if they did not shape up immediately along predetermined lines. He would proselytize on a large scale, in part because, suspecting that his paranoid beliefs were unwarranted or ridiculous, he felt the need to form supportive cliques to help him prove he was right in the face of anticipated or actual individual or systemwide protests to the contrary. He would also proselytize in order to disseminate his beliefs widely so as to get as many people as possible to join his cause for the purpose of giving his adversaries an even blacker eye in the press, thus increasing the likelihood that he could secure those reforms that he believed would do him a good that was both immediate and permanent, although not necessarily fully warranted or entirely deserved.

He was so persuasive in his irrationality that he won many in powerful places over to his unreal view of what was happening to him. He had his ways of throwing people off balance with the sheer force of his convictions and well-rehearsed arguments that challenged elementary principles and put his victims into a kind of logical shock in which they failed to respond rationally and constructively. For example, in a typical unconstructive response, his victims would fire back unthinkingly, "I have the right to hate in this, a free country, and to do so without being branded a bigot" in an attempt to justify their hatred as a personal preference. They might do this along the lines of Barron Laycock "Labradorman," the reviewer of Fone's book *Homophobia* who asserted that gays and lesbians "define any sort of *personal antipathy* [italics added] toward gays and lesbians as constituting de facto evidence of prejudice, disregarding [personal] religious, philosophical, and ethical considerations as just so much smoke screen."[1] Self-justifying, blaming responses like this contain ounces of truth, but they also contain pounds of unreality, and this can amount to nothing less than a counterprovocation, and that tends to inflame negative passions all around.

Not surprisingly, even those in powerful positions were reluctant to defend those whom this man complained about but instead were more likely to bow to the strength of his opposition. So instead of cracking down on this manipulative paranoid gay activist, they went along with him, condemning his victims in chorus, even though they were quite aware that they were allowing incorrect impressions to lead them to false conclusions constituting a cause whose goal was admirable but whose methods were questionable.

Of course, there is a positive side to paranoid activism. Paranoid gays and lesbians can become formidable spokespersons for gay rights and get needed changes made. Only when activists go too far do they become irrational and even dangerous individuals whose considerable negative social influence creates havoc in the system, making it even more difficult for other gays and lesbians to avoid the bad treatment these more manipulative paranoid gays and lesbians are raging against and to get the good treatment that the manipulative paranoid gays and lesbians and their advocates are supposedly lobbying for. For ultimately paranoid activist gays and lesbians can clog the system with too much politics of resentment and rescue, causing the system to become mired in self-defense, so that much of its energy goes into surviving in the face of external forces that are attacking it based on all the false information being provided to those on the outside from the few paranoid heterophobic gays and lesbians on the inside.

Here is what I consider to be an example of false accusations of homophobia, in this case leveled against me, presumably by an activist gay who did not much like a book I wrote and gave it a generally unfavorable review on Amazon.com. I wrote my 1999 book *Treating Emotional Disorder in Gay Men* as a psychiatrist hoping to show that gay men have the same emotional problems as straight men but require a modified form of psychological treatment because of the gay context in which their emotional problems occur—a context that significantly determines and affects the nature, causes, and outcome of their emotional difficulties.[2] The reviewer, who did not seem to get this, my main point—that psychiatrists treating gay men have to be alert to how the gay context of emotional problems can affect diagnosis and treatment—started with a loaded and accusatory subtitle for his review, "Friend or 'Phobe????,"[3] then spent much time analyzing not the book but me. The review started off with a distortion, claiming that I said that "psychotherapists too often fall into two camps with gay male clients: they are either bigoted and only work on 'curing' the homosexuality or they are overly activist and blame all ills on homophobia."[4] He then went on to state, not entirely correctly, "Thus, the author encourages and maps out a therapy which acknowledges that SOME gay men suffer from mental illnesses, regardless of homosexuality or homophobia."[5] It would seem that he at least agrees that this point of view is valid. Unfortunately, soon afterwards he turns personally nasty and begins to attack me as that "'phobe" needing comeuppance. He says that I "feign... objectivity in a postmodern era in which you would think that opinionated writers [I happen to believe that my so-called opinions are in fact thoroughly researched clinically based hypotheses] would not try to hide behind the third-person narrative"[6] (which is, of course, the only one appropriate for a psychiatric text. He probably means that I don't state my sexual orientation). He suggests that my book could "seriously be used as a weapon against gay men,"[7] thus implying that I should alter my clinical means for his strictly political end.

Next, getting even more personal, he muses, "On the one hand, this author may be a straight man laughing all the way to the bank or getting tenure by positing this point"[8] (presumably at the expense of the gay men I supposedly attack). Perhaps he really believes that if I were straight I could not know that much about homosexuals. Or he is simply out to invalidate conclusions he does not like by trivializing my motives as self-serving.

Next, groping blindly, he veers from the possibility that I am deficient because I am straight to the possibility that I am deficient because I am gay—but closeted and refusing to come out. As he says, "On the other hand, though the credits say the author has written a book on homophobia, he never once comes out as a gay man."[9] Is it that only a gay man can know about other gay men, or is it that if I am gay I am being dishonest and possibly a hypocrite in this and so in all areas unless I come out and say so?

He also entertains a third pejorative possibility: "One might get the sense that this is a gay man callous to his community" for he "criticizes leather men and drag queens and sees no political valor in camp."[10] As an example, here is what I actually wrote about drag queens: "There are many reasons to be a drag queen, and many kinds of drag queens.... Although some drag queens are without significant pathology, wearing drag can be a secondary manifestation of a larger syndrome."[11] A fourth negative possibility is that, "If he is a gay man, he is in a long-term, monogamous relationship and can pass for straight and thus dismiss... the rest of us."[12] A fifth negative possibility is that I am not gay, a closeted gay, a haughtily superior gay man, or an out gay in a monogamous relationship and lording it over him and others like him but instead someone who is, whatever my sexual orientation, simply highly unethical. As he says, "The author states that some of his anecdotes were obtained by eavesdropping on other people's conversations. That seems completely unethical to me. I'm surprised his peers haven't said the same to him"—no doubt as the author of the review would wish to do.[13] Of course, many newspaper columns quote random contacts with strangers (that which is overheard has no presumption of confidentiality). I am hardly repeating therapeutic confidences, and if strangers minded my overhearing them, they would have spoken in private or whispered, not yelled, things out to their companions or, if I were writing this today, into their cell phones.

In addition, he asserts that I condemn gay men for avoiding straight therapists, saying that I "dismiss... gay men who would seek treatment from one of their own."[14] Clearly he is suggesting that I believe that gay therapists are inadequate to the task. Here is what I actually said: "A therapist does not have to be gay to treat gay men."[15]

To me this reviewer is a gay man struggling with his own identity and lacking self-respect. He then projects his self-hatred onto me so that "I hate myself" becomes "You hate me and those like me, and that is clearly not because I am defective but because you are deficient." Likely seeing himself in some of my examples of psychopathology he comes to feel put down personally, although clearly my intent was not to criticize gay men but to identify and understand their emotional problems in a gay context as a first step in resolving them. He then deals with the perception that I put him down personally by putting me down in an equally personal way, along the childish lines of "tu quoque," that is, "you call me that, well, you are one too, so there."

It is frightening that his assertions are uncomfortably reminiscent of the ones that paranoid homophobes use to attack gays. Paranoid self-homophobic gays' and lesbians' attacks on others who are not their enemies consist of demeaning accusations originating in projections and proceeding according to emotional reasoning to illogical conclusions. Men like this reviewer likely have negative feelings about themselves already in place. Then they undergo a serious and ultimately self-destructive search for a suitable target to hit, once again proving to me the central tenet of this my book: that, as Freudian psychology tells us, behind every criticism of another is a criticism of the self.

CHAPTER 6

The Negative Effect of Homophobia on Gays and Lesbians

In today's society gays and lesbians live with homophobic individuals on the job, where they suffer professionally, and at home, where they suffer personally. However, not all gays and lesbians react in exactly the same way to the same homophobic provocation. Some deny that they are being mistreated, in spite of serious abuse. In denial they continue to believe that the person abusing them does not mean anything by it or that the society to which the abuser belongs accepts them fully in spite of it all. For example, a gay man who overheard the restaurateur say he "hates all c**ksuckers" excused his words as the ranting of a low-rent ignorant man from the boonies. At first, he did agree to boycott the place. But soon afterwards as I was passing by one day I looked through the restaurant window and saw him, just as if nothing had happened, happily partaking of the alien corn. Gays in denial like him often avoid a serious depression, but they do not thereby avoid the limitations imposed on them by the overall depressing conditions under which they accept living their lives.

Other gays and lesbians recognize that they are being abused but claim that the abuse neither matters nor bothers them much. They just accept the fact that some homophobia will always be present to strike fear into their hearts and that, as a result, they will always have to spend an inordinate amount of time and energy keeping up their guard and lifting up their spirits. They recognize that it is a given that on the whole gays and lesbians will never feel entirely affirmed, supported, and loved by everybody and in many situations will, to some extent, always feel like outsiders. They long ago reduced their expectations so that they no longer anticipate much from anyone and so do not feel seriously disappointed by anybody. What they have done is integrated subtle oppression as part of their daily lives and accepted it in the form of the fish eye from the garbage man, the silent treatment from the neighbor, the gas station attendants who fill their cars but do not wash their windows as they do everyone else's, the crossing guard who lets the cars keep going when gays and lesbians are crossing, and the police who come when called but, annoyed at being bothered by a bunch of sissies and dykes, predictably take the straights' side no matter what the evidence and do nothing for gays and lesbians no matter what crimes others have committed against them. They have accepted that the society they live in, being a collection of civilized animals, will always have a pecking order and that some in society will always consider gays and lesbians to be near or at the bottom of the caste system—second- or third-class citizens whom others might find acceptable under certain circumstances but only so long as gays do not aggressively attempt to challenge straights and try to put them down should they try to pass them on the way up.

A patient claimed that he stopped being a gay activist because he felt that he was at risk for becoming far too aggressive for his own good. He said that he learned that what worked best for him was accepting the world as it was and just getting on with his professional and personal life. "You can't expect everyone to like you," he said, claiming that since he could not change the world, he might as well live in it as it was and work with and around it. He even accepted that not being able to change things would cause him to feel even more like a failure. Not only did he accept that he, like all gays and lesbians, would never get the same love and approval that so often come easily and automatically to straights and that his gay life would in some ways always be harsher than the straight life, he resigned himself to the thought that the sooner he accepted these things, the more quickly he could adjust to the inevitable and take steps to minimize its effects, instead of becoming depressed about his fate each day, as if he learned about it anew each morning.

Other gays and lesbians recognize that they are being abused but are unable to accept or rationalize that. Instead, they feel traumatized and get depressed. They feel depressed because they believe that they are being treated like second-class citizens both at home and at work, never really allowed to fit in, still more rarely allowed to get ahead, and always without the means to fight back. A gay man felt this way when his boss told him that he was wasting time from 8:00 A.M. to 8:30 A.M. having coffee when he should have been working—though she herself, on the same time clock, did not come into work until 11:00 A.M.

Though he happens to be straight, Thomas Couser, in an article about the depressing effects of homophobia on gays and lesbians, describes how he felt (specifically, depressed) when someone, thinking he was gay,

> defaced his car by writing "fag" all over it.... the possibility that I was being watched made me feel paranoid. Is this, I thought, a taste of what it's like to be

> homosexual in America—to fear random harassment by utter strangers? In the space of those few moments I began to appreciate that to be openly gay takes considerable courage...how vulnerable I...felt. For several days I experienced shock and fear—fear that the incident might be repeated or that the violence would escalate. I felt violated, and I was angered by my inability to retaliate....I felt as though I had been conspicuously branded....gender stereotypes and homophobia diminish and dehumanize us all.[1]

Some gays and lesbians are able to live with the resulting depression. They accept it as the wages, cost, or side effect of being homosexual—as part of the homosexual condition, which, as they see it, is, by definition, associated with an inevitable punishment quota. They at least try not to let their depression affect them, or, if they do let it affect them, they more or less successfully fight it with psychotherapy, antidepressants, or the hypomanic denial of sexual hyperactivity and even promiscuity.

Just as often, however, the depression eats away at them. It erodes their self-confidence and lowers their self-esteem, often to the point that they come to blame their sad fate not on the unfair treatment they receive but on themselves. On the job, siding with their oppressors, they criticize their own work performance, although it is their performance in bed that others are really criticizing. They try activism as a release and an instrument for change, only to discover that they are compounding the error by making protest too much a way of life, for, by focusing overly on protesting, they fail to fully attend to their individual creativity and generativity and, at the same time, incur even more enmity than they can handle from those they are protesting against. Others continue to do their work yet have trouble functioning creatively. Some even try suicide, indirectly by having unsafe, unprotected sex or directly by slashing their wrists or hanging themselves by the neck until they are dead.

It should not surprise that many of the homophobes I treated were in their turn active depressogenics, that is, men and women who seemed to want, and knew exactly how, to produce the depressing negative effects they intended in their victims. They seemed to know instinctively how to make gays and lesbians anxious and afraid. They knew that people were most afraid when the enemy is unseen, the attack unpredictable, and the attacker elusive and difficult to apprehend and/or attack back. So they lurked in the shadows, hit when least expected, ran too fast to be caught, then, after waiting a while between attacks so that their victims developed a false sense of security that they could shatter once again, now even more effectively, hit with a new attack, also when least expected.

Such depressogenics seem to know instinctively when gays and lesbians need affirmation, support, and love and when, where, and how to withhold these. They will not let gays and lesbians march as identified groups in their parades, saying that they object to homosexuality on religious and moral grounds, while leaving out how they very well know that less pride can grow where there is less recognition. They know that the best way to get at gays and lesbians is to put them down, and they know that one good way to do that is to criticize them when they are bad while never complimenting them when they are good. They know how to demoralize them in a way that results in their feeling ashamed of themselves. If gays and lesbians try gay pride to compensate for feeling low or depressed, homophobes counter by telling them, "Hide your face, God is looking down and condemning you, for, quoting Leviticus, you are an abomination, to be vomited up by the land." Or they tell them to be ashamed of what their being gay did and still does to their parents, they warn them that their homosexuality threatens the integrity of their society, and they suggest that gays and lesbians alone are the reason for the lack of peace in the world and might even cause the world to erupt in flames that would consume us all, if they continue on their chosen, very sinful, and highly inflammatory path.

In particular, homophobes like to frustrate gays and lesbians. One gay man said to me that the worst experience of his life was being repeatedly called a faggot by a child he could not identify because he or she was dressed head to toe in a Halloween costume. And they equally like to make gays and lesbians feel unloved, unwanted, and all alone. Some police used to raid gay bars not merely to enforce the laws, but also to search and destroy gays' and lesbians' comfortable retreats, as they deliberately set out to deprive them of their home away from home by disrupting one of the few public places where they can potentially comfortably congregate with their own kind.

Many become past masters at the art of passive-aggressively provoking gays and lesbians so that they can justify bashing them as intended all along. For example, in the army, straights ostracize gays and lesbians. Some gays and lesbians then get depressed to the point that they can no longer function effectively. Then the homophobes can justifiably say that all gays and lesbians are unable to function up to par, which is all the proof they need that gays and lesbians cannot now and will never make effective soldiers. As passive-aggressives they act out in subtle ways, by making certain that gays and lesbians cannot get what they need, are deprived of what they legitimately desire, or lose what they already have. A straight woman left her job with a gay boss, telling him that she was leaving on the very day he planned to start his vacation so that he had no opportunity to hire her replacement. She left her job this way because she "wanted to ruin his vacation." Throughout his vacation she deliciously contemplated how her resignation was festering in his mind while he was trying to have fun. She was paying him back for being "one of those queers I hate, who don't deserve any better." He wondered whether he had mishandled her as an employee and asked himself how he could have been a better boss. But he was suffering unnecessarily. He could have reassured himself that she did not see him as a defective boss.

He could have rested comfortably knowing that she "merely saw him as a defective person."

In one case a gay man tolerated his neighbor's dog barking for an hour. It was bothering him and making his own dog bark. When he finally could not stand it any longer, he asked the neighbor to stop the dog from barking, whereupon the neighbor told him, "Not for a faggot." So the gay man called the police. But when the police arrived, the neighbor's dog had stopped barking. Alas, now the gay man's dog, having been sorely provoked by all the goings-on, was barking merrily away. The police knew that the neighbor's dog was a problem barker, for they had received many complaints about this dog in the past. But all they said to the gay man was "I only hear your dog barking, not his"—that is, "I will take the straight man's side any time over yours." This is an example of what is usually dismissed as small-town justice, but it should really not be dismissed out of hand but instead entered in the log books under the heading of small-town passive-aggressive bigotry.

Two gay men complained to the code enforcement agency in their town that the street on which they lived was going downhill. The code enforcement inspector's loyalties, however, were to straights, no matter how much they were destroying the neighborhood. So in true passive-aggressive withholding fashion, the code enforcement agent made an excuse for every one of the straights' actions, however improper or illegal. For example, when the gay men complained about an illegal apartment in the rental units across the street, the inspector defended the owner by falsely claiming that it was contiguous to the next apartment and so not an illegal separate at all. When the gay men complained that the garages in the same house were rented out for commercial use in a residential neighborhood, with loading and unloading of trucks going on all day, their complaint was met with the excuse that it was not illegal to store even heavy equipment and industrial goods in a garage even though the garage was in a residential neighborhood. When the gay men complained that another house next door had installed an ugly jerry-built swing set in the front yard, their complaint was met with beside-the-point sophistry, that is, that that ugly thing had to be installed in the front yard because the back yard was too small for it. And when the gay men complained that the gas station next door was not a gas station but a junkyard piled high with scrap, their complaint was met with "he is doing construction now, and I cannot distinguish construction materials from scrap," although in fact there should have been little difficulty distinguishing spare tires and car seats from four-by-four wooden beams and wallboard.

Most devastating of all is that depressogenic homophobes know full well how to undermine any self-defense gays and lesbians might mount against these attacks. When gays and lesbians complain that they are being treated prejudicially, these homophobes counter that they are paranoid; when gays and lesbians complain that they are being discriminated against, these homophobes counter that their negative response to them is not a discriminatory but an appropriate one; and when gays and lesbians complain about homophobes' saying hateful things to them, they threaten them with a lawsuit for defamation of character. They also know how to get authority on their side. This support is always easy to find, since there are plenty of religious leaders, educators, and even therapists out there who are all too willing to provide homophobes with the intellectual and emotional buttressing they need, want, and cherish and otherwise give them all the imprimatur that they desire to most effectively proceed with all their homohating business as usual.

PART II

Cause

CHAPTER 7

Developmental and Psychodynamic Considerations

In significant ways, homophobia is a symptom of an emotional disorder just as paranoid delusions, phobias, or obsessions are. That does not mean that all homophobes suffer from an actual mental illness. Almost everyone has some emotional symptoms, such as a degree of anxiety, a few phobias, and occasional spells of depression. It does mean that developmentally, dynamically, and structurally homophobic ideas and behaviors, especially when they extend deeply into the individual psyche, closely parallel or exactly match the symptomatic constructs that make up verified *DSM-IV* emotional disorders.

Clearly, before we can diagnose emotional disorder, before we can call a homophobe mentally ill, we have to measure the severity of the problem and do so in context. That determination involves deciding whether or not the individual's feelings and behavior differ significantly from the feelings and behavior of others around him, that is, from the homophobic individual's peers, so that we can discover the extent to which the homophobia is determined, facilitated, and condoned socially and as such represents not individual psychopathology but instead so-called good social adjustment. Of course, the mere presence of social influence and validation does not preclude the presence of individual psychopathology. Individuals can still be personally troubled even though they are just one bird of a feather. Therefore, the antithesis to the homophobia of such individuals involves not only social change via activism but also individual change through therapy. Generally speaking, since homophobia has roots in individual as well as in social psychology, the best ways to effectively combat homophobia usually include both altering the social landscape in which the individual's homophobia flares and flourishes and therapy directed to the homophobic person.

EARLY DEVELOPMENTAL CONSIDERATIONS

Adult gay bashing often starts in childhood. It can begin with sibling rivalry that carries over into adulthood in the form of infantile name-calling, as homophobes fight with gays and lesbians today as they fought with their brothers and sisters yesterday, still cursing each other out by calling each other the likes of "faggot" or "dyke" just as they did when they were kids.

If we look at the developmental history of the people whom some gays and lesbians (referring to control freaks) might still call control queens—individuals who subscribe to the myth that gays and lesbians could simply decide to stop being homosexual if only they would listen—we often find that the parents of these latter-day control freaks disciplined them when they were young by simply demanding that they "cut it out," with no explanation given. Such a parent might, for example, have said, "Just say 'no' to touching yourself down there," issuing that order without making any attempt to help the child follow it by explaining the reasons for its issuance or to advise and support the child struggling against surging passion in attempting mastery for the sake of his or her parents. Furthermore, these parents too readily stuck their noses into the personal lives of their children, especially into matters that did not concern them. Such parents often went into places where they did not belong, intruded themselves into situations that were none of their business, and spoke without having been first spoken to or invited in, offering their opinions without actually having been asked for them. Children with this background often grow up to become adults who get into power struggles with gays and lesbians so that they can dominate and control them just as their parents dominated and controlled them when they were themselves children growing up. They expect gays and lesbians to be submissive and to do, and not do, what they are told, "because I say so," and unquestioningly, because their parents expected the same thing of them when they were young. Much of their present-day gay bashing is a convenient rod on which to drape the curtain of a preachy parental "listen to me." Such homophobes often go on a tear against gay marriage and do so without letup as their way to control gays and lesbians by conditioning them through negative reinforcement, that is, not through reward but via punishment, not by encouraging them but by discouraging them, and never by supporting them but always by humiliating them into submission, with threats not promises, with sticks not carrots.

In general, such homophobes have identified with abusive homophobic parents who created a homophobic child directly in their own image.

Children typically identify with their parents out of both a fear of defying them and a wish to maintain a loving relationship with them. In addition, boys act like their fathers and girls like their mothers as part of their resolution of oedipal conflict—that is, they identify with the parent of the same sex as their way to tell them, "I wish to be like you daddy or mommy" in order to say, "I love you too much to compete with you as a rival or otherwise do you harm." Male children seem at particular risk for becoming gay bashers when they identify with a homophobic father who additionally was dominant, controlling, scrupulously religious, and resolutely nuclear-family-oriented, at least on the surface, and who also condemned the child's early manifestations of sexuality, checking for budding sexual activity and then punishing the child harshly for touching himself down there, creating specific masturbatory guilt that later becomes general sexual guilt.

Adult gay bashers also often describe having had mothers and fathers who attempted to desex them when they were children in order to keep them at home indefinitely. They often describe parental attempts at seduction that elicited a child's feelings of revulsion about all sexuality, creating an adult who grew up feeling that sex is at best an embarrassment and at worst a dirty thing. This was the background of a son whose father gave him the creeps by constantly waking him up all night long to kiss his forehead to take his temperature to make certain that he was not getting a febrile illness and whose mother seriously embarrassed him by giving him enemas and bathing him well past puberty, in spite of his heartfelt requests and firm protests that she stop doing so immediately.

Many of today's homophobes were once unhappy children who felt rejected and excluded from their homes either because they had many brothers and sisters to compete with or because their fathers and mothers simply ignored everyone, not only them, but also their siblings. Such early-rejected homophobes often gay bash in a way that is inherently harshly rejecting; that is, they insist that gays and lesbians be excluded from the army, religious groups, jobs, or doing psychoanalysis, excluding gays and lesbians now just as they themselves once felt excluded in the past by their parents. Now they verbally, and even physically, exclude gays and lesbians as they themselves were once thrust aside—for being a lowly child, a big nobody, too small to be taken seriously, and too insignificant and unimportant to count in any, let alone in all, ways.

One of my homophobic patients had a particularly unhappy home life. He had a controlling, critical, homophobic, gay-bashing father and a distant alcoholic mother. As a child he dealt with his unhappiness by making animals feel what he felt. He burned caterpillars to see them squirm and smashed eggs from the nests birds built around his house so that he could in effect evict the babies from their homes. When this homophobe saw four gay men eating dinner together in a restaurant, he thought, "The different men with a little stretch of my imagination could be mother, father, and their children, brother, and sister." He then became upset because they looked so happy together. That started him on a rampage of condemning gay marriage along the mythic lines of "it will destroy society as we know it." He thought, "That's disgusting, a perversion of the natural order of things, a travesty on humanity, with gays and lesbians who get married no different from circus chimps dressed up as babies and playing house." He was clearly condemning gay marriage as his way to deal with his own unhappy loneliness. He wanted to make gays and lesbians squirm, and he wanted to foul their nests, if only in his thoughts, to get back at them and at the world, for how he felt deprived of a happy home when he was a child.

Children of parents who are less homophobic in specific than they are cruel in general are more likely to develop not only into homophobes but also into total bigots. These total bigots target gays and lesbians but also Jews, blacks, women, and foreigners, especially illegal aliens. Hating people of all sorts as their parents hated them, they put everyone down as their parents put them down; humiliate everyone as their parents humiliated them; and abuse everyone verbally, as well as emotionally and physically, just as they were once themselves abused, often simply because they were there and in the line of fire.

Conversely and paradoxically, adult gay bashing can sometimes start with a counteridentification with kind, nonhomophobic parents along the lines of "all kids hate their parents no matter how good they were to them." For example, one homophobe bashed gays and lesbians verbally not because she had mean parents and turned out to be like them but because she had kind parents and had always wanted to be as much unlike them as possible, especially now that she had entered into a state of (ongoing and enduring) adolescent rebellion.

Gays and lesbians can catalyze homophobia when they unwittingly remind homophobes of their own disliked parents. Typically, these homophobes call gay men queens because they remind them of a wuss of a father whom they believed to be less than a real man. Or they call lesbians lezzies or bull dykes because they remind them of an aggressive, imperious, unloving mother.

STRUCTURAL AND DYNAMIC CONSIDERATIONS (ANXIETY AND CONFLICT)

Structurally and dynamically, much (though not all) of what we call homophobia replicates the structure and dynamics of familiar psychological symptoms. That is because homophobic symptoms are the product of anxiety due to conflict, as well as of the defense mechanisms employed to deal with the anxiety and reduce the conflict.

Anxiety is a signal to the ego, or self, that an unacceptable drive, or instinct, which may be of a sexual or aggressive nature, is pressing for conscious representation and discharge, thus threatening to come into conflict with a stern, unforgiving conscience that is likely to respond by creating an uncomfortable sense of guilt. This signal anxiety then arouses the ego to take defensive action against the internal threatening pressures welling up from below, from the id, that is, from the drives or instincts.

The stern, guilty, unforgiving conscience itself typically originates in messages from homophobic (sexophobic) parents, from homophobic (sexophobic) society at large, and even from an individual's own instincts, as the energy from the instincts is diverted from being discharged and is instead turned around toward, and against, the self. With regard to how homophobic (sexophobic) parents contribute to the creation of the homophobe's stern, guilty, unforgiving conscience, the child who is condemned and punished for manifestations of infantile homosexuality is highly likely to become overly guilty about and erotophobic toward his or her adult heterosexual and homosexual wishes. Just such a patient reported that a librarian was looking on while he was checking out a CD of the Donizetti opera *Lucia di Lammermoor.* A colleague of this librarian joked, looking at the image of Lucia on the CD's cover and then at her colleague, "You look just like her." Lucia, according to the patient, was depicted on the album cover as young, attractive, and sexy. The librarian appeared to become very tense. She did not reply, "Thanks for comparing me to this beautiful person, I am glad to know I look like her." Instead, she said, "I should hope I don't look like her too much, for she is too sexy, if not for her own good, then for the good of the people checking out CDs in our library."

With regard to how society contributes to homophobes' unforgiving conscience, homophobes regularly buy into the homophobic party line they hear in school and in church and read in the media. Ernest Jones explains how an analogy of Nietzsche's illustrates how an unforgiving conscience can arise from one's instincts being vengefully turned back on the self. In his analogy Nietzsche describes the actions of the caged lion who "in the hands of the tamer…beats itself against the bars of its cage [and so] create[s] out of its own self [a] torture chamber" and then, as Nietzsche goes on to say, becomes that "fool…who invented the 'bad conscience.'"[1]

As suggested throughout, homophobes regularly turn their unforgiving bad consciences not only on themselves but also on others whom they go on to repress and bash in much the same way they repress and bash themselves. They turn on others in order to help reduce their own guilt, as they reassure themselves, "I do not have sexual feelings, and to prove it I exclude, punish, and even long to exterminate those who do, especially those whose sexual feelings are homosexual." This form of gay bashing often evolves into pseudoidealism; that is, "I am not bashing you (for wanting to get married), just stating where I am coming from (what I think marriage ought to be), not criticizing you but simply expressing a simple belief as to what I think is ideally moral, traditional, biblically correct, and widely sanctioned."

In addition to anxiety arising out of the conflict between desire and guilt (between instincts and conscience, or id and superego), anxiety also arises from feeling flooded by internal powerful, seemingly uncontrollable and uncontainable, sexual and angry feelings that come too fast and furious to be fully and comfortably integrated. In this case, homophobia represents a way to stem the flood once and for all by shutting the lid on one's inner Pandora's box.

Anxiety (or fear) can also arise from potential or actual unpleasant reality. Homophobes often fear the potential or actual psychological and real losses that might occur if they acted on their impulses—the loss of self-admiration, the loss of masculine identity, and, should they be discovered having gay sex or even gay fantasies, the loss of their friends and family as well as of their livelihood. Homophobes who fear being put down, emasculated, or metaphorically castrated often use their homophobia to protest in a masculine way against any possible hint of feminine taint, and homophobes who fear losing friends, family, and their job if anyone even suspected they were gay often bash gays and lesbians in order to throw their friends and family off the scent.

Furthermore, anxiety can have a biological basis relating to perceived territorial threats to one's basic survival. Some homophobes go on to fight gays and lesbians for power just as the birds in the following analogy seem to be fighting each other for position: There were two seagulls sitting on a street light. Let's call them #1 and #2. A third seagull, #3, flew over and pushed #1 off its perch, whereupon #1 flew over and pushed #2 off its perch and #2 flew away; whereupon #3 flew over and pushed #1 off its new perch, and #1 flew away. There was #3, I thought, master of the street light, like some homophobes I treated, at the top but out there not only all alone but also with very little to show for its efforts.

Anxiety in turn results in defensive actions, which, as is usually the case with defense mechanisms, ultimately create more problems than they solve. These defense mechanisms can be either first- or second-line (auxiliary, secondary, or supplementary) defenses. The defense mechanisms (as well as the conflict and anxiety behind them) generally remain visible and discernible in the resultant homophobic product. To illustrate, a gay man asked a neighbor of his, a patient of mine, to curb his dog, to which the neighbor responded by saying, "Faggot, go back to New York where you came from, with all the rest of the queers." In denigrating the gay man and the big city the man came from as a place full of sin, he was proclaiming his own innocence and reducing his own guilt, while simultaneously getting vicarious pleasure by putting the gay man up to doing something he himself secretly wanted but felt unable to do. Another patient developed the obsessive fear that he would prick his finger on a metal spur on a shopping cart in a Greenwich Village supermarket and inject himself with HIV. He was at one and the same time expressing his wish to be penetrated by homosexuals (his fear of, so to speak, being pricked), his anticipation of punishment for his guilty wishes, and his defense, in the form of his subsequent avoidance of supermarkets in areas of town known to harbor homosexuals. As such, his symptom was structurally akin to the erythrophobia (fear of blushing) of another patient, who could not go out in public because she feared that she would blush and reveal her guilty sexual thoughts, a fear that really referred to and covered her guilty wish to turn red "so that they can all see how hot I am." The first patient's ultimate move out of the West Village in New York City to get away from all the queers, a truly literally homo-phobic act, was an avoidant defense that in many ways paralleled the defensive avoidance of (other) phobics who stay away from something because it has come to symbolize what they really fear. He was acting much like other phobics, such as bridge phobics who avoid driving over a bridge (avowing that "bridges do sometimes fall"—the rough equivalent of "queers do sometimes give you AIDS") because they have made the bridge and driving one's "phallic car" over and though its arch, into a symbol of something they personally both desire and fear—a symbolic condensation of the story of forbidden sexual soaring leading ultimately to even more forbidden and guilt-inducing physical sexual bodily contact and ultimately penetration.

A First-Line Defense

Denial and Suppression or Repression of Unacceptable Homosexual and Aggressive Wishes

An example of this defense is a politician's flat-out and highly laughable assertion that even though he was caught trying to pick up a cop in a men's room, he was nevertheless not gay, subject closed. Suppression and denial of their own homosexual tendencies divert homophobes from their homosexual and aggressive leanings and promote a feeling of intactness by convincing the homophobe that "I have no such, or am above those, personal defects." These defenses also help the homophobe distinguish the self from the hated other, along the lines of "this is clearly what I am not, and clearly what I do not do, and here is what I will say and do to prove that I mean it."

Suppression and denial often take the form of:

- The pot calling the kettle black, that is, condemning others' immorality while overlooking one's own;
- Excusing actual homosexual experiences as temporary aberrations of the moment, for example, as due to the excessive use of alcohol or as part of normal male bonding; and

- Claiming exonerating consensus, as in "all old marines talk that way" or "it's in the culture, and my rap lyrics just reflect that."

Second-Line Defenses

Projection

When denial and suppression or repression fail, projection is commonly brought into play as an *auxiliary or secondary defense.* In a typical example of projection, the politician caught in the men's room might introduce anti-gay legislation to stifle others' homosexual behavior as a way to master his own desire and thwart his own guilt, along the lines of "look, world, I am not gay," proving to himself by proving to others how bitterly he hates homosexuality and is among the very first to condemn it.

As emphasized throughout and as is generally accepted, much but not all of today's homophobia involves such a projection. The projection in question is both a projection of forbidden guilty sexuality, so that "you," not "I," become the sinner, and a projection of forbidden guilty aggressivity, so that "you," not "I," become the dangerous attacking one—out to assault me sexually, rape my children, destroy the institution of marriage, and dissolve the fabric of society.

Homophobes commonly also use the following second-line, supplementary defenses to reduce anxiety and resolve inner conflict.

Rationalization

Rationalization supports the projective solution both by softening it to make it more socially acceptable and by strengthening it to justify its very existence. Homophobes typically rationalize their gay bashing by claiming that their homophobia is a sign of emotional health, not of mental illness, because everyone feels this way and therefore gay bashing must be acceptable, since even our new pope thinks it is a great idea and was, at least until recently, actually and actively recommending doing that very thing.

Reaction Formation

In this, homophobes protest about how straight they are in order to hide the reverse tendency.

Sublimation

Positive sublimation transforms "I hate you" into "I want to help you," that is, "I don't hate you or want to condemn you. I want to help you live the life of a happy, fulfilled straight person, for, believe me, I only have your best interests at heart."

Undoing

Some homophobes who feel guilty about being homophobic take their homophobia back, making it, for them at least, okay to be homophobic as long as they feel bad about it and/or do something to countermand it, such as offering apologies that seem sincere, advancing regrets that appear to go deep, or doing self-destructive things to themselves in penance and to atone. In some cases the homophobia is itself a form of self-flagellation, as guilty homophobes torture themselves for being homophobic with pictures of sexual evil and gays and lesbians burning in hell. Alternatively, some homophobes actually harm themselves. Their tongue slips, and they say something that ruins them politically. Or they commit bias crimes whose real intent is to get them caught and punished, as when teenagers recklessly yell antigay epithets out of their car windows at passing gay men, knowing, at least subliminally, that the police are cruising in a marked patrol car right behind. Or they self-punitively arrange to have their homohating create just the opposite effect, so that a man sets out to avoid queers by joining the army only to find out that, as he secretly desired but is also horrified to discover, he is closer to young, sexually active men than he has ever been before. Or he sets out to cleanse the world of homosexuals only to find that this activity actually increases his contact with them, thus creating the frightening possibility that a relationship might form.

Phobic Avoidance

As just mentioned, homophobes who use phobic avoidant (removal) defenses handle their own feared homosexual longings by steering clear of people and things that appear to represent these. This was the case for the patient who had so much trouble walking near gay bars that he found himself going further and further out of his way to avoid them.

Phobic defenses can actually lead to gay bashing. For example, homophobes may beat up and even kill gays and lesbians as their way to defend themselves against their own homosexual ideation—by destroying its presumed source—as the unlucky homosexual too soon discovers, should he pick up a stranger in a bar or hitchhiking and take him home for sex, only to be assaulted at times before and perhaps more often afterwards.

OTHER ASPECTS

The above discussion is not meant to minimize how homophobia can be a conditioned response or consciously learned. As I will discuss further in chapter 12, homophobia often represents an associative link with what the homophobe at least believes to have been negative prior experiences with gays and lesbians. Homophobes have also learned and absorbed their society's mythic homophobic tenets, often without questioning them. Mass homophobia, which often has a politico-religious cast, can also be the result of kindling in which an emotion spreads from a peer or a leader to infect an entire group, creating that general panic often referred to as group hysteria.

SPECIAL SITUATIONS

The Psychodynamics of Mythmaking

Homophobes create fanciful, imaginative, and mostly negative myths about gays and lesbians that they then accept as a fact that proves a prior point and advances a homophobic agenda already in place. These myths are simple fantasies turned into realities and spread for the purposes of converting impressionable, suggestible individuals to the view that all gays and lesbians are evil, in order to arouse homohating group hysteria in the form of general panic characterized by a widespread suspension of reality in which antigay sentiments prevail, take hold, and metastasize to become an almost psychotic-like social contagion.

These homophobic myths are structurally and dynamically very much like symptoms of an emotional disorder. For one thing, myths, like symptoms, are the product of the unconscious mind in two ways. First, many mythmakers are unaware that they are mythmaking. Instead they think that even their most irrational myths are true, although they are as false as delusions and as irrational as phobias. They hold these ideas just as tenaciously, and reiterate them just as compulsively, as if they were delusions. This unconscious, or unaware, aspect of mythmaking helps explain why conscious argument rarely dissuades homophobes from their myths and so why the stupidest myths can exist in the most intelligent people.

Second, much of what is mythological, though seemingly consciously crafted, originates structurally in the unconscious mind of the mythmaker. That is, it originates in unconscious fantasies about gays and lesbians and reflects the operation of defense mechanisms, especially the defense mechanism of projection, the familiar "I deny I am bad by condemning you for being evil along similar lines." As is true of all products of projection, myths reveal more about the mythmaker than they do about the subject of the myth. For example, the myth that all gays and lesbians are fey theatrical people who want to be movie stars and live on an old movie set, barely in contact with the real world, or in lofts in Chelsea in New York City, surrounded by cats or strange-looking dogs, watching old Judy

Garland movies, and longing nostalgically for a wonderful past to avoid a depressing present and an even more distressing future, partly originates (as a wish fulfillment) in unconscious escapist fantasy lived out on the stages of gays' and lesbians' lives. Similarly, the myth that all gays and lesbians show an appalling lack of self-control, are all impulsive and excessively pleasure-oriented, and are predictably unable to postpone pleasure seeking even when doing so would be life-saving originates in part in unconscious desires and fantasies of personal liberation. The myth that all homosexuals are promiscuous and that gay relationships never last or, if they do, are never monogamous originates in part in unconscious erotic fantasy, revealing a forbidden wish to be whorish (for those who are unattached) or to be unfaithful to a partner (for those who are attached). The myth that all gays and lesbians stink, for example, are stinking buttheads, reveals the mythmaker's own obsessive-compulsive fixation on anality, with the homophobe, like other obsessive-compulsives, first dreaming of anal penetration, then reacting in disgust to what he considers to be dirty sexual desires. The myth that all gays and lesbians recruit in the shower room simultaneously denies and reveals an active wish to be recruited, turning the active and unacceptable "I want to rape you" into the passive and (paradoxically) more acceptable "All gays and lesbians are out to rape me."

For another thing, myths are specific defensive constructs installed, as with all defensive constructs, in order to reduce personal anxiety (what is technically referred to as the "primary gain of the symptom"). The myth that all gays and lesbians are sinners reduces the straight homophobe's anxiety about being a sinner himself by defining sin narrowly, that is, homosexually and so as "not me." Holding the myth that gays and lesbians cannot be soldiers is a hopeful way for homophobes in the military to reduce their contact with gays and lesbians in order to keep from getting close enough to them to feel threatened by them and so by their own homosexual longings.

Myths also serve the defensive function of increasing self-esteem. Homophobic myths give homophobes smug self-satisfaction by making them feel more manly or womanly, as well as more perfect than, more moral than, and holier or closer to God than someone else. As Herek put it in 1986, "Homophobia serves the psychological function of expressing who one is not (i.e., homosexual) and thereby [satisfyingly] affirming who one is (heterosexual)."[2]

In their more conscious aspect, myths are often intended to make an interpersonal statement geared to a practical purpose, such as elevating one's social status. Homophobes make myths that are hurtful to gays and lesbians, maiming significant competitors in the race that is life, so that their equally homophobic friends and neighbors will admire them and so that they can, as a result, become stronger and more competitive, further enhancing their illusion of superiority and in reality helping them come out ahead both economically and personally. (Technically this is referred to as the "secondary gain of the symptom.") If gays and lesbians are perceived as defective, then conveniently straights will get all the promotions and can more efficiently live out a desire to be superior and to enslave others, now not merely in fantasy but in reality as well.

Myths also give vent to hostile sadistic fantasies. For example, the myth that gays and lesbians are child abusers persists because it serves well the purpose of expressing as much homohatred as possible. Child abuse and incest are two of the worst accusations anyone can think of to hurl at gays and lesbians or anyone else. (In fact, most gays and lesbians, like most straights, prefer adults to children. They may like adults who look like children, but statistically they rarely actually go after children themselves. Many even dislike children because children in their helplessness remind them of how they themselves were once, and currently still feel, weak, passive, and dependent. In addition, disliking children reassures them that they are doing all they can to be adults and, as such, people who can take care of themselves.)

Structurally, myths are very similar to familiar symptoms such as obsessions. For example, the myth that homosexuality is a choice and that homosexuals could control themselves if only they would ("you brought AIDS on yourself and could have avoided it if you had behaved better"—an idea that leaves little room for constitutional hormonal sexual drive so strong that it is predictably accompanied by human fallibility, making sexual desire an irresistible force that regularly meets an all-too-moveable object) is reminiscent of the classic obsessive-compulsive's reliance on being in full control as a way to solve all problems, thus "If I do this or don't do that, then this will or won't happen," for example, "If I don't step on a crack then I won't break my mother's back." The fantastical exhortation that "You can control your sexuality simply by taking a cold shower, or doing the equivalent of 100 genuflections a day for 10 years in penance" is reminiscent of obsessive magical no-touching rituals to avoid contamination, as well as hand-washing rituals to atone for presumably dirty past sexual acts and current damnable dirty sexual desires.

Homophobes' most familiar myths include:

- Homosexuality is a choice.
- Abstinence is possible, desirable, and virtuous.
- Gay sex will make you and others physically and emotionally sick.
- Homosexuality is an illness.
- Heterosexuality is normal, whereas homosexuality is abnormal.
- All gays and lesbians have only sex on the brain.
- All homosexuals are promiscuous.
- All gays and lesbians are drunkards and druggies.

- All gays and lesbians are ashamed of being gay.
- All gays and lesbians are personally and professionally self-destructive.
- All gays and lesbians are miserable creatures; being gay is fun for a while, especially when you are young, but basically gay life is the pits, and especially so when you get older.
- All homosexuals make bad, incompetent parents.
- All gays swish, and all lesbians swagger.
- All homosexuals are rapists and pedophiles.

The Psychodynamics of Name-Calling

The names homophobes call gays and lesbians, like faggot or queer, are effectively minimyths and as such also dynamically and structurally like symptoms of an emotional disorder. For example, bad names are *dynamically* wish fulfillments (e.g., when they *deny* personal femininity and the possibility of being emasculated) and *structurally* compromise formations that express both sides of the conflict between wish and fear. To illustrate, a bridge phobia spells out both the wish to soar and the fear of and punishment for soaring ("I will faint and crash my car"), and the dirty name "elitist" similarly refers both to the homophobe's wish to be something he is not and his fearful self-condemnation for breaking through the barriers to achievement that have been set up not only internally but in actuality by his family of origin and the society in which he lives. Therefore, it is not surprising that the name elitist comes across as both a compliment and a criticism, an expression at one and the same time of wide-eyed jealousy ("you are what I would like to be") and of narrow jealous rage ("I hate you for what you have become").

Elitist (Elitist Intellectual)

Elitist intellectual, a common euphemism for faggot, refers mainly to men who like the theater and the ballet, as distinct from real men who, if they go to these things at all, do so only because their wives push them to and then have the good sense to proclaim their dislike for the performance throughout, either by vocally protesting during intermission or by silently complaining, for example, by yawning and falling asleep, so that everyone can see that "I am bored with this stuff." Developmentally speaking, many who use this name have identified with lower-middle-class, often blue-collar parents who never had anything remotely like literary pretensions and who believed that working with their hands was not merely different from, but rather superior to, working with their minds. Manual labor was viewed as masculine and intellectual labor as feminine.

It does not help to tell these elitist-bashing homophobes that gays and lesbians are good because Leonardo da Vinci was gay, for it only affirms their basic premise that gays and lesbians are a priori and always evil; in essence, as one gay man sardonically put it, "All that gays and lesbians do is doodle, invent gadgets, and paint smiles instead of doing the salt of the earth work that has an immediate and lasting benefit for society." Telling them that da Vinci was gay also hits home, reminding homophobes of what they are not, which only makes them even more anxious about what they are, causing them to become even more defensively homophobic than they were formerly.

Instead of seeing his own capabilities as different from but equally valuable as those of his gay and lesbian neighbors in the South Side of Boston, a homophobic patient, who had lived in the neighborhood all his life, from the time before it was gentrified, saw his abilities as inferior to those of his new neighbors, the ones who were doing all the gentrification. He was good with his hands and had become an able carpenter. They were good with their minds and had become able doctors, lawyers, and businessmen. But the suspicion lurked throughout that they had what he did not have, and on that account he felt he was less of a man.

In response, he started to brood about how there are two kinds of men in this world: superior men who are straight and inferior men who are gay. The superior men did the real work of the world and made it go around. They farmed the land and drove the trucks that delivered the milk. The inferior men did the unnecessary work of the world and were basically peripheral to and not needed for its progress and survival. These were the elitist intellectuals like his neighbors, people who sat on their butts all day long playing mind games or the piano.

He concluded, somewhat defensively, that although gays and lesbians had better homes and bodies, more money, and more sophisticated clothes than he did, he was the better person, for he belonged to the class of men who were superior because the world could not do without them: simple, honest, direct, uncomplicated, hardworking people who provided humankind with basic services, however plain, unglamorous, and underpaid. Whereas he went to bed early to get up fresh to do God's work each morning, they arose shortly before midnight for a kind of Walpurgisnacht, to do Satan's bidding. Gays and lesbians, he concluded, were expendable, for they belonged to the realm of the effete, a place where bloodless sissies made designer shower curtains and built beautiful but underoccupied homes in trendy resorts. As he put it one day, "These people have 10 bathrooms apiece, although as near as I can determine, they each have only one large colon."

He maintained his "me-versus-you" and "I am the better person" view of life, in spite of its inaccuracies, because it improved a self-esteem that had been lowered by his envy of gays and lesbians. His homophobia allowed him to see himself as potent, effective, lovable, and chosen by

God, in comparison to gays and lesbians who, as he saw it, were impotent, ineffective, and despicable, for they were not chosen by God but sent to earth by the devil.

DINKS

The term DINKS (double income, no kids) is a favorite among those homophobes who envy gays and lesbians what they have after comparing gays' and lesbians' attempts at achieving success and comfort in life to their own unsuccessful tries at becoming upwardly socially mobile—only, in so many cases, to find themselves unable to go onward and rise upward, often because they ultimately defeated themselves because they felt guilty about betraying their families of origin and their standards. Newly successful politicians of humble lower-middle-class origins particularly like this term because although it has enough positive associations to make it appear nonconfrontational and at least on the surface complimentary, it also has enough negative spin to sound like a condemnation to those who need to hear one.

Queens and Sissies

Competitive homophobes who feel envious of gays' and lesbians' considerable achievements feminize gay men so that they can view them as far less accomplished than they actually are. They call them queens so that they can view themselves figuratively as kings who rule and dominate, exactly as men traditionally do. This term also suggests that gays are superficial and pretentious, giving homophobes the fodder they seek to affirm their own substantiality and sincerity.

One blue-collar homophobe, whom his gay victims called a "member of the unintelligentsia," constantly complained that gays and lesbians were piss-elegant people whose only goal in life was to be as much unlike their peasant parents as possible. He condemned one gay man for being the sort of person who was not able to do any better than hang out at a leather bar down the block to meet handsome strangers costumed in chaps (a kind of leather pants) and fall in love with them just because they were not the homespun working stiffs he himself toiled next to on the assembly line. He also frequently mentioned another gay man he knew as an example of that typical gay excessively enamored of superficialities such as beautiful clothes worn in elegant men's bars and who once even spoke of being in love with a man just because he wore an overcoat with a velvet collar and ate at gourmet restaurants. "In short," he concluded, "all gays and lesbians are wastrels because they live their lives not in the pages of *Popular Mechanics* but in the pages of various decorator magazines." Regarding the latter criticism he had a small point—there is more to life than home furnishings—but he overlooked that although some gay men do favor substitute over real gratification and affirm their identity around matters of very little intrinsic importance, even those who do that usually do so only for fun and are otherwise very serious about many things.

Swish or Butch

These terms suggest that all gays are feminine, and all lesbians are masculine. The intent is to enhance and perfect one's own masculine or feminine self-image—by devaluing another comparatively.

Fag

This is a demeaning term meant in part to conjure up an image of men who are deficient because they are limp-wristed, tired, effete, ineffective nerds, creeps, and wusses. No one seems to know its origins for certain; indeed, its meaning may essentially derive from its sound with its relationships to *flag* and *sag,* hence referring to someone unable to become, or stay, erect when and where it counts.

Sicko

This term reassures homophobes that they are healthy in comparison to gays and lesbians; that is, "I am saner and more effective than you." Naturally, these homophobes define sanity and effectiveness according to their own middle-of-the-road conforming values, which become the social norm.

Queers

This term implies, among other things, a need to isolate gays and lesbians from the mainstream to get them out of the way and so render them less competitive.

Fruits

Fruits symbolize femininity. Like the term *vegetable,* this term also suggests a comatose state of inert, dumb passivity meant to contrast with the altogether admirable bright, active, masculine quality the critic wishes to see in and attribute to himself.

Pedophiles and Child Molesters

These epithets' primary intent is putting gays and lesbians down as harshly as possible by calling them the worst thing one can think of. Also, those using these epithets are implying that somehow they feel vulnerable in the homosexual presence, as if they are themselves unprotected children in danger of being abused or raped.

The following case illustrates how complex are the ideas that become forged into just one simple but overdetermined name one homophobe called gays: "*screamers*, like a bunch of *banshees*."

A homophobic patient of mine complained incessantly during his therapy sessions that he could "not eat out in New York because he always sat next to some queer who is screaming so loudly that I cannot hear myself think or concentrate on my meal." When asked to illustrate one such incident, he described how just the night before he sat across the aisle from a gay man who was "haranguing" his companion about the details of a *Sound of Music* tour he took more than a generation ago. The patient guessed that the man had toured the places where the von Trapp family had lived or the set of the movie that was made about their lives.

As the patient related, "The man spoke loudly and so much that he left no room for his companion to insert any comment. He regularly dropped the name of Julie Andrews, a star of the movie, as if he were somehow gaining by a fantasized association with her. In effect he was bragging that he knew someone who was rich and famous, in contrast to himself, a big unemployed nobody. He also bellyached incessantly as if he seemed to be taking more delight in what went wrong with the trip than in what went right." For example, he described, in what my patient thought was excessive detail, an inconvenience he underwent during the tour: "'They left me for a whole half hour at the hotel with all my baggage, and, imagine this, the place had been closed for months.'"

This gay man's verbosity bothered the patient well beyond what it should have, clearly because it hit a nerve. When I analyzed what nerve the verbosity hit, that is, what conflicts it aroused, I learned that the following were really the things that most upset my patient. My patient was bothered that the gay man seemed to be taking over and taking charge—pinning his companion to the wall, so to speak, and "pinning the rest of us to the wall too." He was bothered that the gay man wanted to be number one, on stage, even if only in a small way. The gay man seemed to want to get the other patrons to pay full attention to him. My patient also secretly wanted to be the number one person at all times. But he found that unacceptable because he feared competing successfully with rivals, as if that meant destroying them completely. In part, this was because he suffered from a fear of success due to the unconscious belief that accomplishing something meant hurting others, and that was incompatible with his self-image as a kind person who would never try to take over and push people around and against the wall, and then completely out of the picture. The patient said about himself, "I am the sort of person who basically best thrives when surrounded by people who are, or at least whom I can perceive to be, already failures, for I fear that in any endeavor there is only room for one, and I can best be a winner if everyone else around me is already a loser."

The patient's thoughts next ran to how, as a child, he always felt left out of things and how the gay man's look-at-me cry, a plea to be noticed, reminded him of his own desperate but unsuccessful attempts to join in family situations from which his brothers and sisters just as clearly wanted him excluded. He was also bothered that the gay man was brashly exposing himself, "talking so loudly we could dance to it." My patient was a shy, retiring man unable to act in a way he felt might suggest being at all shameless. He himself made a habit of never standing out—his way to reassure himself that he would never be rejected and would always belong, at least in some limited way.

That the gay man seemed to be almost perversely delighting in being inconvenienced and abandoned bothered the patient because he considered unacceptable his own need to brush with danger, just so that he could brag about how he managed to survive the harshest of circumstances—and so was not as vulnerable as he and others might at first think.

Of course, he also envied the gay man because he was going places while my patient had to stay home. Even though he would not have wanted to go on this particular tour, he felt he was stuck in the United States with his wife and kids and so was missing out on other, equivalent tours.

He also noted that the gay man was merely touring as an observer. To him that meant that the gay man was only passively appreciating someone else's accomplishments, not accomplishing something on his own. This reminded my patient that his own accomplishments had been modest and that he would always remain the failure who associated with successful people, never the other way around.

That the gay man seemed to be unemployed suggested a kind of laziness, which in turn suggested a passivity that made my patient fear his own feminine tendencies. That the gay man had Julie Andrews as his hero and not, say, James Bond meant that the gay man did not really want to be a real man. That is, as my patient saw it, the gay man was, like most gay men, "just a preening sissy."

Finally, the gay man, by dwelling on the nostalgic past, stirred up the patient's depressive feelings that his future could never be as good as his early years had been. In his case the past that appealed to him most was when his parents were alive and the world was a simpler place, without so many queers (and foreigners) about, to boot, or so much open sex going on just about everywhere you turned.

Clearly, this man's name-calling was self-referential, which is why, in chapter 14 on antitheses, my best hint is to recognize that all homophobia, hurtful name-calling in particular, is a self-statement, a self-criticism, and a self-flagellation, making it unnecessary and even inappropriate to take the homophobia personally; instead, the hearer must think (and say if appropriate), "homophobe, heal thyself," because, after all, "it does take one to condemn one."

CHAPTER 8

Homophobia as an Emotional Disorder: Paranoid Homophobia

In order to fully understand homophobia we must recognize its important origin in and subsequent relationship to emotional disorder. Herek distinguishes three homophobic attitudes according to whether their origins are (1) "*experiential* [due to] categorizing social reality by one's past interactions with homosexual persons,"[1] that is, "accept[ing] gay people in general on the basis of pleasant interaction experiences with a specific gay man or lesbian [or] hold[ing] negative attitudes toward the entire group primarily as a result of... unpleasant experiences with particular gay men or lesbians";[2] (2) "*defensive,* [that is,] coping with one's inner conflicts or anxieties by projecting them onto homosexual persons" to "reduce painful emotions and feelings (e.g. anxiety) that are triggered by gay people or homosexuality... occur[ing due to] the person's own psychological conflicts related to sexuality or gender [and] occur[ing] largely outside of the individual's awareness";[3] and (3) "*symbolic,* expressing abstract ideological concepts that are closely linked to one's notion of self and to one's social network and reference groups."[4] Herek's second type, defensive homophobia, is very much like an emotional disorder because, as Terry S. Stein says in another context, prejudice serves different psychological "evaluative, expressive, and defensive" functions.[5]

In the previous chapter I emphasized how homophobia, like other symptoms, originates developmentally and dynamically in conflict, anxiety, and defense. In turn, the different conflicts, anxieties, and coping defenses spin off unique homophobic patterns that in content and structure resemble emotional symptoms. Thus, homophobia *is* primarily phobic when homophobes mainly view gays and lesbians as "bad luck" and *avoid* them like the plague. It is primarily obsessive-compulsive when homophobes mainly feel disgust with the dirty things (as they see it) that gays and lesbians do to each other sexually, then set out to *cleanse* the world of the filthy queers and dirty lesbians. And, most importantly, it is primarily paranoid when homophobes *project* their forbidden homosexual and hate-filled feelings onto gays and lesbians, come to attribute self-characteristics to gay and lesbian strangers, then go on to persecute them as an alternative to persecuting themselves, so that "I hate and attack myself for being queer" becomes "gays are all poised to attack me, diminish what I stand for, destroy my life and that of my family, try to seduce my underage sons and make them homosexual too, and tear apart the very fabric of the society I live in."

As Herek says, paranoid homophobes who "cope with [their] inner conflicts or anxieties by projecting them onto homosexual persons"[6] view gays and lesbians as persecutors out to destroy their lives and their families' lives. According to Sanford et al., the resultant paranoid homophobia involves "a strong inclination to punish violators of sex mores (homosexuals, sex offenders) [that is less] an expression of a general punitive attitude based on identification with in-group authorities [than a suggestion that] the subject's own sexual desires are suppressed and in danger of getting out of hand."[7] Sanford and colleagues then conclude "that we can learn what is suppressed in the subject," usually strong "unconscious urges of both sexuality and destructiveness, by noting what attributes he most readily, but unrealistically, ascribes to the world around him"[8]—so that, in the vernacular, "it takes one to know one." In Adorno's words, projection "point[s] in one direction . . . that prejudice . . . is but superficially, if at all, related to the specific nature of its object [so that the resulting prejudice] is more a subjective experience, for example about 'power fantasies' . . . completely independent from interaction with reality."[9] Thus, when we hear that Representative Bob Barr says that "the flames of hedonism, the flames of narcissism, the flames of self-centered morality are licking at the very foundation of our society, the family unit,"[10] we should immediately suspect that Barr is projecting an inwardly condemned personal feeling outward, perhaps in order to deal with how hot he gets in the presence of gay men and how he begins to fear that *his* unconscious sexual fantasies are licking at his ego and threatening to overwhelm it and him.

Some more severely ill paranoid homophobes, those suffering from paranoid schizophrenia or a (paranoid) delusional disorder, develop actual delusions and/or hallucinations about gays and lesbians, with homosexual content in the delusion itself. For example, a severely paranoid patient became convinced that "I am being accused of doing homosexual things by the Angel of Suck sitting on my shoulder." He also developed classical delusions of the influencing machine: thinking he was being controlled by people who were inserting a computer chip in his head to manipulate him; on close inspection, this "insertion" clearly referred to oral penetration. He became suspicious of all technology, really fearing not technology per se but technologists, whom he believed were out to use science to disrupt the order of things by modifying his genes, part of their plan to modify the gene pool of the world, with their intent to have him participate in their scheme of siring a generation of men, women, and children all of whom would turn out to be as queer as he was.

A patient entered treatment because he felt depressed because his mother had not given him her power of attorney, so he feared he would not be able to take care of her financial needs if she became senile, an event no more likely to occur to her than to any other individual of her age. Soon it turned out that he was beset by a number of irrational worries, not just that one. One of them was that men were staring at him in the elevator, looking at his crotch, with dishonorable intentions. He lived in Greenwich Village in New York City, which, he reminded me over and over again, was full of homosexuals, and he felt that he would be the next to fall into their predatory paths. He did not seem to consider that he was a very old man who had in any case never been physically attractive and now had become completely unattractive, not so much because of his advanced age but because he did not take care of himself physically. He had actually become dilapidated because, although he had the money to buy new clothes and did in fact buy them, he would not wear them, fearing that they would get soiled and be ruined, should he, for example, go out on a sunny day without an umbrella, only to have it turn cloudy without warning and rain on his custom-made attire.

Soon this man became excessively preoccupied with the possibility that he would be seduced by homosexuals. He spent an inordinate amount of time walking away from every gay bar in Greenwich Village so that he could not be cruised by someone coming out the door. But being in the Village made it likely that in walking away from one gay bar he would merely be walking to another. Eventually, he could hardly go out of the house at all for fear of being attacked by queers. Soon enough, and of course expectedly, he began to feel that I was one of them too and became tortured by the possibility that I, like the others, would grab and seduce him against his will. Once he told me a joke and then spent days worrying that I would tell it to someone he knew who would recognize its source and connect him with me, at best revealing that he was seeing a psychiatrist and at worst raising the possibility that he was not one of my patients but one of my lovers. So he stopped going to his favorite restaurant because he knew that I occasionally ate there. However, with the typical flair homophobes have for displaying the latent homosexuality that gets through all the defenses, he instead began eating at another restaurant, this one right down the block from where he knew I lived—which was, not coincidentally, right around the corner from what was, at the time, the most notorious gay bar in the Village!

He felt somewhat better after joining a loose-knit political group dedicated to taking symbolic antihomosexual stands. For example, he particularly favored one heterosexist group that was suing the appropriate agencies to force them to allot more space in local building projects to sports facilities for the children of West Villagers. At this point, his symptoms improved because he felt part of a holy mission, as well as because he felt a sense of safety in numbers, supported and validated by those of like mind, and loved in a safe, at least manifestly nonhomoerotic environment, if not for himself, then because of what he was doing: verbally bashing the "amoral conditions certain people create in the city we would all like to live in without shame." Not surprisingly, he received a lot of support from the locals. But he might have received less if they had recognized that his "save the Village for the children" campaign really originated in a desire to "keep the queers out of my part of town."

Another patient was an erythrophobic individual, that is, a man who feared being seen, and caught, blushing. He believed blushing was a sign of heat that gave his homosexuality away. As a result, he was unable to readily leave home to walk the streets. He said, "I fear all the crime in the city." But the crimes he really feared were "those against nature, perpetrated on him by all the queers running about."

Projection commonly results not in developing full paranoid ideation but in developing *ideas of reference,* that is, a false feeling of centrality, in which the subject believes that he or she has assumed a primary place in the minds of gays and lesbians who are looking at or talking about and even secretly cruising him or her, or, as is very common these days, are planning a hostile challenge of straight values or straight life. So we hear, in effect, "We have to stop gays and lesbians from marrying each other because it reflects badly on the institution of *my* straight marriage and will bring *my* institution down entirely, and with it *my* happiness and social stability will be entirely gone."

An erotophobic patient was trying to suppress his overt homosexuality by invoking the "gay sex is dirty" mantra. Nevertheless, he found himself, in spite of himself, constantly preoccupied with and brooding about what gays do in bed. Each time he saw someone he believed to be a gay man he found himself staring at his pudendum, wondering where it had been and turning over in his mind what it had been doing there. He reminded himself over and over again to be angry at and disgusted by what he saw, and saw all too clearly. One day he attended a concert of American music. When a famous out-of-the-closet homosexual American composer appeared on stage for applause after a premier of his work, he could do no better than imagine this man not writing at his desk but writhing in sexual positions. As he put it, he was turning him over in his mind, each time with a shudder over the possibility that such complicated beautiful music could come out of such a simple ugly animal. As a result, he stopped attending concerts of American music entirely "because they might foist another gay guy like this one, one just as amoral as he, on me."

This man also feared being indoctrinated by activist gays and lesbians who were presumably out to spread the homosexual word and recruit him, blowing him kisses until he yielded. The aforementioned paranoid schizophrenic who complained that a computer chip had been inserted into his head had as his counterpart this homophobe with paranoid tendencies who, as it turned out, felt that all queers were, figuratively speaking, body snatchers—out to occupy his person and turn him into a duplicate of themselves. He recognized this idea as truly crazy, so he sanitized it to become "I can't be too careful to avoid gays and lesbians because they might snatch away *my* morality, *my* society, and *my* way of life."

Sometimes paranoid personality traits develop such as the one Sanford et al. described: a readiness to "think about and to believe in the existence of such phenomena as wild erotic excesses, plots, and conspiracies" (e.g., Bill O'Reilly's conspiracies against the Catholic Church).[11] Less severely ill paranoids, those with merely paranoid tendencies, not only do not become overtly delusional or hallucinate but are also, on some level, both generally at odds with the homosexual content of their false delusional-like beliefs and ashamed enough of it to clean it up for public consumption. So they either censor the beliefs out of their homophobia or censor their homophobia out of their beliefs, hiding homophobic thoughts from others and sometimes even from themselves. They still bash the gay "enemy," only in a more derivative and indirect way, as I describe in chapter 9 on passive-aggressive personality disorder homophobia.

Some *straight* bashing is actually a paranoid phenomenon homophobic in its intent if not in its manifestations. Some men who appear to be pathologically jealous individuals *straight bash* their wives for cheating on them. Further analysis shows that they have, in fact, projected their homosexual wishes and fears onto their wives to the point of developing Othello-like pathologically jealous fears that their wives are cheating on them. They are not so much condemning their wives for the cheating as they are condemning themselves for having fantasies of cheating on their wives with their wives' lovers.

Not surprisingly, paranoid homophobes on all levels have a hypocritical ambivalent quality to their homophobia that results from constantly having to struggle with their own homosexuality, so that one day they condemn others who have same-sex relationships, only the next day, losing the struggle, seem to have something like same-sex relationships of their own, for which they then go on to condemn themselves, then others, ad infinitum. The simulated homosexuality that is often part of hazing (a recent image sticks in my mind of army men hazing each other by simulating anal insertion) exemplifies ambivalence associated with conflicts about underlying forbidden homosexual desire—as these men at one and the same time do it, then take it back by making a joke out of it. Put differently, on the one hand, they might say "join the army to get with real men and away from the queers," whereas, on the other hand, they might say "join the army because that way you will be with people who are the same sex as you are," hence it is highly important that we "keep the queers out of the army and away from me." (For this reason, it is proper to raise the following question about some homophobic recruits: "If you wanted to avoid everything homosexual, why did you decide to join up and live with all those men in the first place?" and to answer the question, "Should gay men and women be allowed to serve in the armed forces?" with, "Sure, and just as important, straight recruits should be discouraged from dealing with their own guilty homosexual desires by attributing them to others, then becoming excessively fearful of people who are not actually attempting to seduce them or otherwise do them harm.)

True projective homophobia develops in a stepwise fashion. Identifying these different steps in turn helps us understand, explain, and contest the commonest homophobic tenets in circulation today, such as a fear of seduction by out-of-control gays and lesbians, the belief that gays and lesbians are dangerous enemies (men who give you AIDS and women who destroy your marriage by seducing your wife), and the conviction that all gays and lesbians are sickos and need to be cured or, since that is unlikely, quarantined, an even better plan.

Sometimes the steps are sequential, while at other times they occur simultaneously. I suspect that the men who killed Matthew Shepard, issues of possible drug usage aside, were taking multiple steps at once: feeling homosexually aroused, projecting their forbidden homophobic wishes outward and killing the messenger for having conjured up their homosexual desires, feeling hate after catching Shepard up in all their general bitterness and rage, and projecting their hatred outward so that Shepard became the enemy about to do bad things to them. Additionally, some believe that in tying Shepard to a fence the way they did they were symbolically crucifying him—perhaps an overdetermined act that simultaneously contained elements of cleansing themselves of sin (by killing the sinner) and sinning themselves (by doing something hatefully satanic—the very thing that was done to Christ).

The steps described in the following sections trace how the fully delusional or delusion-like beliefs that characterize paranoid homophobia are formed along classic psychoanalytic lines first set forth by Freud in the Schreber case,[12] which still has meaning and impact today.

ANXIETY AND GUILT APPEAR

The process starts with one or both of two prime feelings ascendant: sexually excited homophobes feel "I love him," and angry homophobes feel "I hate him." Either the love or the hate elicits anxiety because of guilt or fear of what society might think, say, or do. Due to anxiety these feeling are then transformed defensively, both internally and by projection onto the outside world.

In a typical sequence these individuals internally change "I love him" to "No, I don't love him, I actually hate him," then, because of anxiety and guilt, project that hatred externally onto the outside world so that they feel persecuted by gays and lesbians. To them, that persecution, as Fenichel says, "represent[s] the homosexual temptation, turned into a fearful threat, threatening independently of the patient's will."[13]

Conflicts over hostility toward gays and lesbians may not, however, appear. There may only be expression, not projection, of anger, so that we have not a paranoid but a sadistic homophobe, as discussed in chapter 10.

REPRESSION, DISSOCIATION, OR DENIAL IS ATTEMPTED

Homophobes generally first attempt to handle their anxiety over their unacceptable sexual and aggressive feelings by repressing or dismissing them. With respect to their anxiety over their unacceptable aggressive feelings, they often repress their hatred by instead avowing that "I love homosexuals, and some of them are even my best friends." Repression is close to dissociation, as when a politician recently in the news might truthfully proclaim, "I am not gay," because he represses his gayness to the point that afterwards he can even be a bit (calculatedly) amnesic for anything gay he might have thought, said, or done.

OTHER NONPROJECTIVE DEFENSES ARE TRIED

When repression, denial, and dissociation do not work, the following nonprojective defenses are attempted and brought into play:

Avoidance

Those who resort to avoidance feel nothing; as far as they are concerned, gay people do not even exist. Not only are they untouchable, they are unmentionable because they are invisible.

Sublimation

Sometimes, latent homosexuality and homohatred are not discharged raw but are instead transformed (sublimated) into negative or positive social behaviors. A homophobe can sublimate negatively by changing forbidden homosexual desire into so-called socially desirable antigay proselytizing, for example, closing down shows by gay photographers to bust obscenity, not incidentally giving vent to guilt about and expressing hoped-for absolution for voyeuristic impulses. Or a homophobe can sublimate positively by changing forbidden homosexual desire into homoerotic asexual bonding, laudatory charitable work with AIDS patients, or supposedly laudatory reparative therapy for the purpose of curing homosexuals of their disease.

Reaction Formation

Like sublimation, reaction formation can go in either one of two directions. Homophobes who feel erotically attached to gays and lesbians often handle their forbidden attachment by protesting too much that they hate them, whereas homophobes who hate gays and lesbians often preach one day that homosexuality is an abomination and then, the next day, feeling guilty about being so hostile, become crusaders for the gay cause.

Undoing

In this reaction, homophobes cover their homophobia by saying just the opposite of what they mean and doing just the opposite of what they are tempted to do, to obscure what they really think and deny what they really feel.

Intellectualization

Here we find the use of hypercognition as the favored defense. This is characteristic of contemplative homophobes who say, in effect, "Do not hate, instead debate." These individuals handle their passions (and try to cope with those of others) by brooding philosophically about them—not so much turning words into feelings as defensively turning feelings into words.

Displacement

Personal antipathies are displaced onto impersonal institutions, such as the ballet or Public Broadcasting Service (PBS), which become symbols or stand-ins for individual highly charged emotional complexes. These homophobes are attempting to deal with an inner personal sexual or hostile threat by challenging the value and denigrating the status of an outer, impersonal, sociocultural institution. For example, with this in mind, homophobes complain that PBS is an elitist organization and contrast this elitism with the masculinity they associate with, and personally approve of, in the Sports Channel.

Suppression

This is a conscious attempt at self-control along the lines of taking a cold shower to feel less hot and bothered—while vocally recommending that others do exactly the same thing.

PROJECTIVE DEFENSES ARE REQUIRED

In many cases, the process stops with such nonprojective defenses. The potential homophobe first erupts, then dismisses and forgets about the whole thing and goes about his business. For example, a social worker told me of a colleague who refused to deal with a married couple after he discovered that their first names were John and Marvin. He complained to the social worker and asked to be taken off the case. The social worker responded by telling her colleague that she herself was a lesbian, whereupon the man felt so threatened that he handed in his resignation the very next day. Similarly, a kitchen worker recently told his boss, a lesbian who ran a small café frequented by gays and lesbians, that he hated serving queers. She told him that she hated homophobes and warned him to shape up or be fired, whereupon he just quit.

However, too often homophobes discover that all the aforementioned defenses only incompletely suppress their erotic and angry feelings toward homosexuals. The inner closet door will not stay closed. Instead, their homosexuality and anger, if these do not actually explode, come oozing out around the edges. Even the oozing ultimately tends to reach fever pitch and break through, especially in homophobic men whose masculinity is challenged in real life, say after an attempted gay seduction, which they may or may not have brought on themselves. In either event, the eruption attracts the most inner attention and ultimately requires radical countermeasures in the form of breakthrough projection. This routinely attaches itself to the ounces of truth buried underneath pounds of paranoid elaborations and uses these to defend, really justify, the homophobia as provoked, that is, as the second, not the first, strike. These individuals call their homohatred not offensive but defensive. They say that they are merely responding to real adversaries, although they are actually creating straw men and scapegoats and are less the passive victims they would like to believe themselves to be and more the active perpetrators that they deny that they are or have ever been.

In effect, these projecting (paranoid) homophobes are using gays and lesbians as blank screens or inkblots on a psychological test. They blame the victim in preparation for victimizing those they blame. They transform an internal struggle into an external struggle between themselves and another, so that we hear, "I am not prejudiced, you are difficult to get along with, and so my antagonism toward you is not something that comes from within me, from me, but is provoked by your antagonism toward me. So I ought to hate gays and lesbians because they are irresponsible to dangerous, and it follows that gays and lesbians could avoid most of my and everyone else's opprobrium, if only they would live their lives differently and not do all those evil things that they do and won't stop doing, no matter how many complaints they get from me."

The distortive process follows these projective pathways:

I hate him. No, I don't hate him, he hates me (projection of the hatred). This path leads to the belief that gays and lesbians are dangerous enemies out to hurt and harm straights by seducing their sons, defiling their straight marriages, contaminating the whole world with the HIV virus, or, at the very least (or most), passing on their gayness, which is catching. Seriously troubled paranoids believe that as a group gays and lesbians will gang up, band together, and keep the world from experiencing lasting peace. Exactly how gays and lesbians might do that does not matter very much; what matters is the retained primary (delusional) belief that "when gays have a will, they will find a way."

I love him. No I don't love him, I love her, and no I don't love her, she loves me (changing of homohate to heterolove and projection of the heterolove). This can result in erotomania, where the manifest object of a purportedly straight man's affections is a woman, but the real intent is to resolutely pursue a "her" as a diversion from the overwhelming forbidden desire to pursue a "him."

I love him. No, I don't love him, he loves me (retention and projection of love). In this process one's own temptations are retained but converted into being tempted, predictably causing one to yield to living the homosexual life and having homosexual sex. The cry is "I am not being seductive, you are out to seduce me," and "I do not want to have gay sex with you, you are emotionally and physically raping me." This kind of thinking leads to such a belief as, "since all gays and lesbians are sexual menaces out to recruit me, I must be especially cautious to not support homosexuals in any meaningful way, because that just encourages them." So when two lesbians were elected couple of the year and their coupledom enshrined in their yearbook, right-wing talk show hosts complained that that was a bad idea because it could only encourage the recruiting of teens into becoming lesbians and choosing the lesbian life. Typically, those who project this way deny their paranoid homophobia and instead cite reality as the reason for their beliefs, for example, "my sister became gay after a lesbian came onto her."

A latent homosexual patient, when psychologically compensated, insisted that his interest in men was only platonic. He admitted that he admired men in uniform, but he said that was only because they best represented the ideal kind of man he wanted to be. Either things changed when he began decompensating into paranoia, or he began decompensating into paranoid when things changed. His interest in men in uniform became an adversarial relationship with them, as if he were saying, "I do not love them, they love me, and that's unacceptable." Once he sued New York City, complaining that he felt constant pain in the groin because of something he was convinced happened when he rode a city bus. He insisted that when he fell asleep on the bus, "the bus driver got up out of his seat, walked to the rear of the bus where I was sitting, took out his sharp pencil, and stuck it into my testicles." When he was better compensated, he became a vocal opponent of admitting gays and lesbians into the armed services. He presented all the usual rationalizations for this purportedly realistic position, but, not unexpectedly, his stance was really a personal one—if he were in the army he would not want to be exposed to gay men living in such close quarters with him, who would therefore be out to seduce and attack him "with their pencils."

I love him. No, I don't love him, she loves him (retention of the love projected onto a hetero-object). This leads to straight-appearing pathological spousal jealousy. A straight wife, husband, or partner is accused of having the affair the accuser actually wants to have. Often, a man who is spying on his wife to see whether she is having an affair is really hoping to discover that she is in fact having one—so that he can get lucky with her lover. When such men kill their wives' lovers, as they sometimes do, they are often just killing the messenger, the one who makes them aware of their own homosexual desires.

Sometimes the projection involved is of the feeling that one is decompensating emotionally due to strong instincts breaking loose and getting out of whack. When this occurs it can lead to the belief that gays and lesbians are crazy lunatics out of control who en masse cannot think or behave in a rational fashion and so are part of society's lunatic fringe.

Sometimes the projection involved is one of guilt. When this occurs, it can lead to the belief that gays and lesbians are bad, amoral people just like oneself. Or it can lead to the development of litigious delusions. Thus, according to Fenichel, projecting homophobes develop litigious ideas or delusions when they "consider the outward establishment of their integrity and innocence as the most important thing in the world," and, after a "homosexualization" of the "spheres of guilt and punishment" take things to the top to "verify their innocence [as] an attempt to defend [themselves] against homosexual impulses."[14] Such paranoid homophobes first become secretly convinced that the world has condemned them as guilty for being homosexual. Second, displacing their guilt from their presumed homosexuality onto some derivative matter, they set out to prove to the world that they are innocent of being homosexual, specifically, by taking that derivative matter all the way to the Supreme Court, seeking exoneration and absolution purportedly for civil or criminal acts they feel unfairly accused of, when the exoneration they seek is actually for their own guilt-laden homosexual transgressions.

In sum, hateful gay bashing should, until proven otherwise, be considered to belong to the paranoid spectrum of homophobia. Among the more current manifestations of paranoid homophobia are the belief that gays and lesbians are dangerous out of all proportion to any real danger they present, some examples of pseudoheterosexual stalking of famous people, the fantasy that all homosexuals want to do is seduce straights ("gays and lesbians are out to rape me") and their children ("all gays and lesbians are pedophiles"), the belief that all queers and dykes are crazy, and some examples of take-it-all-the-way-up-to-the-Supreme-Court fanaticism that appear to be asexual but are in fact homosexually driven. Freud saw this many years ago and wrote about it in the Schreber case.[15] Today we seem to have forgotten what he said and, in forgetting that, have pretty much overlooked the conceptually important and therapeutically significant relationship between homophobia and paranoia.

True paranoid homophobia must be differentiated both from manipulative paranoid homophobia and from Pollyanna paranoid homophobia. True paranoid homophobes attribute their own unwanted homosexuality to others to disavow any possibility that they are gay. In contrast, manipulative paranoid homophobes concoct delusion-like ideas not to disprove a point about themselves in order to reduce their inner anxiety but to prove a point about gays and lesbians in order to increase the possibility of real, often political, personal gain. Whereas true projective paranoid homophobia is a way to improve one's prospects by reducing one's anxiety, manipulative paranoia is a way to improve one's lot by improving one's prospects.

Whereas projective paranoia looks mostly like a disease, manipulative paranoia looks mostly like a talent. Projective paranoids are relatively disinterested in worldly accomplishment. Social advancement is either a secondary matter or is entirely unimportant to them. The world that these paranoid homophobes are most concerned with is the internal one, where they suffer from anxiety about their own homosexuality. If they attempt to alter the world, say by enticing others into the fray, their goal is not so much to struggle and triumph in the real world or to enlist people as aides in achieving common cause but to obtain inner relief through altering the external landscape, by suckering others into becoming pawns in their psychological dealings with their own personal, unacceptable, inner fantasies.

In contrast, manipulative paranoid homophobes use paranoid mechanisms primarily for purposes of direct, palpable, personal (that is, interpersonal and political) gain. They simply use gays and lesbians when and as they need them. They do incidentally benefit somewhat from reducing their personal anxiety. But that benefit is secondary to the one they get from improving their personal lot.

In typical fashion, manipulative paranoids use and abuse gays and lesbians for gain, then drop them when they are no longer needed or when they ask for something back for themselves. A straight individual expects a lesbian to throw a baby shower for her when her firstborn arrives and to provide babysitting services so that she can return to work. But when the lesbian's mother dies and the lesbian asks her close friend to attend her mother's funeral, she decides, "This lesbian is trying to seduce me," her way to avoid inconveniencing herself by having to make the trip.

In the workplace, manipulative paranoid coworkers gay bash chiefly to render gays and lesbians less competitive. Such gay bashing was rife in a psychiatric service where I once worked. A few workers claimed, without substantial evidence, that a gay mental health worker, who was in fact innocent of the charges, was trying to seduce them in his office after hours. These coworkers were not so much denying individual latent homosexual trends by criticizing an overt homosexual as they were trying to get the gay mental health worker out of the running so that they could get more of the pie. It was not primarily a complex intrapsychic matter. It could be simply put: "With shared out-of-control suspicion leading to the firing of a talented gay man, there were more referrals for me."

Politicians regularly use paranoid mechanisms manipulatively, with gays and lesbians as their victims, in order to fuel their campaigns. They act paranoid about gays and lesbians and put them down not so much to feel psychically vindicated and personally grand as to promote intragroup cohesion in their ranks by concocting a common enemy for all concerned to rally against. In decrying how gays and lesbians are evil, they are not primarily ridding themselves of a feminine taint. They are primarily proclaiming their oneness with an in-group with similar ideas and values—the majority of voters who are still to this day by birth, intellect, and inclination fearful of gays and lesbians. Male politicians of this ilk are not primarily out to deny the possibility of psychic emasculation. They are primarily interested in avoiding the possibility of real castration, that is, the possibility that they will lose an election. Radio talk show hosts and Internet bloggers who egg their audiences on to condemn queers may incidentally be offering themselves and their audience of other paranoids the opportunity to get some latent homosexual poison out of their systems. But in the main they are using the audience not to reduce their personal anxiety but to increase their actual ratings.

For some newspaper columnists, gay bashing is the hot topic that sells. One well-known columnist is a manipulative paranoid of the gentle contemplative type, a pundit who uses butter (persuasive reasoning) not guns (threats of intimidation or murder) against gays and lesbians. He is not mainly in business to prove that he is not himself gay. His primary purpose is to get and keep a homophobic audience's attention. He is not mainly out to prove anything to himself to reduce guilt about his own sadistic feelings or to find reasons to admire himself more, not less. If there is any admiration to be obtained he mainly wants it to come from without, not from within, from his audience, not from his conscience. He cites references such as the Bible or certain homophobic psychiatrists to prove that all homophobia (as he sees it) is understandable, excusable, predictable, justifiable, and inevitable because it is little more than a rational response to what gays and lesbians are and do. But by so doing he is not trying to portray gays and lesbians as troubled sick people to prove himself healthy or as criminals to prove himself law-abiding by comparison. He is merely trying to produce a daily column, and he needs to have something controversial to write about. He is not so much a closet queen as an overt opportunist.

Even our homophobic society recognizes, however covertly and to a limited extent, that true projective paranoids have emotional problems. But certain segments of society are regularly fooled into viewing manipulative paranoid homophobes not as troubled psychopaths but as rational beings, not your "usual neurotic homophobes." Manipulative paranoid homophobes fool these segments of society into seeing them not as excessively homophobic but as appropriately antihomosexual—and their homophobia not as a mental disorder coming from below, from their instincts, but as an orderly process coming from above, from a higher power. Their paranoia seems less compulsive than preferential, for their dislike of gays and lesbians is not a sign of personal mental disturbance but part of a conscious plan to favor straights made to look like appropriate heterosexism that is the product of free will, that is, not determined for but by the (reasonable) individual. They transform their homophobia into a respected religious belief or a mainstream secular philosophical vision on a par with existentialism, all in a free country where everyone is entitled to dislike gays and lesbians without being shamed or humiliated for doing so or having their arms twisted to the point that they, becoming irrational, agree to accept gays and lesbians as equals and as perfectly normal.

Manipulative homophobes get away with their homophobia because they hold two trump cards: the king of being (mainly) straight and the ace of so-called belonging to the ruling class. They also get away with it because, being manipulative by nature, they can be manipulative about their manipulativeness. They know how to manipulate society into believing they are sincere and how to convince those whose ear they want to get that they are right, with no other possible explanations and conclusions even remotely as valid as their own.

Being a true paranoid is not at all incompatible with being a manipulative paranoid. Internal rumblings easily combine with external considerations, for many of these individuals have every reason to want to reduce their anxiety about being homosexual themselves *and* to pick up a little advantage along the way. Thus, many serious homophobes put gays and lesbians down for two reasons. First, they do it for emotional gain. They are projecting their forbidden homosexuality and condemning others' homosexual sins to feel less sinful themselves, while ridding themselves of guilt about their hostility by viewing their hatefulness as second strike—a response to having been provoked by all those troublesome gays and lesbians out there. Second, they are also strivers who emasculate others for gain by indulging in the sort of behavior we are familiar with from the Wild Kingdom shows on television, where the animals attempt to establish dominance and seize control. These individuals set out to vanquish those gays and lesbians whom they (at times correctly) perceive to be the competition so that they can win in a battle where, as they see it, gays and lesbians are the enemy, because, just by being there, they represent a barrier and threat to the homophobes' own peaceful existence and personal advancement.

Another group of individuals, those suffering from Pollyanna paranoia, are less paranoid than they are depressed. Their message is likewise "I hate and fear you because you are queer," but in this case it really means, "Because you are queer you don't love me, but reject me. And I cannot get used to that or take it lying down, from anyone." These homophobes then go on to exclude and reject gays and lesbians because they feel, not always entirely without justification, that they have been excluded and rejected by them.

Alcohol-related homophobia starts with the use of alcohol and other substances to manage latent homosexual desire and quash it chemically in order to live more comfortably in the queer world inside and out. Unfortunately, soon enough alcohol disinhibits homosexual desire, for alcohol use instead leads to a churning of the very discomforting feelings that the homophobe is trying to suppress. The following scenarios are typical: the guys get together and get drunk at a go-go bar, all the while concentrating on the fantastic dancers so that they do not have to notice each other. Or they attend a ball game and drink beer, then afterwards pile into a car. Homosexual desire, which has already increased due to the drinking, becomes even more intense when their legs touch. Fantasies grow, previously adequate defenses are overwhelmed, and a homosexual panic ensues. To relieve that panic they act vociferously straight in ways ranging from shouting antigay slogans from the car at passing men believed to be homosexual to picking up and beating up queers. In unfavorable cases they go on to develop delusional ideas in which they deal with their forbidden sexual fantasies by attributing them to others, whom they perceive to be seducing them, and set out to hurt and destroy these others to stop all the immorality. In time some even begin to suffer from alcohol hallucinosis or delirium tremens, hallucinating that gays and lesbians are after them or even that God for His own purposes is calling them queer. In such cases a vicious cycle occurs in which the homosexual fantasies promote even more defensive drinking, and the defensive drinking, along with the closeness to buddies that often accompanies it, in turn promotes even more homosexual fantasies.

Parents who drink may give birth to children suffering from a fetal alcohol syndrome, that is, children whose brains are damaged in utero by alcohol (as well as by tobacco and other toxic substances). Emotional dyscontrol is a possible symptom of fetal alcohol syndrome in the adult. That emotional dyscontrol can take many forms, one of which is excessive irrational hatred of everyone, a kind of universal bigotry that more often than not in some subcultures takes on a predominantly homophobic cast.

CHAPTER 9

Homophobia as an Emotional Disorder: Passive-Aggressive or Subtle Homophobia

Overt violence against gays and lesbians still exists today, but it is less common and less tolerated than it used to be. Today the operative concepts for expressing homophobia are politely, nicely, and in a refined manner. In part this is due to an increasingly gay-friendly social climate that requires homohaters to become more refined—if not in their secret homohating thoughts, then at least in their overt homohating actions. As a result, much homohatred has become less directly aggressive and more passive-aggressive. Homohaters generally think and feel much the same way they always did, but they cover it up better and have become more resourceful in expressing their homophobia. But that does not mean that they love gays and lesbians any more than before, and it does not mean they hate them any less.

Today much homohatred is not the hostility of the homophobic patient who tried to bomb a woman's college because she believed that the women there programmed the computers to send out rays beamed at and meant to penetrate her vagina. Something of an anachronism is the scenario where two lesbians were forced to sell their house in a middle-class neighborhood and move because they were unable to deal with people driving by calling them dykes from the car windows, having their house windows broken and eggs thrown at their house, and having their new car first scratched with sharp objects, then dented by fists punching in the hood, while the police failed to respond to their calls for help or, if responding, did not arrest the real criminals for crimes of violence but instead harassed the lesbians for having reported them.

Today, homophobes are less likely to gay bash openly and more likely to insinuate the bashing, that is, bash covertly. Today impeachable crimes have been replaced by unimpeachable logic. We rarely hear crude anti-gay jokes in public places. The guys down at the sports bar still tell them, but mostly they limit themselves to sneaking in a few while looking over their shoulders to make certain that only simpatico people are listening. Rude accusations hurled by homophobes at gays and lesbians have been replaced by indirect and refined attacks consisting of indelicate points made delicately, then rationalized cleverly: "I didn't say anything bad," or "if I did, it wasn't *so* bad," and "if it was, I am truly sorry, but they deserved at least some of it anyway."

Today, we mainly hear things like comments of the personal trainer who said that though many of his clients are gay, at least *his* clients know that he is a happily married man, so *they* never try to cross the line with *him*. We hear less in the way of critical accusations and more in the way of concerns and worries, such as the worry that gays and lesbians will tear the moral fabric of the nation apart by getting married and adopting children. From the president of the United States we hear not about how bad gay and lesbian relationships are but about how good straight marriage is. Talk show hosts deny they are homophobic, and at first they do not seem to be, unless you follow them over time, in which case it becomes clear that they are always taking the gay-unfriendly side in controversies where one stance is just a tad more homophobic than the other, such as the controversy about who should have the final say on gay marriage—the judiciary (likely to look on it favorably) or the voters (likely to vote it down). When we find gays and lesbians ignored, it occurs in a courteous and subtle manner, as when a cooperative apartment building changed the locks on its front doors, simply forgetting to contact two gay men who were temporarily out of town, so that they came back from their trip to find themselves locked out, baggage, pets, and all. These days homophobes still install ceilings meant to keep gays and lesbians from rising up too far. But because they make the ceiling out of glass, they are able, when gays and lesbians protest, to point to the heavens and say, "Stop complaining, for you see, there is no barrier whatsoever up there."

The rational, subtle, indirect, passive-aggressive hostility of today is not necessarily good news, however, for it is actually the most dangerous and destructive kind. In part, because of its modest import, it becomes very difficult to identify, which has several distinct and unique adverse consequences. First, gays and lesbians are left feeling that something is wrong but not knowing *what*. They then naturally suspect that something is wrong with them; that is, they blame themselves for their own victimization. Typically, they come to think that if they were better people, others would not treat them so shabbily, as did the woman who felt, "If I were a better scholar, then I would not have been denied tenure," and as did the man who felt, "If I were a better doctor, then I would get more referrals." They think they are paranoid for falsely believing themselves abused when in fact they are right to perceive others as hostile to them; they are not imagining it and are wrong to conclude that they are making it up and worrying too much about what other people think because they are too sensitive for their own good. Soon they become convinced that they are the ones with the problem, and so they are the ones who have to make all the changes. Next, when they finally see through it all, they get twice as angry as before, because now they feel like big fools for accepting the attacks on them without having even tried to defend themselves. They get upset that, having failed to realize what hit them until it is too late to do anything about it, they have once and for all lost the chance to protest, repair the damage, or seek revenge. Furthermore, as they soon learn, fighting what you only suspect is always harder than fighting what you know for certain. Thinking that those who despise you do not hate you or actually love you leads to serious miscalculations, such as investing in relationships that go nowhere and winding up unexpectedly dumped or applying for jobs that are out of reach or, if available, are entirely the wrong jobs, in what are, for some gays and lesbians, completely the wrong professions.

Not surprisingly, being passive-aggressive does work to the homophobes' advantage. It helps homophobes rationalize their homophobia and so advance their long-term cause. It helps them reduce their guilt about being homophobic so that they can continue homohating guilt free, business as usual. It helps them keep homosexuals involved with them, looking and hoping for something better, hence still around and available to be attacked once again. Gays and lesbians tune in repeatedly to passive-aggressive homophobic talk show hosts, hoping that this time they will recant at least a little and let up on them. They might not do this if the hosts came out and said that "gays and lesbians are an abomination." Instead of openly declaring their homophobia, they sucker gays and lesbians in, putting specific diversions in place—all the better to hit them again with a subtle homophobic remark that is so well crafted that their victims do not even realize that they have been put down in the first place.

It follows that the comeback for much that is homophobic today involves using antidotes suitable for dealing with passive aggression in general as well as for dealing with passive-aggressive homophobia in specific. Here I would like to refer the reader to my book, *Passive-Aggression: A Guide for the Therapist, the Patient and the Victim.*

What follows are some classic ways passive-aggressive homophobia and homophobes present.

CLAIMING UNCERTAINTY

These homophobes *wonder* whether but do not *firmly conclude* that gays and lesbians might be a threat to society, subverting as they do the natural order of things. In claiming this uncertainty, homophobes put forth their homophobic ideas tentatively, as if querying their own declarations makes it acceptable and entirely invalidates any hostility they might feel and show.

DOING AND UNDOING

First, these homophobes express reservations about or hostility toward homosexuals openly and, second, they take these back, often through a rationalization. They admit to being homophobic, then apologetically note that that is not wrong, for everyone has mixed feelings about gays and lesbians; after all, most gays and lesbians are, like everyone else, imperfect. They note that they are entitled to express justified antagonisms in a country with free speech. They go on to support their homophobia with logic, in the process employing selective inattention to that which might disprove points they want to make, or they split hairs, creating differences without true distinctions, as in "I hate the sin but love the sinner." They also rationalize their homophobia by practicing junk science persuasively, as when a psychoanalyst claims that gays and lesbians are too brittle emotionally to become psychoanalysts because homosexuality is caused by a perverse oedipal fixation, one that predictably disqualifies gays and lesbians from helping the many similarly fixated patients every analyst has to work with. They also undo their negativity by claiming positive motives; for example, one psychoanalyst suggested that she would not let gays and lesbians become psychoanalysts but only because she wanted to protect them from too much stress due to having to listen day in and day out to the rants of homophobic patients!

CITING SO-CALLED REALITY AND CLAIMING "I AM JUST BEING REALISTIC"

In the homophobic view of reality, human beings are stratified in a rigid class system consisting of *Übermenschen* and *Untermenschen,* with gays and lesbians intrinsically on a lower position on the scale than the one homophobes themselves occupy. Whether or not the homophobes will be accepted by gays and lesbians is no more a question that needs asking than a patient of mine who named his delicatessen "I'malocal" needed to ask, "Do the tourists in town accept me?" When these homophobes cite the innately nontraditional nature of gay marriage, their intention is not to affirm some truly inherent distinction that they embrace philosophically but to devalue gay relationships through stratification, as in "straight marriage is a sanctified institution to which heathen lowlife gays and lesbians need not apply."

USING EUPHEMISMS

Euphemisms consist of refined code words for gays and lesbians, like the word *elite* on a lamppost sign in a heavily gay town that reads, "Run those elites out of town." Euphemisms involve a displacement from the major to the minor, for example, from "you are a sexual predator" to "you are a social undesirable" to "yours is an alternate lifestyle to mine (and not the other way around)." Homophobes also speak euphemistically in reverse, such as when they use the word *faggot* as a euphemism for wimp ("when I use the word faggot, it's not about being gay, for I just really mean *wuss*").

BLAMING OTHERS/EXTERNALS TO MAKE THEIR HOMOPHOBIA "NOT ME" (AND DO NOT KILL THE MESSENGER)

Claiming to be misunderstood, homophobes say, "You are taking what I say out of context" or "You are just being hypersensitive and falsely accusing me of being a homophobe." Identifying with the aggressor, they become disparaging, but only because they were disparaged first. They blame the Bible for their homophobia, after overlooking the overall loving tone of a book that in its entirety welcomes all men and women. Speaking about professional issues they note that their homophobia just makes good business sense, for gays and lesbians are as erratic professionally as they are personally, stating that "while I don't mind working with gays and lesbians, I happen to know that my colleagues at work just won't be as accepting of them as I am." A boss will not advance gays and lesbians in his company. He denies that that is because he dislikes homosexuals or because he thinks that they are not up to the job. He says it is because *others* in the company dislike them, and he cannot afford to alienate everyone who works for him. Or we hear "I am just following the crowd," as in "Everyone says that gays and lesbians are unreliable" or "My homohating rap lyrics only reflect what is going on in my community and my culture." Or they wear homophobic T-shirts that make a statement that is obviously not theirs alone, for "all I did was buy a mass-produced item that says, 'Silly fags, dicks are for chicks.'"

PROVOKING OTHERS TO ACT OUT FOR THEM

At work, as in their personal lives, homophobes get others to act homophobic (and violent) for them. They discriminate against gays and lesbians or hamper their development not directly, by putting them down, but indirectly, by setting them up—with other homophobes. For example, talk show hosts know exactly what to say to fire up homophobes around the world to take up the cudgel and do their emotional and physical gay bashing for them.

In one clinic a nurse encouraged whatever patients she could approach before anyone else got to them to refuse to see the gay doctor and to instead pick the straight one who was his colleague. For his part, the straight doctor not only did nothing to discourage what was in essence an unethical practice but also actively used the nurse as a tool to undermine the gay doctor both personally and professionally, to use the gay doctor's homosexuality against him to win a popularity contest, and to get the business he needed by shattering the competition so that he could come out on top at promotion time and be first in line for patients at referral time.

Parents often incite their children to act out for them to avoid feeling guilty themselves or to avoid having criminal charges leveled against them. The father eggs his child on to kick in a neighboring gay's fence so that the father can avoid guilt and prosecution by saying, "I do not have that much control over my kids." Proselytizing homophobes pass on their homophobia to friends and family, including to their children, not only because they want everyone to agree with them but also because they want to stir others up to become disciples to go forth and do their dirty work for them.

CLAIMING ULTIMATE FAIRNESS

Denying that two wrongs do not make a right, homophobes justify their homophobia by claiming that they treat everyone, not just gays and lesbians, badly, so that gays and lesbians are supposed to tolerate their abuse because these homophobes also abuse straights. A boss yells at everybody, not just gays and lesbians. The Psychoanalytic Institute rejects 90 percent of all applicants, straight as well as gay. The armed services, as a news commentator might say when told that the army threw out 10,000 gays and lesbians last year, evicts not only gays and lesbians but also straight men and women, even though far more of the evicted straights than the evicted gays and lesbians actually had work-related problems and even though the armed services frequently throw out gays and lesbians just for being homosexual but never throw out straights just for being heterosexual.

ACTING TOLERANT, BUT ONLY SELECTIVELY

If their most prominent tolerances are at the same time the most trivial ones, homophobes can be fair, balanced, and supportive of gays and lesbians but only when that does not count for much. This group can be represented by the individual who will not buy goods in a certain state because it will not pass the antidiscrimination laws she believes in but only enforces that rule when she does not really need anything that that state happens to make.

BEING HOMOPHOBIC, BUT ONLY INTERMITTENTLY

Intermittent homophobes lead double lives. They are liberals by day (for public consumption) but bigots by night (for private self-realization). Their homophobia only comes alive under certain rather specific conditions or associatively, when something bothers them because it locks into one of their very personal complexes.

HITTING YOU WHEN YOU ARE DOWN

Passive-aggressive timing consists of launching into an attack just when it hurts the most. When the younger man of a gay couple had to have a serious operation, his mother came to the house to help out and babysit the pets, freeing up the older man to stay with and take care of his lover. This nice gesture, however, came at a price. The mother got the older man's ear when he was at his most anxious because his partner was in surgery. She then proceeded to attack the older man in the midst of all his worry. She told the older man that at one point she had deeply resented his taking her son away from her. (Early in the relationship she had actually barred the older man from the house and later tried to convince her son to attend a far-off medical school just to get him out of town and away from this man.) As she now announced, she had at first rejected the older man because of his age and sexual orientation, but two years ago she bit the bullet and accepted the relationship: a backhanded compliment that in effect said, "I used to devalue you, but lately I changed my mind and came around not to valuing you more highly but to accepting the inevitable fact that you would always be here."

Then, in so many words, she accused the older man of making her son gay and of liking him only for his youth (implying that her son's youth was the only thing going for him, although in fact it was a negative factor for the older man, who actually chose to ignore it in favor of the younger man's other qualities). She then went on to embarrass the older man about a previous relationship he had with another younger man, the son's former friend, citing this as proof that the older man was robbing the cradle on a regular basis, although he was not doing anything of the sort, for the older man had simply met her son through the younger man's former best friend, and these two were, not unsurprisingly, of the same age. She then picked on the older man for his advanced age. Using the pregnant-question technique to couch her attack in the form of mere curiosity, she asked him, with an obviously critical inflection, "Just how old are you anyway?"—too often the kind of question you ask not if you are looking for negative information but if you already have all the negative information you need and are simply looking, on the one hand, to confirm it and, on the other hand, to rub it in.

ACTING SUPERIOR

Clearly, as a straight woman and as a mother, this woman felt doubly anointed and higher up on the pecking order than others. Therefore, as she saw it, she could be the one to decide whether or not to accept gays and lesbians in general and her child's partner in specific, never mind the other way around. Her view, of course, only reflected a society-validated view that straights are tops and gays and lesbians are bottoms, and that this was, is, and always will be the natural order of things, period.

ABUSING GAYS AND LESBIANS SECONDHAND THROUGH THEIR PARTNERS

Passive-aggressive homophobes typically maintain an at least superficially loving relationship with one member of a couple but abuse that individual indirectly through his partner. Two gay men, one considerably older than the other, had been partners for 25 years. The mother of the younger man, one of my patients, told me she could not accept her son's being gay. But she never mentioned that to the son. All she told him was "I love you and want you to be happy, whatever you do and are." But she told the son's partner something different entirely: in a quarter of a century she had never accepted their relationship and still wished her son would wake up, get married, and have children.

UNDERMINING GAYS' AND LESBIANS' RELATIONSHIPS BEHIND THEIR BACKS

To his face, a gay man's sister told him how much she loved him, then attempted to undermine the relationship he had with their mother by reporting back all the passing negative comments her son made about her to his sister, even when these were not positional statements but wisecracks just designed to blow off a little steam, made only in the anger of the moment and told to someone believed to be both sympathetic and discreet. The sister also told all the relatives that her brother did not want to see them. She did this because she did not want them to see him with his lover, for she believed that his homosexuality reflected badly on her and the family. Then, when her brother bemoaned the fact that the whole family seemed to be rejecting him, she, playing dumb, just said, "I can't imagine why that is happening. They never said anything to me about it."

DEVALUING ONE BY PRAISING THE OTHER

The common expression "Some of my best friends are gay" can be interpreted in one of two ways: as a compliment or a criticism, with the ambiguity, of course, calculated. Does the statement mean "I accept gays as well as straights as friends," or does it mean "While mostly I prefer to hang around with my own kind, I make exceptions for gays and lesbians, but only when they are exceptional" (and they are not always)?

ACTIVELY PROVOKING GAYS AND LESBIANS

Many passive-aggressives actively provoke the very gay and lesbian behavior that they say they most disapprove of and are just condemning passively and justifiably. Recently, I sat near the booth of a man eating dinner in a mixed gay and straight (but predominantly gay) restaurant in Greenwich Village in New York City. The man chose the occasion of the St. Patrick's Day Parade (an occasion on which New York's gays and lesbians are particularly sensitive to criticism and exclusion given the ongoing prohibition against their marching as an identified group) to take his female date to this restaurant and then announce, so that anyone within earshot could hear, that he agreed with the powers that be that gays and lesbians should not be allowed to march in the parade. This not unexpectedly caused the gays and lesbians in the restaurant to have, as one loudly put it, a "hissy fit." That in turn seems to have influenced the straight man's impression of how gays and lesbians behave in public, which further justified his wanting to deprive gays and lesbians of their right to march in the parade. This became obvious from his next comments, made in a stage whisper, along the lines of "such behavior shows you why we are intolerant in the first place and cannot let gays and lesbians push the envelope of equality too far." Throughout he was only aware that he was criticizing gays and lesbians for how they behaved, which was, in his opinion, a given. In fact, he was provoking them to behave badly so that they could merit his criticism of them and in that way validate his preexisting negative thinking about them.

SIMPLY AND OFTEN TOTALLY, BUT ALWAYS POLITELY AND JUSTIFIABLY, IGNORING GAYS AND LESBIANS

Many homophobes avoid even associating with gays and lesbians. A gay man's family does not invite him and his lover to any family events. They deny prejudice, citing seating limitations, financial constraints, and other convenient excuses. Revealingly, the truth will out, as it did one day in church when the pastor suggested the equivalent of "Today, everyone express love to those from whom you previously withheld it." At this time, the whole family turned to the gay men sitting behind them to shake their hands—to discharge a debt they most certainly owed.

A book author is happy to accept a gay editor's editing her book but will not acknowledge his work in the book itself because she does not want to be associated in any way with someone gay. A literary agent, one of my patients, is told of a talented gay author, and he writes to her, but she keeps postponing responding because he is gay and she has a "reputation to uphold." Another literary agent, also a patient of mine, would never look at gays' and lesbians' productions at all. If he thought he had one at hand, he would put it right back into the enclosed SASE or email a rejection immediately so that it would not prove offensive to him and almost literally contaminate his desk. (This agent was also an erotophobe who responded to a woman's offer of a handshake by chanting to ward off what he perceived to be a serious threat and make it go away fast before it could somehow do him harm.)

Ignoring gays and lesbians often consists of giving them a chilling reception in the form of the cold shoulder or treating them as if they are invisible—the secular equivalent of religious excommunication, a kind of declaration of death in which another, although still very much alive, is proclaimed deceased and treated accordingly.

In a veterans' clinic where I worked, two social workers were on the staff. One wrote a paper on hysteria and was gay. The other did not write anything and was straight. When the clinic needed a lecture on hysteria, it simply and without fanfare chose the social worker who was straight to give the lecture. At one all-too-typical office reception for this clinic, the straights gathered in little clusters, while the gays and lesbians roamed around them, unable to break in, in effect relegated to being lost in space.

A doctor refuses to specialize in proctology because too many of the clientele are gay and he dislikes "working with people of that sort." The sister of a man's lover subtly humiliates both her brother and his lover by making dates for occasions, then canceling them. In addition, she does not call them unless she has a problem she wishes to discuss or unload or needs them to do something for her. When invited to join them, she says, "I'll let you know," then never calls back. She rarely accepts invitations in the first place, and if she does she never returns them. One reason she does not accept them is that there are too many gays and lesbians in the town her brother lives in, not something she wants to expose her teenage daughter to, lest she become contaminated in some way.

A neighbor refuses to nod back at a gay neighbor's hello, thinking, as the old joke goes, "I wonder what he meant by that?" But in this case it is no joke.

GIVING BACKHANDED COMPLIMENTS

Backhanded compliments such as "Some of my best friends" are an effective way to make exactly the opposite point. Other examples of backhanded compliments include "You make a great neighbor; you are hardly ever home" or complimenting the straight person as a way to criticize the gay one, as did the woman who raved to a gay doctor about how her doctors were wonderful because they had big families and lots of children. Many homophobic straights compliment lesbians by saying that their relationships are significantly better than the relationships gay men have, that is, supposedly closer, more long-lasting, and characterized by fidelity, as their roundabout way to criticize gay men (as well as all men) for "not being able to keep it in their pants."

WITHHOLDING THE POSITIVE IN FAVOR OF THE ALL-NEGATIVE VIEW

For example, in contemplating the social problems gay marriages might cause for straights, homophobes overlook the social benefits gay marriage would confer on gays and lesbians who might, in turn, no longer fit negative stereotypes and so (as some might hope) better acclimate themselves to and even benefit straight society. Homophobic doctors, overlooking the healthy side of gays and lesbians, view them as sicker than they actually are. For example, a psychiatrist called a gay man paranoid simply because he worried aloud about the outcome of his lover's surgery—and he had reason to be worried, because his lover was being operated on at a second-rate hospital. Indeed, gays and lesbians, like most minority groups, typically find themselves being called paranoid when they are in fact simply being persecuted and actually have real enemies. Then, when they try to defend themselves with a "But you don't understand what subtle homophobic prejudice is like because you are straight," they are put down further but now for a supposedly different reason—for being hypersensitive, which is in this case just another word for paranoid.

SUBSCRIBING TO AND PROMULGATING MYTHS ABOUT HOMOSEXUALS

Many homophobes subscribe to the myth that sexual practices and nonsexual abilities are closely related, so that homosexuality means being defective not only sexually but intellectually. Of course, the idea that evil sexual practices make one intellectually defective, as well as its twin, the idea that only intellectually defective men and women indulge in evil sexual practices, are cherished homophobic myths on a par with another equally cherished erotophobic belief, the one found in adolescents and some of their parents: that masturbation makes you insane. (Myths about gays and lesbians that homophobes find worthy of accepting and promulgating are listed in chapter 7.)

CONTEMPLATING NONASSERTIVELY, INTELLECTUALLY, AND RELUCTANTLY

Homophobes ask themselves difficult unanswerable questions such as "What is the essence of sin?" They particularly favor intellectual arguments about what constitutes "equal rights" as compared to "rights that are more equal than others." (As they see it, clearly gays and lesbians want to be more equal than others when they demand special rights in the form of hate crime laws that provide them with special treatment that straights do not get.) They also like to argue that any form of affirmative action is not justified to repay gays and lesbians for past injustices because it creates new injustices (for straights) instead, so that antidiscrimination laws do not make gays and lesbians less unfairly disadvantaged but more unfairly advantaged. They suggest speciously that the gay rights movement actually stirs up violence against gays and lesbians, so that gays and lesbians should retreat into the shadows if they are to avoid getting hurt. Moreover, I am still wondering what exactly they mean when they claim, "Our society is founded on the principle of marriage being between a man and a woman." That may be a principle that has existed in our society from the very beginning *as a tradition,* but some traditions do not participate in the foundation of society but rather develop in a society already under way.

Homophobes also convert raw anger into intellectual concern. They do not come out and openly accuse gays and lesbians of being child abusers. Instead, they brood about the possibility that their children might be in danger of abuse from gays and lesbians. They do not express overt death wishes toward gays and lesbians. Instead, proving that pity is often little more than sublimated sadism, they *worry* about gays' and lesbians' physical health in the face of the tragic epidemic of AIDS. They ask and seek penetrating answers to already-loaded questions. One homophobe asked, "What do two earrings stand for?" and "Are all gays and lesbians promiscuous?" and "Do you think it is okay for a gay man to be a sports coach?" and the familiar "Should gays and lesbians be allowed to marry, then be allowed to adopt children, because isn't bringing up a child in a family of same-sex parents contrary to the laws of nature and likely to condemn the children to lives of comparative impoverishment?" Although (contrary to the assertion of some excessively activist homosexuals) it *is* scientifically valid to try to research the developmental origins of homosexuality, psychoanalytic theories that rigidly posit that homosexuality is the result of a developmental lag, such as an oral fixation or regression, are often little more than subtle attempts to promulgate hostility disguised as pseudoscience—just a way to express the all-too-common homophobic sentiment that all gays and lesbians are primitive, backward individuals. Rife these days are talk show slippery-slope hypotheses of the "where does it all end?" variety, postulating that when it comes to recognizing gay marriage, not enough external controls exist to assure that allowing gay marriage will not lead to recognizing polygamy, then bestiality as well, and then who knows what, as if society cannot distinguish among such things.

All such contemplative arguments and debates only appear as if they are intended to prepare for discovering and advancing the truth. In fact, they are meant to take the homophobic side in an ideological controversy; those who do the brooding plan all along to resolve the debate in favor of a homophobic rationale, one that is already firmly in place and in mind.

BEING CONTROLLING

All homophobia, especially passive-aggressive homophobia, at least in part represents a vehicle for ordering others about. Passive-aggressive homophobes decide what gays and lesbians should want and do and then go on to impose their own strict standards on them. Not surprisingly, these homophobes, eschewing level playing fields, openly decry the probability that gays and lesbians are trying to control *them.* As Richard Merkt, a New Jersey Republican, suggested, "In the end, the truth is, the homosexual lobby wants same sex marriage for one reason—to use the power of the state to force heterosexuals to approve of homosexual activity and relationships."[1] (Merkt once again provides us with an example of how straights think that first-class citizens like themselves should be able to set the rules for second-class citizens like gays and lesbians.) Similarly, homophobic parents know that the straight life is best for their children and even know what their children should wear, and they do not hesitate to try to overrule their children's wishes in the matter. In this they remind one of the mother who gave her lesbian daughter and her partner gifts of clothes that were inappropriately frilly, then complained that they never wore any of them.

WITHHOLDING

Homophobes withhold help when they sense that gays and lesbians need it the most. Even a doctor might unconsciously avoid a right diagnosis as his or her way to say, "You as a second-rate citizen don't deserve first-rate medical care." I know of a case of misdiagnosed back pain that was, according to a highly respected internist, inferentially attributable to homophobia. He guessed that the emergency room doctor, almost consciously wanting to be sadistically punitive, diagnosed a gay man's back pain as due to muscle strain when it was in fact due to a herniated disc and then, instead of admitting the man to the hospital, sent him home on a painful and dangerous journey in a taxi and on foot. Surprisingly, the emergency room doctor worked in a hospital located in New York's Greenwich Village. "Even there," as the internist says, "if you are gay you don't always get the same level of medical care you get if you are straight."

In like manner, passive-aggressive homophobic friends refuse to come to dinner on time or to a party that gays and lesbians are giving. Then they typically blame the traffic when the tie-up results not from the traffic but from their personality, for the traffic was a known factor they deliberately chose to ignore. Often passive-aggressive bosses keep gays and lesbians but not straights on tenterhooks by saying, "I have a bone to pick with you," then make an appointment for "later next week," not stating in advance what they have in mind and refusing to have the planned discussion earlier to relieve the tension. Passive-aggressive bosses drag their feet when it comes to promoting gays and lesbians on the job. A homosexual teacher and his lover moved from a small town back to the big city not only because they were unable to handle having their friendly good-mornings met by stony silence and because they were refused entry into the block alert program because that was "for families" but also because they discovered that on their jobs they were being given bad evaluations and held back, in spite of their superior training, experience, and teaching ability, because, even though they taught children well, they produced none of their own.

Police who withhold typically remain unavailable to gays and lesbians who become crime victims. In one town, when teenage gangs beat up gays and lesbians, the police tended to express their own feelings about the matter by "never knowing who did it," although they were the only ones who seemed confused. The local populace also took the side of these teenagers indirectly by taking the side of their parents, even when the parents knew all about what their children were doing and did nothing to stop it. One person commented about the father of one of the teenagers, "Poor man, he has so many problems, he can hardly be expected to also solve those of his sons." In a similarly passive-aggressive manner, a local woman in the town I live in, when told the story I related in my introduction of the shopkeeper who called gays and lesbians the double-f words for complaining that he was not cleaning up his excelsior fast enough, withheld affirmation as she responded with a defense of the homophobe: "It's so hard for someone who doesn't know the area is gay to move in unawares, then to discover to his complete surprise exactly where he has landed."

Homophobes often withhold help even from their best friends, even when these friends are brutally attacked. Instead, they become suddenly unavailable, both as an expression of a disapproval that was simmering all along and out of fear of being identified with gays and lesbians and in turn being abused because of the association. As a result, gays and lesbians have friends until they need a friend, when they turn to their friends only to have them turn away. Finding strength from within becomes the order of the day because that is the only order likely to be filled.

A patient asked a gay doctor for a prescription for valium. She wanted it immediately, and she did not want to wait in line to register for the clinic, although registering was clinic policy. The doctor refused to see her unless she registered because his superior had told him, "If you treat patients without their registering you are in effect in private practice, and the hospital will not cover you for malpractice." The patient responded by complaining about the doctor's uncaring behavior: "He made me wait, and he was rude to me too." Then, when the doctor told her that if she would only register, he would be glad to write the prescription for her, she accused him of trying to bribe her to shut her up and blackmail her to spare himself further indignity. In the administrative struggle that ensued, everyone took the patient's side, not because the doctor was wrong and the patient was right, but because withholding support from a gay man was a good way to express already-existing hostility toward him and by extension toward all other gays and lesbians.

Homophobes also typically withhold respect and recognition from gays and lesbians. A gay psychologist was acceptable for confiding in informally, such as in the elevator or in the clinic. But when he suggested following up by coming for counseling in his private office (and paying for it), the response in effect was "What? Pay for something that is all talk?" This gay psychologist also made a good (informal) sounding board, but no one ever had the time to listen to him, because they felt that what he had to say to them was necessarily of no importance, not at least compared to what they had to say to him. In many workplaces straights who willingly act as expert consultants for gays and lesbians are unwilling to consult gays and lesbians as experts in turn. They advise gays and lesbians but never take their advice, even when the gays and lesbians are recognized authorities in their field. (In my experience many minority group doctors and other professionals like money managers often experience and complain about this kind of mistreatment and feel barely tolerated and frozen out professionally because others refuse to take them and their work seriously.)

A lesbian I know has a friend whom she has known for 20 years, who, as she put it, has "never ONCE complimented her on anything." When this lesbian, an author, had a new book come out, her friend did not even acknowledge it or go to any of her book signings to support her. Whenever she had her hair cut or a new outfit or anything, she would remark about it, noticing, "You have a new outfit." And it would end there. Once she told the lesbian that her husband and she were flipping through the channels and saw she was being interviewed on television and that they both thought the suit she was wearing was okay (that is, "some things about it they liked") but that she should do some shopping at another store.

ALWAYS TAKING THE STRAIGHTS' SIDE

I know of a case in which a bartender with a large family seduced a gay man, then the whole town blamed the gay man for seducing him and being a house wrecker and, in order to punish him, virtually exiled him, to the point that he had to leave town.

BEING HYPOCRITICAL

One way to be passive-aggressive is to be a wonderful human being with straights, putting on a good show, but only with straights, so that when gays and lesbians complain about how they are treated, everyone wonders whether the problem lies with the gays and lesbians, who "are undoubtedly as paranoid as everyone knows them to be." Such homophobic individuals have a double standard according to which they treat straights differently from gays and lesbians. At the veterans' administration where

I worked everyone who lost a parent received flowers but not one gay man. When his mother died, only one person gave him anything, and that was a card. Of course, they continued to ask him for funds when they wanted flower money for others who had suffered similar losses. This clinic also gave a straight man time off to attend his professional meetings, but when the gay man asked for the same consideration, he was told that his (equally academic) meetings did not qualify.

ACTING DEPRESSED

The homophobic cry "What is the world coming to with all these gays and lesbians around?" is the depressive passive-aggressive homophobe's way to express anger at gays and lesbians by turning the anger inward, in true depressive fashion, making an explosion into an implosion ("I am angry with you" becomes "I am disappointed in you"). An example is one homophobe's sad public complaint at a town meeting that she was heartbroken that gays and lesbians altered the complexion of the family town she thought she was going to live in when she first moved there. We are all familiar with the kind of mother who, upon discovering that her son or daughter is homosexual, proclaims, perhaps in a letter to an advice columnist, "While I am heartbroken, I will give my child my undying support." At first, reacting to the second part of her statement, we feel, "I admire any parent who does not reject the child when he or she discovers the child is homosexual." But second, reacting to the first part of her statement, we do a double take and feel, as we should, "Heartbroken? It is not as if the child has just been branded as a criminal." Or is it?

Depressive homophobes suffer masochistically in order to hurt gays and lesbians. Typically, to "send the bastards a message," they beat gays and lesbians over their heads with their own bloody bodies and cut off their own noses to spite gays' and lesbians' faces. Antigay small towns advertise themselves as family oriented to discourage gays and lesbians from coming there and are willing to go broke just to tell the world how much satisfaction they get from doing what they consider to be the right thing, even though they have little to show for their efforts other than the Pyrrhic victory of empty stores. In effect, they do not mind killing Oscar Wilde to tell the world they hate gay men, even though that means they never get to see or hear the beautiful things he could have written, had they just let him live in peace.

Some straights accept or even sadistically provoke an attack on themselves as part of their deliberate plan to launch a counterattack on gays and lesbians, guilt and consequence free. They deliberately take antigay stands, for example, against gay marriage, because they know that homosexuals will protest, and then they can act the part of the wronged party, get the reactionary sympathy vote, and build a power base from there, using the common gay enemy as their stepping-stone.

The question is often asked whether women are more homophobic than men. Some say that women are better disposed toward homosexuals than are men. In my personal experience, women do at least seem to be less homophobic than men. But that may only mean that they are more passive-aggressive about their homophobia. Possibly this is because women tend not to abuse gays and lesbians simply to cleanse themselves of their own latent forbidden homosexuality. Therefore, for them, personal involvement deriving from rancor is less of an issue. As a result, when they put homosexuals down, they do so in a less trenchant and more carefully crafted way—and one that is at least less obviously derived from prejudice.

CHAPTER 10

Homophobia as an Emotional Disorder: Other Forms

DEPRESSIVE HOMOPHOBIA

Depressive homophobes suffer from personal feelings of worthlessness and a sense of inferiority. They then prop themselves up by putting gays and lesbians down as second-rate citizens simply not comparable to them. Underneath they are typically jealous of gays and lesbians, many of whom they believe to be smarter, richer, in better physical shape, and more artistic than they are. They deal with that jealousy by making negative stereotypes to even the playing field and the score, so that they themselves can grow comparatively in stature. They condemn all lesbians for their grotesque hairdos and tendency to swagger, and they condemn all gays for swishing and for being loopy, effeminate, superficial people interested only in money and sex, unable to do their work by day because they party all night, always acting sick, crazed, and obnoxious in public by being seductive at inappropriate times and in inappropriate places, for example, when teaching a class, attending family functions, or just lying on the beach vulgarly discussing their sex lives too openly and making passes at people who do not wish to be touched or seduced. For depressive homophobes, even their bigotry itself becomes a source of self-pride, for by discriminating they convince themselves that they have the good taste to discriminate, and that although they are bigots, they are at least the biggest bigots of them all.

A patient of mine once stared bullets at groups of gay men who were obviously enjoying each other's company. He contrasted their being together with his own isolation and loneliness. When he railed against "those faggots," he was really condemning them for having the fun he felt he could never have. When he called them elitists, he was really condemning them as bad for simply being too good—he hated the intelligence and sophistication that they had but that he felt he completely lacked. Not surprisingly, gay pride defenses often fail with such depressive homophobes, for these defenses only further reduce these homophobes' low self-esteem. When gays and lesbians tell them, "I am as good as you are," it inspires them to gay bash even more in a frantic attempt to reestablish at least parity and, whenever possible, superiority.

Many depressive homophobes bash gays and lesbians in response to the loneliness that they believe regularly affects this group, as if it could affect them as well. After putting themselves in the place of homosexuals, as one saw it, "Cruising lonely hours among strangers, with no children to be my comfort in my old age," they attack the lifestyle that they feel might produce such an undesirable result. So these homophobes come to hate gays and lesbians because they make them feel as if "the gay fate is one that might await me," a "there but for the grace of God go I" mentality, relieved by homohatred in the service of homoavoidance used to isolate themselves from contact with someone whose sad fate could somehow be catching and so become the homophobes' very own fate.

Many depressive homophobes are also guilt-ridden, self-destructive people who condemn all pleasure in others in the same way they condemn any pleasure they might obtain for themselves. They are often strict moralists who do not like to see anyone, themselves included, enjoying themselves in any way. Displeasure-oriented individuals, they think that anything joyful is bad and that anything sad is good. For them, suffering is the main or only way to achieve a state of grace. As such, they condemn gays and lesbians as pleasure-oriented hedonists who regularly indulge in a frenzy of immorality and corruption—reserving their harshest criticisms for those gays and lesbians who are trying to lead, and succeeding in leading, fulfilling lives. For these sadomasochistic moralists, the term gay is not merely a term of opprobrium with a deeper meaning; it is also a term of opprobrium that stands for itself.

Byrne Fone, referring to a "moral purity movement," describes such a displeasure orientation as follows: this movement "prescribed dietary and sexual abstinence for those vulnerable to sensual excess . . . [particularly the] adolescent male, beset on every side by the lures of rich food, masturbation, seductive women—and sometimes seductive men. Since sex outside of marriage was a sure path to ruin, young men were counseled to seek the safe haven of the bourgeois home and marriage—even, once the duties of procreation were completed, sexless marriage."[1]

Edward Gibbon, in his book *The Decline and Fall of the Roman Empire,* also describes a form of displeasure orientation:

> In their censures of luxury [such individuals] are extremely minute and circumstantial; and among the various articles which excite their pious indignation we

may enumerate false hair, garments of any colour except white, instruments of music, vases of gold or silver, downy pillows (as Jacob reposed his head on a stone), white bread, foreign wines, public salutations, the use of warm baths, and the practice of shaving the beard which... is a lie against our own faces and an impious attempt to improve the works of the Creator.

These individuals impose whimsical laws... on the marriage bed [which] would force a smile from the young and a blush from the fair. It was their unanimous sentiment that a first marriage was adequate to all the purposes of nature and of society. The practice of second nuptials was branded with the name of a legal adultery; and the persons guilty of so scandalous an offence against... purity... soon excluded from the honours, and even from the arms, of the church.

[For] ascetics [of this kind] the loss of sensual pleasure [is] supplied and compensated by spiritual pride... the merit of the sacrifice [is estimated] by its apparent difficulty; and... in the praise of... chaste spouses [is] poured forth the troubled stream of... eloquence.[2]

Some depressive homophobes are Pollyannaish individuals who come to feel personally worthless because, in wanting to be loved by everyone, they cannot escape feeling rejected by many. They feel gays and lesbians are rejecting them sexually, when a lesbian tells any man "no," and nonsexually, when they view the joyous diversity of being gay as a criticism of their own monotonous lifestyle and so as a rejection of their own moral and value system. To them, gayness becomes a stubborn elitist individualism involving a rebellious transgression virtually directed as a personal snub. They feel not so much attacked by gays and lesbians who threaten them as deprived by gays and lesbians who ignore them—by snubbing the homophobes' value system just because they have their own gay ideas about what is and what ought to be right, good, and fun.

The more paranoid depressive homophobes project their self-critical feelings of badness onto gays and lesbians, coming to view them as monstrous fellow human beings, just like themselves, as if gays and lesbians, like them, reflect badly on the human race as a whole. They then go on to murder gays and lesbians for the same reasons that some mothers with postpartum depression murder their children: they feel that their children are their bad seed who need to be destroyed. For such depressive homophobes gay bashing or murder is a personal suicide that has become a homicide, with roving gay bashing reflecting a mass-murderous desire to "wipe everything evil" off the map. Not surprisingly, then, such homophobes, in the midst of their own flames, speak of and justify their homophobia as a cleansing of the world by fire.

SADOMASOCHISTIC HOMOPHOBIA

Sadomasochistic homophobes tend to be angry people who hate everyone—gays and lesbians, straights, and themselves. They hurt everybody, straights as well as gays and lesbians, themselves as well as others, in the process.

As sadists, sadomasochistic homophobes are hardly in conflict about their homohatred. Rather, they convince themselves that gays and lesbians deserve being hated and should by definition be the objects of their scorn and the subjects of their violence. In other words, unlike paranoid homophobes, who project their hatred outward due to anxiety and guilt, the hatred of sadomasochistic homophobes is virtually guilt and anxiety free. They actively enjoy making gays and lesbians suffer and also like the fallout from doing so. As teenagers they cruise in cars around a gay resort or so-called gay ghetto, yelling insults out of the car windows, and as adults they pick up and murder gays and lesbians. Sadistic homophobes who say they disapprove of gay adoption on moral grounds and for the sake of the children, who supposedly do not do well if brought up in households without a parent of each sex present, often thoroughly enjoy not only not letting gays and lesbians be parents but also depriving innocent, needy orphans of a home.

Such homophobes are like piranhas who move in for the kill whenever they sense vulnerability. They view homosexuals as being particularly "flawed," and that "flaw" as a "wound" that spills first blood. Not surprisingly, they tend to bypass proud gays and lesbians and attack those who plead for mercy, for mercy pleas give them the sign they seek that here is someone who is weak and whose weakness makes them desirably vulnerable.

An example of how sadistic homophobes use angry words and behave in an angry way toward gays and lesbians can be found in the words and behavior of the homohating man who verbally demonized his gay neighbors by comparing them to Hitler, Satan, and warlocks. He also displayed his anger toward them concretely by deliberately keeping his yard full of junk just so that he could cause them further dismay. Not one to actually assault anyone physically, except in his dreams and daydreams, he confined himself to looking bullets at those he believed to be gay. For example, he haunted the local diner not only to eat but also to pick out groups of men eating together so that he could stare a withering murderous stare at them, the kind one stares through a gun sight. He thought of this stare as a way to make a fist with his eyes, to visually beat up on his victims, even to burn them alive with the hot rays that were emanating from his head. He also saw his staring at them as a cleansing ritual, intended to rid himself of rays of hatred inside. Had this man chosen to go on to kill queers, as he might have done if he went off his antipsychotic medicine, he would no doubt have done so to prove something to himself: how serious he was about ridding the whole world of all queerdom.

Looking for reasons to retaliate against gays whom he believed were trying to seduce him, this man would regularly pick fights with men who brushed against him accidentally in the subway. Once he even started a fistfight with a man who merely walked in front of him in the aisle of a supermarket, who was, as he put it, "Acting as if he were looking at a display case, but in fact blocking my view of the merchandise, and probably just trying to give me a good view of his ass." This man once even said of himself that he modeled his life on some of the more familiar examples of police brutality and that, without individual homosexuals for him to have as enemies, he could easily have become an enemy of the entire state. Not surprisingly, gays who tried to pick up, argue with, or otherwise tangle with him (he could sometimes be quite seductive), would too soon and too often discover how dangerous it could be to come on to a stranger.

As masochists, sadomasochistic homophobes hate gays and lesbians as part of their plan to hurt themselves by depriving themselves of the pleasure of having homosexual friends and family. They also do destructive things to gays and lesbians as a way to do destructive things to themselves. They make inept, politically embarrassing, or disastrous slips of the tongue. They overinvolve themselves in petty self-destructive vendettas against gays and lesbians, wasting much time and effort in abusing them, draining energy that they might have otherwise used for creative thought and constructive action. They would rather be lonely than have gay or lesbian friends. And they would rather see their businesses fail than hire gays and lesbians as workers or serve them as customers.

PHOBIC OR TRUE HOMOPHOBIA

The literature tends to question the applicability and appropriateness of the term homophobia since phobia implies fear, whereas *hatred* of, not fear of, gays and lesbians is supposedly the core dynamic in homophobia. As Kort says, homophobia "does not fit the definition of a true phobia: an uncontrollable, irrational, persistent fear of a specific object, situation, or activity."[3] Even so, in many cases the homophobe truly *is* phobic of gays and lesbians, making the term homophobia a model of specificity. Phobic homophobes avoid gays and lesbians just as true acrophobics avoid heights, and for most homophobes fear and anxiety are just as significant as hatred in their feelings toward gays and lesbians. Also, speaking dynamically, true phobia does actually contain a component of hostility, so that the phobic's fear contains and expresses a retribution for unacceptable angry, even homicidal wishes. Thus, classically, a boy projects his rivalry with and hostility toward his father to become "my father hates and might kill me for hating and wanting to kill him." Only the lad finds it uncomfortable and unacceptable to think, "My father hates and wants to kill me," for that threatens the father-son relationship. As a result, he displaces from his father to a father figure like a ferocious animal, perhaps developing a phobia of dogs or, as with Freud's Little Hans, a fear that horses would bite off his "wiwimacher" (the term Hans used for his penis).[4]

A similar mechanism is involved in the creation of true homophobia, along the lines of "I hate and want to kill gays and lesbians" being transformed to become "They hate and want to kill me by giving me AIDS or seducing me, so they are dangerous people, people to stay away from, and it would help a great deal if I never had to run across one because all were quarantined, exiled, or entirely removed from the face of this earth." In a stepwise process, phobic or true homophobes first become anxious and fearful in the presence of gays and lesbians. Then they reduce their level of anxiety via their main defense: avoiding gays and lesbians, much as bridge phobics reduce their level of anxiety by avoiding driving over bridges. In other words, for such homophobes, homosexuals represent a "trivial prompt." The prompt is trivial because it makes the homophobe anxious not so much for itself but because of what it signifies: something personal and highly symbolic. In the case of homophobes the prompt symbolizes something they despise, like femininity, passivity, and weakness, or something that elicits their very special fears, such as a fear of emasculation. For such homophobes, by symbolizing something meaningful, gays and lesbians call up strong emotions that represent an excessive response to an inconsequential stimulus. That is, these homophobes fear and avoid gays and lesbians not because of who gays and lesbians are but because of who and what they stand for. The homophobic fearing, disliking, and avoiding occur not only because the homophobes are bothered by homosexuality itself but also because they are bothered by what homosexuality means to them. Thus, to them being penetrated means being emasculated, so that a homophobic man condemns gay men because thinking of gay sex makes him feel like less of a man, then avoids gays much as a phobic avoids dogs that might bite or high bridges that might collapse. For example, it is possible that the composer Charles Ives, allegedly a notorious homophobe, avoided writing consonances and preferred writing dissonances to avoid feeling castrated. According to Stuart Feder, Ives said he wrote "masculine music" to avoid hiding behind "silk skirts." Ives supposedly asked, referring to the preference for easy listening he saw as a current problem, "Is the Angle [*sic*] Saxon going 'Pussy?' [then proclaimed that his music was] greater [because it was] less emasculated than any of the [music of the] so-called great masters [like Wagner and Mozart]."[5]

Many true homophobes, like most phobics, have multiple fears and so avoid more than just gays and lesbians. For example, a male homophobe avoided gays and lesbians to reduce his fear of having his feminine side exposed. In addition, as an erythrophobe who feared blushing, he avoided strangers because he feared that his blushing would reveal his sexual thoughts to everyone. As a social phobic, he avoided public speaking because he feared embarrassing himself by fainting and wetting his pants. As a claustrophobic, he avoided going to the theater or church if he had to sit in the middle of the room but would go if he could sit on an aisle instead so that he could leave unobtrusively if strong feelings took over and got out of hand, possibly causing him to weep visibly and uncontrollably. This homophobe said he responded negatively to homosexuals because he consciously viewed homosexuals, homosexuality, and homosexual acts as per se unpleasant and because he had many negative associations to all the homosexuals he had met in the past. But he mainly responded to homosexuals negatively because they aroused forbidden erotic and hostile fantasies in him, and these enlivened the homosexuality, making it a more frightening stimulus for him than it actually needed to be. Like phobics afraid of bugs, he had endowed gays and lesbians with magical powers to the point that he saw them as capable of doing almost anything bad, ranging from undermining society and influencing the world's morality in a negative way to desiring to take over the world and ultimately doing so much as, according to Tony Wharton, Pat Robertson said, "Bring[ing] about terrorist bombs... earthquakes, tornadoes and possibly a meteor."[6]

Speaking psychodynamically, phobic homophobes use the same defense mechanisms true phobics use to handle the unpleasant feelings and fantasies they experience in the presence, and sometimes even in the absence, of homosexuals. In each case the defensive operation comes through as a unique homophobic construct.

As with all phobics, *avoidance* is the primary defense mechanism of phobic homophobes. After identifying homosexuals as the presumed source of their discomfort and the presumed reason for the danger they believe themselves to be in, they avoid them to achieve long periods of sustained inner peace, well-being, and freedom from fear. A core preoccupation of homophobes who use the avoidant defense involves making certain that gays and lesbians do not invade their space. They achieve this by passing laws against gays and lesbians designed to put and keep them in their place and get them out of their way, for example, laws to keep them out of the military service, to obscure their presence once they are there ("don't ask, don't tell"), or, when these things fail, to evict them from the premises even after they have become established. One reason behind passing laws against gays and lesbians getting married is to thwart the possibility that gays and lesbians will move to the suburbs and live next door to them. In short, these homophobes advocate antigay legislation to curb gays and lesbians for much the same reasons dog phobics advocate leash laws or elevator phobics attempt to defeat every high-rise building put before the planning board in the town where they live.

Like all defenses, avoidance achieves pleasurable feelings associated with the anticipated or actual relief of homophobic anxiety. These pleasurable feelings are often so intense that sometimes these homophobes even come to love to hate homosexuals, accounting for some of their paradoxical preoccupation with homosexuals even when others' homosexuality is actually none of their concern and even less of their business.

However, the peace and well-being that result from the relief of homophobic anxiety through avoidance are illusory, exacting as they do a price. That price involves complications of avoidance, especially those arising from elaborate, exhausting precautions that limit the homophobe's movement, compromise the homophobe's capacity for enjoyment and reduce the homophobe's ability to love and his potential pool of love objects. Furthermore, all homophobes have to ante up eventually. They cannot avoid gays and lesbians forever, either in fact or in fantasy. Sooner or later the devil comes by to collect his due. The homophobe encounters a trivial prompt, and because undischarged anxiety has built up over time, a crisis occurs in the form of breakthrough anxiety—which consists of an anxiety attack so intense that it undoes all the pleasurable peace and freedom from fear the homophobe until then had managed to sustain.

In addition, as with most defenses, the avoidance itself contains a self-destructive, self-punitive element. It is almost as if homophobes are deliberately and guiltily removing themselves from life in order to salve their guilt about their secret sexuality. That parallels how the bridge phobic arranges not to get from here to there, how the phobic with stage fright sees to it that he or she does not give the speech that would establish their reputation, and how the better-safe-than-sorry agoraphobe, afraid of venturing outside of the house without someone to protect him or her, allows a fear of being mugged to keep him or her from ever going someplace interesting and thrilling, in particular taking the plunge into the exciting crowds of the big city.

A phobic homophobe's supposed preoccupation with the raging immorality of gays and his fear that gays would overpower and rape him, forcing him to yield to their forbidden passions and pleasures, originated in his own fear and condemnation of his sexual feelings. So he defensively avoided such Sodom and Gomorrahs as San Francisco because of what he considered to be their secular progressive excesses, as if just being there would cause who knows what instincts of his to break through. Avoidance was also his way to reassure himself that he was a moral person who would have nothing at all to do with the immoral people gays and lesbians were. Ultimately, after therapy he was able to strike up a kind of tolerance bargain with gays and lesbians, itself a form of phobic pact that said, "Gays and lesbians are okay as long as they don't move into my neighborhood or my home town, that is, as long as they keep their distance from me and do not come so close that they act as a constant irritant and reminder of what makes me anxious."

A second defense involves mastering vulnerability by surrounding oneself with a *protective homophobic cocoon,* a shell that serves figuratively as a suit of armor. Homophobes develop a phobia of gays and lesbians for much the same reasons that agoraphobics have a companion in tow when they venture forth. The homophobia, like the companion, is an aide that helps protect them from their enemies.

A third defense involves the *seeking of consensual validation.* True homophobes typically form homophobic societies to keep themselves from feeling isolated and to enable them to enlist others to help them rationalize or deny the phobic nature of their avoidance, along the lines of reassuring them, "You are right to be afraid."

Seeking consensual validation often involves *proselytizing*. Homophobes often do what they can to convert others to become equally homophobic. They try to get everyone to be as afraid as they are. Typically they try to convince others to agree that gays and lesbians should not have any rights at all because, if they got some, they would want it all. In this they are much like other phobics who warn the world against lurking dangers from phobic objects, such as dogs that bite, planes that crash, and rickety ladders that drop cans of paint on the heads of those who dare walk under them. All concerned are indulging in a kind of phobic advocacy composed of misery liking company and a wish to normalize their own fear by making others equally afraid.

A fourth defense is the *counterphobic* defense. This involves identification with the aggressor along the lines of "you can't fire *me*, I quit on *you*." In this case, gay bashing becomes a way to firm up the straight journey in order to convince oneself that one is not heading in the opposite, gay direction. These homophobes are like the counterphobic individual afraid of heights who takes up parachute jumping or the counterphobic individual afraid of being killed who becomes a killer, but only to make the world a safer place.

A fifth defense involves *anticipating anxiety* in order to master it. These homophobes become preoccupied with homosexuals in order to better hone their homohating coping skills implicitly. They are also taking their pulse to determine how exactly others' homosexuality is affecting them and what precisely they need to do about that before it is too late.

A sixth defense involves mastering fear by *belittling* its nature, magnitude, importance, and significance. Just as bridge phobics attempt to master the bridge by belittling it, saying something like "You can make it across that little bridge; after all it's not exactly the Golden Gate," homophobes belittle gays and lesbians, saying, "They are all sick" or "all second-class citizens" in order to reassure themselves, "You have nothing to be afraid of; they are just big nobodies, too weak, defective, and unimportant to do you any harm." A man, characteristically condemning his phobic trivial prompt to cut it down to size, savaged gays and lesbians for refusing to honor the family tradition and trying to change the natural order of things, with men wanting to be women, women wanting to be men, and gays and lesbians wanting to get married like straights, instead of piously leaving things just the way nature made them. His condemning them was his way to convince himself that he did not have to fear gays and lesbians because, as outsiders, they did not need to be taken seriously, for they were not even part of the civilized world to which he belonged and so did not even have to be reckoned with in the first place.

A seventh and primary defense involves *displacement*. In displacement something that makes the homophobe anxious is shifted from the more to the less significant, as when a symbol is substituted for the real thing. The result of this defense is that homophobes fear not homosexuality itself, which they can neither avoid nor do anything about, but instead what they believe homosexuals and homosexuality stand for, such as femininity, which they can safely skewer, or being a loopy wuss, which they can readily satirize. Just as another phobic might substitute a fear of flying for a fear of a sexual encounter, the phobic homophobe might substitute a feared threat to the natural order of things by a dissolution of the accepted male-female identity, dichotomy, and design for a fear of the real thing: an attempted seduction that would undermine his heterosexuality and that he simply would not be able to handle.

An eighth defense is *secondary rationalization* of one's homophobia. Homophobes, like all phobics, deny that they are phobic. They deny because they need and want to keep their phobia, because they are ashamed of it, and because society encourages them to hide any hint of what society too readily misinterprets as unacceptable. So they rationalize their homophobia as an acceptable wish, a natural preference, an admirable personality trait, or a normal biological condition. They say, "fags are after all revolting and to be avoided at all costs," just as phobics afraid of flying claim they take the train not because they fear the plane but because they like the scenery on the ground or otherwise disguise their fear of flying as a general dislike for public transportation, then disguise that as a wish not to travel; phobics afraid of going out into crowds proclaim a preference for the country over the city; phobics afraid of success proclaim a liking for the simple life; and phobics excessively afraid of contamination claim they do not have a germ phobia but are merely taking sensible precautions—the ones that we all need to take against the germs that lurk everywhere in life and are lying there, just like all the world's gays and lesbians, waiting to go on the attack.

OBSESSIVE-COMPULSIVE HOMOPHOBIA

Obsessive-compulsive homophobes are strict moralists making certain that others do only what coincides with their own high or excessively high principles. Gays and lesbians in their view are unprincipled sinners, and gay sex is a dirty thing because it is not like their own sex: out of necessity and in the family way, in the missionary position, in the dark, within the confines of marriage, and for the purpose of procreation.

Obsessive-compulsive homophobes are also rigid individuals who develop repetitive homophobic rituals meant to magically tame homosexuality and homosexuals. For example, a patient of mine would say a long prayer of salvation for each man she believed to be "a homosexualist" as if her mind could control their matter and her own mental exercises and mantras could change their behavior. As if they believe in magic, out of mind means out of sight for them, as they deny that homosexuality even exists by invoking the "don't ask, don't tell" principle—a personal two-monkey approach that in essence says, "I accept evil but only so long as I don't have to see or hear it."

These homophobes also favor influencing through contemplating. They worry as if they can thereby control the outcome of what they worry about, for example, "If I worry enough about gays and lesbians taking over the world, it won't happen." They favor brooding about imponderables as their royal road to salvation through enlightenment, so they try to determine whether designating antigay crimes as hate crimes would mean giving gays and lesbians equal or more than equal rights. Brooding is their way to detach themselves from feared and hated emotions as they transform passion into persuasion and feelings into words so that "hate" becomes "debate." They do not beat gays and lesbians up, but instead they argue gays and lesbians down; they do not get mad, they do not get even, but instead they just get philosophical, hoping that precise definition will lead to gays' and lesbians' complete contrition and full submission.

As controlling individuals, homophobes feel entitled to tell, and responsible for telling, homosexuals what they should do, even in private. Control gives them the gratifying feeling of power that comes from being in charge of those others they place firmly under their thumb. For them, homosexuals are defiant, errant children who simply must follow their orders to disavow their personal gay inclinations, hopes, and dreams and to become straight because "that is what I, as your new, self-appointed parent, think that you ought to do." Not surprisingly, obsessive-compulsive homophobes set forth specific conditions under which they will and will not accept gays and lesbians. They are willing to accept gays and lesbians into their fold if they renounce their filthy homosexual activities and remain celibate throughout their entire lives. They will accept gays and lesbians who submit to them by staying in their assigned closet, but they will not accept those who do not listen to them and instead continue to go their own way—being sexually active, right out in the open, regardless of "how much I disapprove of that and warn you to stop." They also view gays and lesbians favorably if they are in conflict about their homosexuality because, although they have sinned and continue to do so, they at least seem willing, and eager, out of a sense of laudable guilt, to atone for their sins, even in, or shortly after, the very act of committing them. In short, these individuals sit in judgment over much that is none of their business, micromanaging gays and lesbians to macromanage the threats they believe gays and lesbians constitute to their personal morality and even to the safety of their persons.

Additionally, obsessive-compulsive homophobes are excessively perfectionistic individuals who view gays and lesbians collectively as flawed people who mar a world that would otherwise be flawless. We hear, "The world would be a *perfect* place if it weren't being *completely* spoiled by queers." Likewise perfectionistic is their compartmentalizing of gays and lesbians into neat little positive and negative packets, so that some gays are their *best* friends, whereas others are their *worst* enemies.

As neat freaks, these homophobes believe that the body and its functions, particularly its sexual functions, are dirty. After deciding gays and lesbians do especially dirty things with their bodies, they set out to cleanse the world of its dirty gays and lesbians and wash their own hands of any possible contamination by the filthy homosexuals. When they speak of gays and lesbians corrupting and so destroying the moral fabric of society, they are really, however, speaking of their own overwhelming fear and condemnation of fecal contamination, so that for them gays and lesbians are little more than "disgusting buttheads," with being gay not only catching but also as frighteningly repulsive as the filthy plague. Some even hesitate or actually refuse to touch gays and lesbians or as a precaution wash their hands thoroughly after shaking hands with them. Taking matters to the next level, they often demand that society protect them by quarantining all gays and lesbians as if each and every one of them has a communicable disease—ranging from the open sores of AIDS to the moral sickness of just being queer.

A homophobe was disgusted with gay men because he felt that they were all covered with a thin layer of feces. He did, however, accept and pardon gays and lesbians who were in conflict about being gay, because, as he saw it, at least they were making an effort to clean up their act. He particularly hated homosexuals who were very sexually active not only because he viewed them as morally bankrupt and homosexuality as morally wrong but also because he saw them and their homosexuality as particularly dirty and diseased. A complete bigot, he not surprisingly also disliked Jews for accumulating "filthy lucre," blacks because they were "brown like feces," foreigners because they were "the great unwashed," and women because they "soiled their panties, with regularity, once a month."

When dining out, this man could hardly go to the bathroom if he suspected that there was a gay man anywhere in the restaurant because he feared he would contract AIDS if he used the same washroom. When he had to use the restroom, he developed a severe hand-washing compulsion upon leaving. Convinced that he could pick up HIV from a contaminated door handle, he had to return to the sink to wash his hands over and over again—only to find that he was recontaminating his hands each time he touched the doorknob when he tried to open the door on the way out, so that he had to go back to wash yet again. He also did not defecate as often as he needed to because he felt that defecating was dirty. He even ate lightly in order to avoid making excessive feces and once developed bulimia, unconsciously put into place as his method of colonic cleansing.

In his therapy sessions this man could not say the word *asked* (one that came up frequently in his conversation) without immediately adding, "Doctor, that sounds like assed." In the supermarket he more than once stood in the middle of the aisle turning the prune jars upside down to watch the prunes fall, ostensibly to see which jar had the thickest syrup but really, as he came to realize, "my way to have fun watching turds drop." On each trip to the supermarket he bought as many rolls of toilet paper on sale as he could carry home on his arms. At one time he had 135 packages of multiple rolls stored in, really stuffed into, the closets of his small apartment. The neighbors saw him coming and going with what one called a big "shit-eating" grin on his face fresh from the triumph of having gotten another shopping bag full of toilet paper at bargain prices. When it came to disposing of his garbage, in order not to have to go to the incinerator, which he avoided because he was afraid that soot would back up and get on and blacken his face and clothes, he virtually gift wrapped his garbage to make it presentable enough so that he could take it down on the elevator without its being discovered and safely deposit it in the wastepaper baskets on the city streets, in violation of (or really because of) the laws against the use of city trash baskets for household waste.

Once he invited a gay colleague to share his office, then threw him out because his own colleagues were complaining about his association with someone gay. The excuse he used to get rid of this man was that he had dirtied the premises. What did he do? He soiled a 59-cent desk blotter because he ate a sandwich and a piece of coleslaw fell on it, staining it irretrievably, as he put it, and he ruined a pair of 28-dollar blinds because he simply did not know how to swing a window on pivots closed without catching the blinds in the window frame and bending them. Clearly this was not a financial matter, because a few dollars would have covered the damage nicely. It was a personal matter—one that involved a gay man soiling and contaminating his office—which was not just an office but rather a place he saw as an extension of himself.

As a therapist this man even expressed his personal fears of contamination in the way he analyzed gays and lesbians and the reasons for which he analyzed them. He was not analyzing them for being gay so much as he was analyzing the gayness out of them. It was as if he were purging them of being gay, figuratively cleaning them up by giving them the equivalent of a psychic enema.

For obsessive-compulsive homophobes, gay bashing or even murdering gays and lesbians is an unconscious act of self-cleansing. As an example, two men picked up a soldier hitchhiking in California and had sex with him in the back seat of a car. After complying, the soldier pulled out a knife and threatened to kill both of them, saying he felt dirty and needed to clean himself up after what he felt was the big bad thing he did. They saved their lives by talking him down—really talking to and soothing his guilty conscience—by telling him to give everyone a break and just chalk this big nothing event up to experience.

As doers and undoers, these individuals manage their own unacceptable feelings by turning them into their opposites. They typically cover their anger with an almost compulsive saccharine, condescending charitableness that implies the reverse; that is, you are needy enough to warrant help from me, pathetic enough to require my pity, and in sufficient personal disrepair to require my reparative therapeutic endeavors. Their overwrought claims that they really like gays and lesbians are their way to absolve themselves of guilt-laden conflicts about hating them, as they turn their sadism into understanding or pity but never really into love. They pray for gays' and lesbians' salvation for hours at a time, repeating themselves often enough to be certain that the prayer covers all their anger and expels all their sinful thoughts. One such individual, in an evangelical fury, closed his eyes and tightened his facial muscles as if to both give his prayerful thoughts more amplitude and momentum and, in effect, squeeze the evil in his insides out, like toothpaste out of a tube. When he finished, a beatific look came over him as if he had emptied himself of sin. Then he became unctuously loving. Soon enough, however, the first signs of a frown spread over his face, signaling that his anger and evil thoughts were returning, popping back in the seams that he could not keep from showing between the prayers he was offering constantly.

These homophobes are also purists for whom there is nothing between love and hate—no happy medium, no tolerance, permissiveness, acceptance, or even the benign neglect that many gays and lesbians would settle for. Instead, we see criminalization taken back with the priestly ritual of forgiveness, as gays' and lesbians' sexual acts are first made into crimes even though there are no victims, and they are then offered full salvation and forgiveness, even though there has been no crime.

Developmentally speaking, these homophobes tend to have suffered under rigid controlling parents who did not want their sons and daughters to grow up and leave home. As they grow to maturity these homophobes find both straight and gay adult sex to be a threat because it represents just another alluring but forbidden stepping-stone away from home and mother. Mother often plays into this laggard development. One boy's mother sued a dermatologist for taking a mole off her underage son's abdomen near his genitals without her permission. Clearly, the boy had wanted the surgery in order to improve his sex life, and that threatened her. As an adult gay man he called into and supported the party line of right-wing antigay talk shows—from home, in his mother's presence, so that she could overhear him and be reassured that he would never leave her for a lasting liaison but instead would stay at home and be with her forever.

PERSONALITY DISORDER HOMOPHOBIA

Passive-Aggressive Personality Disorder Homophobia

In passive-aggressive personality disorder homophobia, the main way homophobia presents today, gay bashing is expressed not in a raw or open but in an indirect, refined, subtle way. Passive-aggressive homophobia tends to be both low-key and constant, to the extent that it becomes a full way of life as it is deliberately applied indiscriminately, on the principle that the wider the net, the larger the catch. Passive-aggressive homophobes typically express their homohatred by withholding, by being neglectful, or by supporting or even encouraging others' homophobia as a way to express their own indirectly. For example, although Bob Grant, according to Bob Herbert, said of participants in a gay-pride march that "ideally, it would have been nice to have a few phalanxes of policemen with machine guns and mow them down,"[7] upon his retirement in 2006 a number of conservative luminaries wildly praised him, including former New York governor George Pataki, the conservative columnists Ann Coulter and William F. Buckley, former Speaker of the House Newt Gingrich, and even New York's former Mayor Ed Koch, according to the Newsmax.com staff.[8] The more moderate homophobic talk show hosts rarely say anything that can be construed as openly homophobic. Rather, over months and years they simply appear to be regularly taking the "anti" side more in legitimate pro/antigay controversies, as when they express their opinion that it is best to take the issue of gay marriage out of the courts (where it will pass) and give it back to the voters (where it will fail). Passive-aggressive homophobia was discussed in detail in chapter 9.

Histrionic Homophobia

Histrionic homophobes see what they believe as they let their emotions guide their logic and their perceptions determine their reality. The days are not completely gone when, as Joyce Purnick relates in her article "Recalling a Gay Rights Non-Crisis," after passing the gay rights bill in New York City in 1986, "lawmakers bickered and wept; Rabbis cited the Talmud, priests quoted from the Bible... and Mayor Edward I. Koch—sounding like an upside-down Chicken Little—intoned: The sky is not going to fall, the sky is not going to fall."[9] Even today the extreme worrisome fear prevails in some circles that giving gays and lesbians their rights cannot help but unleash terribly destructive social forces and start us all down the slippery slope to complete anarchy in a world that will never achieve lasting peace.

Like true histrionics who imagine footsteps in the dark, ghosts in the mansion, or their name being called in a lonely place, these homophobes see gays and lesbians everywhere, then, making much too much of homosexuality the same way they make much too much of everything else, develop exaggerated visions about what gays are and do, misevaluate the extent to which gays and lesbians realistically can or want to influence things, and become emotionally overwrought and panicky as if the world is going to come to an end just because it has gays and lesbians in it. For example, they get hysterical about the possibility that gays and lesbians by loving other gays and lesbians will undermine or completely destroy organized, civilized society as they know it.

Histrionic individuals are also particularly attuned to competitive issues, especially where "I stand" relative to where "you stand." Gays and lesbians make them anxious because they view them as competitors who will put them down and show them up. As Byrne Fone, writing about Jake Barnes, a character in Ernest Hemingway's *The Sun Also Rises,* puts it, "whatever homosexuals are supposed to be in the eyes of middle-class observers like Barnes—lonely, loveless, sexually inadequate, unfulfilled, unhappy—is given the lie by their public assumption of easy superiority and confident worldliness. When Barnes sees his own life reflected in this highly polished mirror, it seems drab and lacking in style.... Homosexual panic turns to rage, and homophobia is not far behind."[10] In *Moby Dick,* Herman Melville might have been describing a competitive histrionic homophobic patient of mine when he wrote, "When a person placed in command over his fellow-men finds one of them to be very significantly his superior in general pride of manhood, straightway against that man he conceives an unconquerable dislike and bitterness; and if he have a chance he will pull down and pulverize that subaltern's tower, and make a little heap of dust of it."[11] Victor Hugo in *Les Miserables* might have had the same patient in mind when he wrote that "genius invites hostility."[12] For, as Raymond Hernandez says in another context, histrionic homophobia is "something that can often mask larger insecurities, frustrations, petty rivalries, hostilities and other emotions that are part of coming of age" and in particular part of the process of "jockey[ing] to fit in among...peers."[13]

Histrionic homophobes famously put gays and lesbians down because they envy everything from their hard bodies developed in the gym to their freedom from family responsibility. They criticize gays and lesbians for what they perceive to be their flaws so that they can view themselves, and in turn be viewed, as comparatively flawless. They devalue gays and lesbians so that they can overvalue themselves. They resist giving up their homophobia because it is a refuge from feeling inferior—and gays and lesbians are for them an ideal foil because, like Achilles, they make a worthy competitor but one with a desirably fatal flaw. They do not want same-sex marriages not only for the moral and religious reasons they cite but also because they want to be the only ones legitimately married, with their straight marriage bigger and better than the gay kind.

One of my homophobic patients was a flag-waving jingoist who proclaimed "being gay is un-American." He waved the American flag less because he wanted to wave the flag and more because he needed to display his flagpole. He waved the flag and raised the flagpole for much the same reasons he tattooed his arm with a logo that read "I love Mary" and regularly wore his favorite T-shirt, the one that proclaimed he was participating in coed-naked basketball—that is, he was affirming his fidelity to the United States far less than he was reaffirming his masculinity to himself.

This homophobe accepted certain gays and lesbians but only the ones he could view as big nobodies because he could see them as in some way inferior to himself. He hated proud, successful gays and lesbians, especially the ones who came out as if they were not ashamed of being who and what they were. It followed that he mostly hated gays and lesbians not for what they did wrong, as he claimed, but for what they did right. For example, for many people, being an intellectual is not a bad thing. But for this man gays and lesbians were elitists, by which he meant not superior but inferior, for, as he told himself, though they seem intelligent and sophisticated, what good is that, because they do not do the real work of the world, like hunting for game, foraging for grain, or raising the roof beam high. Not surprisingly he also disliked lesbians. He claimed that he disliked them because they were unlike real women. In reality, he disliked them because they were like men and, being like men, represented even more competition for him.

Developmentally speaking, for this man gay bashing was in large measure the continuation of an old sibling rivalry. The homosexual of today was a stand-in for the brothers and sisters that he envied in the past. He competed with gays and lesbians in the present for the same reasons that he competed with his brothers and sisters long ago. He had always wanted to be number one among his siblings and had regularly tried to get all the available parental love for himself by convincing his parents that he, and he alone, was the worthiest child of them all. Consequently, in his adult homophobic role he was like a gladiator in combat. His homophobia was meant not only to kill off the opposition but also to favorably impress the spectators.

One brother, a successful physician, was not someone he felt he could ever match or surpass. For him, all male homosexuals were brother substitutes, with gays making particularly satisfying objects of scorn to pick on because as queers, being already one down, they made easy and readily available bull's-eyes. A recurrent theme of this man's life was "I wish the world was a place where my brother was gay, for if that were the case I could lick him with one hand tied behind me."

Once, after a gay man whom he had formerly liked built a house bigger than his, this man first added such a large new wing on his old house that his friends said he had not one but two houses. Then he dropped the relationship completely to avenge himself on this man for having beaten him in the house competition.

Anatomically, he was so poorly endowed that he could but view his penis as so teeny and shrunken that it lay somewhere toward the female end of the continuum between men's and women's genitals. He condemned so-called gay hypersexuality as threatening because, as he saw it, all gays were winners who had more between their legs than he did.

So he set about branding them as losers just to emasculate them so that they did not show him up as someone with comparatively nothing at all down there. Gay men who allowed themselves to be penetrated also reactivated this complex because he thought of them as formerly men now become women. Therefore, I was not surprised to hear him during one session congratulating himself for having bought a big new truck and bragging about the extra-large tires he put it up on as well as the fishing rod holder he installed on its front so that he could proudly display his rods in all their phallic glory as he plowed through traffic. But he was not merely out to get somewhere. He was also out to demonstrate his equipment. He was less driving and going fishing than he was in effect showing the world his goods.

Psychopathic Homophobia

While true paranoid homophobes are guilty-feeling people who externalize blame to diminish their own guilt, psychopathic homophobes are guiltless people who externalize blame so that they can grab the good things to which they feel entitled. We might say that whereas paranoid homophobes like and need to rearrange facts so that they can see themselves in a more favorable light, psychopathic homophobes prefer to be seen in a more favorable light so that they can rearrange facts—so that they can get while the getting is good and take the money while they can still run. In other words, psychopathic homophobes externalize guilt and blame onto others not so that they can deny an aspect of themselves, not to reduce anxiety, but so that they can diminish the standing of others and increase their chances of extracting something from them.

When such homophobes bash gays and lesbians, it is part of their plan to use them, for example, to win an election or obtain a coveted job. They devalue the gays' and lesbians' services so that they do not have to pay for them, much as some people find reasons to complain about the service in a restaurant at the end of an enjoyable meal so that they can reduce the size of the tip. Psychopathic homophobes as patients suddenly learn that their doctor is homosexual so that they do not have to pay a bill they ran up. As bosses they conveniently suddenly discover that their workers are homosexual so that they can avoid having to increase their salaries. As colleagues they become homophobic to backstab to get ahead, as did a man who, himself gay, got married to hide that fact, then outed an unmarried rival, a former beloved mentor, just so that he could get a coveted job both of them were vying for.

Psychopathic homophobes set out to enlist the support of others in their goal of forming powerful antigay sociopolitical coalitions. They are often personally appealing salespeople who easily mesmerize others into forming the large groups with clout they need to help them become the winner who takes all. Of course, being manipulative by nature as well as by design, they know how to cleverly excuse their gay bashing after the fact with various tricks of logic, so as to convince themselves and others that they have a mission that is admirable and deserving because they are not homophobes for evil but homophobes for good, in particular for the good of civilization, mankind as a whole, and of their Lord.

Although many psychopathic homophobes are covert and sly, others are openly aggressive. They do not simply reason contemplatively that same-sex marriages will destroy the fabric of society but instead provoke pitched battles between gay and straight social factions, because actually tearing the social fabric apart serves one of their main purposes—being able to be the ones to put it together again. They incite to riot, so that they can rush in on their white horse to quell the resultant disturbance.

Narcissistic Homophobia

Narcissistic homophobes see themselves as representing the standard everybody else should follow. They have the chutzpah to believe that who they are gives them the right to criticize those who are in any way different, just for being so. Just as the xenophobe's definition of a good American is "who and what I am," for the narcissistic homophobe "my heterosexuality, family standard, and straight marriage" define "who and what you should be." They define marriage as "innately an institution between a straight man and a straight woman for the purpose of having children" simply because that is what their own marriage is, and anything else is comparatively flawed or entirely immoral.

No matter how much their qualifications are mainly self-conferred, narcissistic homophobes still believe themselves uniquely qualified to judge others—in preparation for converting those whom, as they see it, do not match up. One goal of all this judging is to remake gays and lesbians in their own image, in particular to have them conform to their own family standard. Another is to grandiosely deny any homosexual and related trends they might discover within themselves so that they can become flawless in their own eyes and in the eyes of others. To this end, they even vocally condemn gays and lesbians for things they themselves are and do, so that they condemn gay promiscuity while hypocritically overlooking, conveniently forgetting, or comfortably dissociating away equivalent behaviors in themselves and in straight people in general. For example, using selective inattention that is deliberately unfair to the objects of their scorn, they complain about gays and lesbians being sexually preoccupied, ignoring the content of their own locker room conversations and their own life indiscretions, which they keep secret from everyone, sometimes including themselves. Not surprisingly, unless someone actually brings them up short, it does not bother them at all to tell others to do what they say, not what they do. The most homophobic man I ever treated was a straight doctor who preached sexual, particularly homosexual, restraint, only to have his patients find his name listed in the newspaper for soliciting a prostitute in a run-down area of a Jersey Shore community—most startling, shortly after his wife had a baby.

These homophobes also derive a great deal of their pleasure from the dominance involved in sitting in judgment, for it makes them feel like royalty wielding the scepter. Feeling like royalty is especially reassuring to men whose self-esteem is low because they condemn their feminine side and to women whose self-esteem is low because deep down they believe it when others imply or actually tell them that a woman is a defective man.

One narcissistic homophobe criticized gays and lesbians as his roundabout way to congratulate himself. An opera buff, he would boo not to say, "*you* are a disaster beyond belief" but to say, "*I* have the good taste to recognize lack of talent where I see it, and the good sense to want to criticize those who don't see it the way I do." Along similar lines he condemned gays' and lesbians' heretical blasphemy in order to brag about the extent of his own faith and condemned gays' and lesbians' sins in order to proclaim himself free of sin and guilt. In a general way, he wanted to reduce gays' and lesbian's status in society in order to reaffirm his own high social value and status both in others' eyes and in his own.

Particularly narcissistic are the prolonged self-indulgent temper tantrums these homophobes have against gays and lesbians. These tantrums are of the puerile kind children have when they feel angry with their parents for having deprived them of something they want or for having criticized them for doing something they supposedly ought not to have done. Narcissistic homophobes want gays and lesbians to buy into their own lifestyle; when gays and lesbians do not, they act hurt, as if the gays and lesbians are bad children who have minds, needs, and goals of their own. They then have a social temper tantrum as if the kids are growing up and defying them and about to leave them all alone, at home in an empty house.

Homophobic narcissists further maintain and elevate their self-image by finding ways to rationalize their homophobia. They are mostly too narcissistic to admit that they are prejudiced. So they tie themselves in knots using plausible excuses to deny their own homohating tendencies. They typically emphasize how their homophobia is a response to the so-called negative doings of gays and lesbians. One homophobic boss justified his homophobia by saying that gays' and lesbians' sexual preoccupations clearly made them difficult to get along with personally and that their sexual promiscuity clearly made them unreliable professionally. For example, to hear him talk, all gays and lesbians regularly kept late hours during the week because they were constantly looking for sex. As a result, they predictably could not do the work he wanted them to do because that required them to get up early the next day; this meant that they made unsuitable employees in his office, for that was a place that required regular attendance and demanded an especially high degree of concentration.

Other self-soothing narcissistic rationalizations include "Some of my best friends are gay," "What I say is only words," "I just had a temporary lapse into carelessness or stupidity," "I am not homophobic because I make some trivial sacrifice, like refusing to ski in a hate state," "I am homophobic in my thoughts but not in my actions (such as my hiring practices, that is, I am prejudiced, but that is okay because I do not discriminate)," "I am homophobic, but I do not mean it personally nor about you, for you are an exception," "There are worse homophobes in this world than I," "Everybody is slightly homophobic, they just don't admit it like I do" (the child's tu quoque or "you are one too" argument), "I am only homophobic when sorely provoked by gays' and lesbians' bad, inciting behavior," and the all-too familiar "I am only a reflection of my society," an attitude that is well on its way to the infamous Final Solution rationalized as "I am only following orders."

Narcissists often use their homophobia as the basis for joining a group where they can feel admired and loved by other homophobes with whom they have a great deal in common. These groups are mutual admiration societies where the more bigoted the group members, the more external victims they have, the more love and approval they get from their peers, and the less lonely, depressed, and guilty they feel as individuals. Many ultimately go public in their attempt to glean consensual validation, hoping to garner even wider support along the lines of "Hey buddy, we all know where you are coming from," said loud, clear, and often.

PSEUDOHOMOPHOBIA

Schizoid Pseudohomophobia

Whereas paranoid personality disorder homophobes are more uncomfortable in the presence of homosexuals than in the presence of heterosexuals, schizoid homophobes are highly uncomfortable in the presence of almost everybody, heterosexuals as well as homosexuals. Paranoid homophobes avoid relationships with gays and lesbians to avoid recognizing their own homosexuality, but schizoid homophobes avoid relationships with everybody to avoid the anxiety that closeness brings.

Borderline Pseudohomophobia

These individuals dismiss gays and lesbians the same way they dismiss straights from their lives. They get deeply involved in a close relationship, then suddenly, without warning, drop the person, sometimes after years of what at first appeared to be at least a peaceful intimacy. A social worker is still mystified by how a psychiatrist friend of hers, someone she had known for 20 years, dropped her in just this way. The only provocation was that she once asked the psychiatrist a personal medical question, only to have the psychiatrist tell her off, saying, "Don't you ever call me again. I never mother dykes."

Gays and lesbians involved with such people think they have been victimized by a homophobic attack. In fact, they have not been treated prejudicially at all. They have been treated all too equally, only that means that they have been treated all too badly—like everyone else.

CHAPTER 11

Homophobic Cognitive Errors

This chapter describes some of the main cognitive errors comprising the illogical ideology of homohatred. Homophobes make these tenets seem, in spite of their underlying distortive nature, superficially persuasive enough that they have a chilling effect on their victims. It follows that gays and lesbians can best protect themselves against homophobes by understanding the faulty logic underlying the homophobe's supposedly correct and authoritarian pronouncements, whether these come from the church, the president of the United States, bloggers on the Internet, or right-wing talk show hosts. For example, gays and lesbians who understand the projective processes that make up paranoid homophobic cognitive distortions can recognize that the attacks on them that seem so personal are usually little more than self-statements, with the paranoid homophobic criticisms of others representing self-criticisms, because when it comes to homophobia, as we might say in the vernacular, "It takes one to bash one."

Speaking generally, homophobic thought relies heavily on the use of sophistry, which Merriam-Webster defines as "reasoning that is superficially plausible but actually fallacious."[1] Homophobes who use sophistry are often shrewd enough to have learned precisely how to start with a false premise and carefully reason their way to a plausible predetermined and, for them, utilitarian conclusion. Moreover, they become skilled at their false reasoning because they are preoccupied with their homophobic sophistry, regularly practice getting their fallaciousness exactly right, and additionally have an emotional need to devalue gays and lesbians that is strong enough to motivate and guide them to come up with newer and cleverer ways to do just that.

The different errors I describe in the following tend to overlap conceptually and occur together. As an example, homophobes often combine selective abstraction with part = whole cognitive errors (both of which I define below) to create the homophobic logical fallacy particularly in vogue these days that all homosexuals are sick and so should take the cure, a conclusion homophobes arrive at by selecting the outlandish gay behaviors that do admittedly occur from time to time in gay life and taking them out of statistical context, making the partial into the whole view, so that homophobes now come to see exactly and only the negative things they already believe. An inability to like gays and lesbians and a need to dislike and abuse them are already in place. Then homophobes, in a form of backward reasoning, find one or more ways to justify the dislike with so-called facts so that they can proclaim, "I think scientifically, sense morally, and act out of social awareness, while at all times retaining my basic sense of kind humanity."

One homophobe's backward reasoning started with an emotionally driven homohating premise that consisted of postulating the primary hypothesis that gays and lesbians were second-class citizens, then building on that by looking for evidence, always available, that all gays' and lesbians' loving relationships were somehow second rate (some are, but hardly all), so that while gays and lesbians might be entitled to form civil unions (second best), these must both in name and substance fall short of actual marriage (best of all). Often he started with the premise that homosexual acts should be criminalized, then, to support that view, took what he needed from the Bible, overlooking the many biblical statements that he as a Catholic could not buy into, such as "Ye shall make you no idols."[2] To prove his homohating premises he cited Leviticus's prohibition not to "lie with mankind, as with womankind; it is abomination,"[3] but he himself did "go up and down as a talebearer among [his] people"[4] and allowed to "come upon him a garment of two kinds of stuff mingled together."[5] He also postulated a fixed predictable relationship between effeminacy in men or masculinity in women and sexual preference and then, although observation told him that any such relationship was an inconstant one, found a way to prove that, so that his "I see you as gay because I see you as effeminate" really meant "I see you as effeminate because I see you as gay."

The following are some classes of cognitive errors homophobes make to create and justify their homophobia.

EMOTIONAL REASONING (TAKING THINGS MUCH TOO SERIOUSLY)

Homophobes using emotional reasoning turn fancy into fact via "inexact labeling," which according to Robert J. Ursano and Edward K. Silberman consists of the "tendency to label events in proportion to one's emotional response to them rather than according to the facts of the situation."[6]

Homophobes do not actually care what gays and lesbians are, say, or do. Instead they feelthink, making things up along the way and according to desire. Predictably, homophobes take everything much too seriously. Thus, according to an article in the *New York Times*, "Attacks Show Easygoing Jamaica Is Dire Place for Gays," "the Western Mirror, a Montego Bay [Jamaica] newspaper ... published an article [nonsensically condemning gays and lesbians for being] responsible for a shortage of women's underwear in the city"![7] One predictable result is that these homophobes have end-of-the-world feelings when they see gays and lesbians acting counterculturally to any degree and in any way. For example, the commentator Bill O'Reilly on July 29, 2008, on his show *The O'Reilly Factor* seems to view two gays taking communion in drag as a full invasion of the church and that invasion as the beginning of a national takeover—although the gays are likely to be merely having a bit of antisocial fun and just getting a little gender-bending relief from what one of my patients called "my Church-induced depressing reality." Those who do not have a sense of humor or who suspend it become excessively literal and, failing to appreciate the triviality of camp, respond not as if a few benign gays are camping but as if hoards of malignant gays are bivouacking.

The more manipulative psychopathic homophobes reason emotionally on a more conscious level in order to attain a specific advantage or competitive edge. Theirs is a put-on hysteria, meant to impress and convince. Typically, when challenged, they innocently but insincerely justify their attitudes by claiming ignorance, inadequate schooling, and/or poor briefing.

AD HOMINEM REASONING

In ad hominem reasoning, criticism of the producer leads to a falsely negative evaluation of the product, so that work is judged by a preinstalled negative opinion of the worker. Citing the damage done by the homophobic play reviewer George Jean Nathan, Lyle Leverich, in *Tom*, a biography of the playwright Tennessee Williams, writes, "Nathan ... was outspoken in his loathing of sexual deviation. He was first among a few critics to let their homophobic feelings prejudice them against not only the playwright but his plays, as well. Nathan would ultimately give *The Glass Menagerie*—as a play ... a sneering review and finally, despite the great success of *A Streetcar Named Desire*, dismiss the playwright as 'a Southern genital-man.'"[8] In effect, in psychoanalytic terms, homophobes like Nathan, equating ego with id, equate gays' and lesbians' higher intellectual with their supposedly lower instinctual behavior and judge them accordingly.

STEREOTYPING

Stereotyping involves the simultaneous use of a number of overlapping cognitive errors.

Part = Whole Reasoning

In part = whole reasoning, homophobes promote unwarranted extensions from the specific to the general. They take a slice of reality and make it the entirety so that they come to view rare, uncharacteristic, and exotic behaviors on the part of gays and lesbians not only as more significant but also as more widespread than they actually are and as typical not just of a few gays and lesbians but of the whole homosexual class. In the view of bigots, *all* Irish drink and talk too much; *all* Jews are cheap, money-grubbing hoarders; *all* blacks (but especially those encountered on a dark street) are dangerous; *all* Puerto Ricans are lazy and shiftless; *all* Italians are gangsters and buffoons who wear gold chains or dark-colored Zegna suits; *all* Asians are sinister individuals not to be trusted; *all* old people kvetch because they are too labile to remain calm; and *all* gay men are sinners, sissies, and child molesters. Practically speaking, stereotypers create and then define a whole class according to one or a few assumed negative (more rarely positive) characteristics, creating a false entity that, if it does exist at all, exists only in their minds.

Homophobes who judge gays and lesbians as a whole according to a few, admittedly sometimes negative characteristics gays and lesbians can have typically favor using the sexual yardstick as the sole one by which they measure gays and lesbians and so judge them not only personally but also professionally. They do this even though, as they must already know from their own lives, sex comes from a different part of the brain than does work. (Other bigots do the same thing when they theorize that a straight politician's patronizing of prostitutes is a sign ipso facto that his judgment is too defective for him to govern.) When homophobes judge gays and lesbians entirely by the sexual yardstick, which is only one measure of any person, they come to view homosexuality as a disability, and they conclude that a disability in one area is a disability in all, in effect claiming that a homosexual's sex life necessarily spills over into his or her professional life as if no compartmentalization exists, certainly not one that spares the ability to function occupationally. Then they reason that queers do not make effective army pilots or, as one troubled veteran patient of mine suggested, that "the only thing all gays do in the trenches is their nails."

There are several subcategories of part = whole reasoning, which are described in the following.

Similar = the Same Thing Reasoning

In this kind of reasoning, homophobes conclude that a few shared characteristics make disparate into identical things or behaviors. In a grotesque example of this kind of reasoning, given by Steven Froias, a planning board hearing was in progress to determine whether an ice-cream parlor that was housed in a lighthouse "would be permitted to move from their current location across [from the beach] to a more residential part of the city" of Long Branch, New Jersey. In response, one of the planning board's members suggested that the lighthouse would be "inappropriate for the more residential location because children in the area would be exposed to the . . . phallic looking lighthouse," and another planning board member cautioned, "Before [everybody] start[s], I would like to remind you that this is an application for a child's dessert shop and (in) your commentary, if you could, please refrain from making any statements extending from your own possibly inappropriate sexual preferences in this matter."[9] In similar manner, not a few homophobes confound occasional cross-dressing with full transvestism. Some, confusing gay male sexual with gay male personal passivity, conclude that all male homosexuals are personally as well as sexually passive, then assert that gays can never be effective professionally outside of certain so-called gay professions because they are all supposedly not forceful or masculine enough to take charge fully. They apply a similar kind of reasoning to lesbians, confounding lesbianism with wanting to be a man and that with being excessively abrasive and forceful, thus disqualifying all lesbians from entering such women's callings as nursing and suggesting that professionally all lesbians stick to being police officers or truck drivers.

Selective Abstraction

According to Aaron Beck, selective abstraction involves drawing full conclusions about a situation or event based on "a [single] detail taken out of context ignoring other, more salient features of the situation, and conceptualizing the whole experience on the basis of this element."[10] Homophobes typically use selective abstraction to equate all gays and lesbians with the most easily identifiable gays and lesbians, making these the only ones homophobes (who generally do not have a wide circle of gay acquaintances, friends, and family) recognize and whom they therefore view as epitomizing the entire existing group.

As politicians homophobes justify opposing gay marriage as if the (somewhat) nontraditional nature of gay marriage entirely invalidates its full sanctity. As psychoanalysts they cite developmental lags and unresolved dynamic conflicts to explain homosexuality fully, although these are neither necessary nor sufficient and are as frequently found in the histories of straights as in those of gays and lesbians and so are less likely to be causal than incidental and trivial.

Selective abstraction typically overlooks the true value not only of homosexuality in general but of certain homosexuals in specific. One homophobe complained that a certain hairdresser was overly sissified. Perhaps he was, but what about his volunteering his services one day a week in nursing homes setting the hair of elderly ladies who had nothing else to look forward to in life? In particular, selective abstraction overlooks the social value of gay marriage—that the salutary effect on gays and lesbians of getting married could well affect their behavior positively and, if nothing else, could have social value for straights. It also overlooks how being homosexual can be an advantage, for example, for therapists doing psychotherapy, making the homosexual therapists better therapists by motivating them to help others avoid experiencing the same pain that they as homosexuals have experienced in their own life due to social prejudice and discrimination.

Overgeneralization

Like selective abstraction this consists of drawing conclusions about all gays and lesbians based on only a few examples, then changing "some" to "all." Prejudiced people select the few gays and lesbians whose actions prove a negative point they wish to make, then tar all gays and lesbians with the same brush, forgetting that there are gays and lesbians of all types and in all walks of life. There are many familiar examples of this type of thinking, including the well-known statements to the effect that all gays and lesbians belong to a kind of raunchy underworld, that all gays molest children, and that all are recruiters regularly trying to enlist straights in the gay cause and make them gay in turn.

Magnification

Magnification enlarges the point that selective abstraction creates until part of the picture becomes the entire scene. For example, straights feel complete disgust and revulsion toward gays and lesbians as the result of seeing only the baser aspects of their sex acts up close, unsoftened by the loving, erotic bath that covers animalistic behavior with ethereal emotion.

Selective Inattention

This leads homophobes to overlook all positive attributes of gay life, including how some so-called typical negative gay and lesbian behavior is in fact situation specific. As one patient said to me, "I walk my cocker spaniel every day past a lesbian bar in New York City. When the weather is warm, there are probably what some view as stereotypical bull dykes sitting outside, but even the ones that can be imagined to fit that description break the stereotypical aggressive mold by fawning all over the dog, and cuddling her, proving how readily the stereotypical bull dyke role is undercut under certain circumstances. I am forced to conclude that 'dykiness' is to some extent an acquisition of the moment, according to the whim and passing need of the minute."

Paralogical Predicative Thinking

In this kind of reasoning, according to Jules R. Bemporad and Henry Pinsker, "the slightest similarity between items or events becomes a connecting link that makes them identical,"[11] once again for the purpose of creating a new reality along desired lines. For example, many bigots reason falsely that if A can be meaningfully equated with B in any respect, and C can be meaningfully equated with B in any respect, than A = C. Thus I (A) am a virgin (B). The Virgin Mary (C) is a virgin (B). Therefore I (A) am the Virgin Mary (C). According to this way of thinking, "some gays and lesbians are pedophiles; you are gay; therefore, you are a pedophile." In like manner, homophobes who want to stereotype gay men and lesbians as making inferior soldiers, sailors, and marines use the slightest (justifiable or, in this case, unjustifiable) similarity and force it into a connective link, concluding that gay (A) = feminine (B), girl (C) = feminine (B), so that gay (A) = girl (C) (and girls cannot fight). Thus, homophobes effectively judge gays' and lesbians' work performance on the basis of their performance in bed when they reason: work is a performance; sex is a performance; therefore, sex = work. They also reason that sex involves seduction, that homosexuals are sexual people, and that, therefore, homosexuals seduce other people. They further conclude that homosexuality is unique, that sick people are unique, and that, therefore, homosexuals are sick.

Stereotyping leads overall to prejudice and discrimination both in and out of the workplace. So often gays and lesbians go through life striving to do well professionally, but they do not, because they do not stand a chance. They do not stand a chance because they try to improve their work, thinking that they are being judged fairly according to the work they do, when in fact they are being judged unfairly according to the sex they have. Ultimately, their self-esteem falls when they come to believe others' negative evaluations of them. Some get angry, whereas others, feeling cowed and defenseless, develop such somatic symptoms as stomach pain or high blood pressure and, perhaps even more frequently, become depressed and possibly even suicidal.

Tangential Thinking

Homophobes think tangentially using minor, incremental logical distortions that string part concepts together, implication after implication, in order to crawl rather than leap not to where their thinking ought to go but to where they want it to go, as they turn a series of semilogical baby steps into one large, disastrous homophobic dyslogical leap.

To illustrate what I mean, consider the example of one schizophrenic patient who was asked, "What are you eating?" and, although he was eating a bowl of cereal, answered, "A bowl of confines." He wanted to talk not about what he was eating but about getting out of the hospital, so he bridged "What are you eating" to "my confinement" via a part concept that had a personal meaning for him. A bowl is many things, one of which is "an item that has sides and holds its contents in so that they cannot get out." This patient chose to speak only of this aspect of bowl, that is, this part concept or single implication of the whole, multivalent concept bowl, because that was the aspect that allowed him to initiate and veer toward the discussion he wanted to have—of how he felt imprisoned by hospital walls, just as his cereal flakes were imprisoned by the sides of his bowl.

As with this patient, homophobic distortions of logic are each so small, the resultant falsifications each so gradual, and the logical shifts each so imperceptible that the overall irrationality of the whole process is disguised by easing towards its conclusions stealthily. For example, homophobes use tangential illogic in an attempt to concoct dangerous slippery slopes and persuade others that all the slippery slopes they warn about do exist, in order to get others to readily buy into the illusion that all gays and lesbians are poised to get out of control and strike fear into the hearts of the general public and significantly and permanently undermine the social fabric. This illogic of "that's how it starts" and "one thing leads to the other" often goes something like this: Gay marriage is unacceptable because it breaks the social mold. Breaking the social mold (which gay marriage does do but only in some, not in all ways whereas it, in many more ways, even affirms and reaffirms this mold) involves breaking with tradition; that means creating a generation of nontraditionalists who will create a new antitraditional society, and that will overthrow the old established world order, leading to polygamy, child marriage, and even bestiality, and to anarchy complete and total—proof that if you give gays and lesbians a finger, they will take an arm, so that gay rights will lead to gay marriages, gay marriages will lead to a violation of the sanctity of the family, and a violation of the sanctity of the family will lead to the downfall of society, if not of the human race, so that there will never be peace and the end of the world will soon be upon us.

This particular kind of slippery-slope thinking and its cleverly slow-but-sure off-course deviation ignore a very important reality, which is the very good possibility that society without any trouble at all can establish external controls on gays and lesbians based on the same commonsense criteria society uses to establish external controls on straights. Just because you allow two gay men to marry does not mean that you have to allow two children to marry (you can set the same age minimums for marriage with gays as with straights) or polygamy (you can keep the same "one person, one partner" rule for gays and lesbians as for straights).

Absolutistic and Dichotomous Thinking

In this, homophobes indulge in a form of black-or-white thinking in which they divide individuals into all good and all bad and, pigeonholing them that way, judge them accordingly, although real life is not so simply nor so easily compartmentalized. These homophobes populate their world with angels (straights) and devils (gays and lesbians), leaving little or no room for mere mortals between the two extremes, even though things only work that way in opera, which in its turn approximates real life about as closely as does homophobia.

Delusional Thinking

Homophobes thinking delusionally, especially in a primarily paranoid way, create characteristic *primary* delusions—which are a priori flat assertions in which opinion supplants fact and there is a simple refusal to entertain rational arguments to the contrary. Gay bashers deem gay bashing right because homosexuality is wrong, and that is where the matter begins and ends. Just as some emotionally troubled individuals think that they are in love with a famous movie star and make their case for being in love by announcing, "We are simply fated to be together," then refuse to entertain rational arguments to the contrary, homophobes deem their bashing to be right and justified because they are certain that their targets are defective, as in "it is obvious that... because everyone knows that... and because God says so." As homophobes see it, they are right to devalue others because in their definition of things others are devalued. They offer no persuasive argument in justification, cite no specific evidence to the contrary, and ignore even the best evidence that counters their beliefs. Instead, they respond to even the most cogent counterarguments by simply repeating themselves. It does not fluster the homophobe to be reminded that the composer Aaron Copland was gay, any more than it flusters today's Napoleon to learn that we have the original's dead body.

Sadly, it is easy for victims of homophobia to allow such confident assertions to lend these delusional homophobes an air of complete expertise. These homophobes' own unquestioning self-certainty and need for self-deception almost magically impact others persuasively, making it possible for such homophobes to stun and mesmerize their targets, who docilely buy into what they have heard, without even a small shake of their head in wonderment or a strong impulse to gag on what they have just been fed.

Zero-sum thinking is in effect delusional thinking, for it is nonsensical to believe that there is a finite amount of morality in the world and that it is quantifiable, as if viewing gays and lesbians as moral, after giving over morality to them, somehow takes away some or all of that pool of morality from straights.

Inconsistent or Hypocritical Thinking

Homophobes use inconsistent and hypocritical thinking to condemn others for doing the very same things that they themselves think and do, after conveniently forgetting that they themselves also think and do them. Their ideation conveniently overlooks or dissociates itself from even glaring internal inconsistencies that might subvert their own contentions.

They call gay marriage unnatural because it is against nature, yet they defy or improve on nature every day in small ways (e.g., they walk with a cane) or in large ways (e.g. they are monogamous). One hypocritical psychoanalyst I know would not admit gays and lesbians to his psychoanalytic institute because they "had an oedipal fixation that rendered them too developmentally primitive to re-parent patients and bring them up right" but seemed to ignore the fact that one could reasonably opine that, also oedipally speaking, his cheating on his wife because he was looking for a better mother left him in almost exactly the same theoretical and actual position.

Inconsistency and hypocrisy often involve a projection (discussed in the following). By projecting their own unacceptable attitudes and desires onto others, homophobes automatically become hypocrites, for they are by definition condemning others for being homosexual when clearly they themselves have not fully overcome or integrated homosexual feelings of their own.

Projective Thinking

Homophobes often use projective thinking for the express purpose of dealing with their own personal failings by blaming gays and lesbians for having caused them to fail. They scapegoat gays and lesbians so that they can deny that their own problems are due to their own shortcomings. So we hear, "The reason I am not working is not that no one will hire me because I do not have the skills but because all the queers around here took all the good jobs" or "Who can get anywhere in Hollywood when gays and lesbians control the whole town?"

Homophobes also blame gays and lesbians to justify hateful things they themselves did in the past or are about to do in the future. First, they feel like gay bashing for reasons of their own, then they gay bash, and then they rationalize their gay bashing as if beating up faggots is acceptable because they deserve it; as the *New York Times* article "Attacks Show Easygoing Jamaica Is Dire Place for Gays" states, gays "flaunt their sexual orientation" and that, and only that, is what gets the mobs mad and "provoke[s] a violent breach of the peace."[12]

Guilt by Association

Here homophobes put their targets in an excessively negative light by grading them based on the people who surround them. Guilt by association assumes that if you are gay, you are necessarily part of the gay underground and therefore must have pierced nipples or have a foot fetish—which, even when true, should not matter so much because these things are generally softened by other nonexploitative, loving behaviors.

Circular Reasoning

Homophobes use circular reasoning to vote against gay marriage. They stereotype marriage homophobically as a hallowed institution between one man and one woman, then condemn gay marriage, as ranging from unacceptable to heretical, simply because it does not fit the definition they just assigned to it. Similarly, in their view, homosexuality becomes an illness because it is not mainstream, and it is not mainstream because it is an illness.

Personalizing

Homophobes who personalize are often referential narcissists who believe that everything the homosexual says and does is somehow relevant to them, so that homophobes make gays' and lesbians' behavior their business, concern, and source of anxiety. Personalization leads directly to ideas of reference; that is, individuals think that gays and lesbians have them in mind at all times. For example, they believe that gays and lesbians are cruising them when they are not or, when gays and lesbians actually are looking at them, that they are in fact not seducing but condemning them. One of my patients complained that some homosexuals were staring at him in the gym looking at him in a sexual way, although they were merely looking to see whether he was (finally) finished with the machine he was using, so that if it were free at last, they could finally get on it.

Denial

Homophobes favor saying the most bigoted things, then proclaiming, "I am not a bigot." They pass antigay laws, then we hear, "This is common sense, not homophobia or gay bashing," although gay bashing is exactly what it occurring, for that is exactly what they intended.

CONCLUSION

Cognitive errors do not arise de novo. Rather, they are thoughts created out of specific feelings to satisfy unique emotional needs. For example, one homophobe, in proclaiming that "the only valid marriage is between one man and one woman in a union blessed with children," was defining marriage that way out of his need to condemn himself for his own secret wish to defy family tradition by striking out on his own and doing things his own way, refusing to listen to what he considered to be all the overly harsh strictures his family and society placed on him. Another homophobe who flatly asserted that gay marriage violated the holy sanctity of matrimony did so to quash her own conflicts about rebelling against her parents' values, with homophobia her way to continue to carry on the family tradition by guiltily proclaiming, "I submit to my parents' idea of what is the one right thing to do and what is the wrong, immoral way to act." For many homophobes the idea that all, not just some gays and lesbians are promiscuous expresses a personal erotophobia: a need to condemn gays and lesbians for being sexually wild in order to keep their own similar but forbidden wishes under better control. Once again, homophobes, like most bigots and indeed like everyone else, are not so much criticizing others as they are affirming themselves.

Cognitive errors also serve the emotional purpose of allowing homophobes to discharge anger guilt free. They also serve a defensive purpose, such as the defensive hypocrisy that enables people who are themselves adulterers to unabashedly and as a diversion criticize gays and lesbians for being promiscuous. Often they express a personal emotional conflict as well as its pathological resolution. For example, a man justified his not walking down Christopher Street in New York's Greenwich Village by concluding that *all* gays on the street were criminals not only trying to steal his wallet from a fanny pack he wore over his crotch but also intending to fondle his genitals in the process. The same man could not shake any gays' and lesbians' hands because he wanted to avoid having to touch them and thus get too close to them and be contaminated. He wanted but was refusing to "press skin" because, as he saw it, gays' and lesbians' skin was infested with scabies.

Finally, mistakes of logic due to cognitive errors have to be distinguished from dissimulation for effect through the deliberate creation of illogic intended to gain specific practical advantage, for example, to provide a competitive edge. Illogic due to cognitive errors also has to be distinguished from misstatements made out of ignorance (which itself can be motivated) that leads to getting the facts wrong. Thus, a number of observers aver that sexual bipolarity is the norm, although, however sincere they may be and nonprejudicial their thinking, they are ill informed, unaware as they are (or want to be) that many species of animals have been observed to engage in homosexual acts, at least by those who actually registered what was right there for them to see.

CHAPTER 12

Other Perspectives

As previously noted in chapter 8, Herek described three categories of homophobic attitudes that he distinguished according to the social psychological function each serves. These are:

1. "*Experiential,* categorizing social reality by one's past interactions with homosexual persons." (This category overlaps with the learning/behavioral perspective of Kirk and Madsen, as discussed below.)[1]
2. "*Defensive,* coping with one's inner conflicts or anxieties by projecting them onto homosexual persons," thereby "imbuing homosexuality with a variety of symbolic meanings [so that] cultural heterosexism enables expressions of individual prejudice to serve various psychological functions,"[2] such as enhancing one's self-esteem or resolving one's emotional conflicts.
3. "*Symbolic,* expressing abstract ideological concepts that are closely linked to one's notions of self and to one's social network and reference groups."[3]

I discuss Herek's second category, the defensive aspects of homophobia, throughout this book, especially in chapters 8–10, where I relate the different homophobias to the different emotional disorders from which they arise. In this chapter, I focus on Herek's first and third aspects of homophobia: the experiential and the symbolic and sociocultural. Additionally, I discuss a fourth aspect, the biological perspective, not included in Herek's list.

THE EXPERIENTIAL PERSPECTIVE

I interpret Herek's notion of the experiential origin of homophobia to mean that negative past and present experiences with gays and lesbians, which do occur, can act as a potential source for and foment later homohatred.

I believe that past experience is almost always a part of but never the sole reason for homophobia. Certainly, some gays and lesbians, like anyone else, can put people off by their in-your-face confrontational and countercultural rebellious attitudes, which can be hard for some straights to accept, leading them to retaliate in kind—by rebelling back. This is especially the case with those straights who, being themselves rigid, prudish, erotophobic, or scrupulously religious individuals, are already vulnerable to finding anything out of the mainstream, sometimes even anything at all sexual, off-putting and even offensive. It is also especially true for straight men preoccupied with their masculinity and therefore already prone to react to a mere hint of gender bending not as if it is merely goofy or unamusing but as if it is morally reprehensible and socially dangerous. Such straights, overlooking their own vulnerability, will likely deny that it takes two to make one homophobe and, claiming that their homophobia is entirely provoked, will say that it is completely reactive when it is in fact at least partly essential; their so-called negative experiences with gays and lesbians are at least partly self-created and so determined less by what they experienced than by what they themselves brought to their experience.

To illustrate, one of my straight patients saw sexual provocation in what were mainly overtures of friendship. He also regularly worried unnecessarily that gays and lesbians threatened his dependent status by attempting to insert themselves into his ongoing heterosexual relationships, and constantly complained that gays and lesbians put him down by thumbing their noses at his straight lifestyle, competed with him too successfully for the world's limited available supplies, were so different from him that they challenged his identity, and actually existed in his town in such large numbers and were so vocal that they represented a potential threat to his own and to the townspeople's moral integrity and even the personal safety of all concerned.

Kirk and Madsen, in their book *After the Ball*, answer such common questions as "Why are people bigoted?," "Why do people not like homosexuals?," and "Why is it humiliating to be told that someone of the same gender has a crush on you?" in behavioral terms that have an experiential component. They say that homohatred develops in the individual as a learned reaction with

> anger and/or fear in response to an arbitrarily defined out-group: fags [learned] in accord with certain fundamental laws of behavior conditioning—specifically, two: *Rule 1: Associative Conditioning.* When a person experiences, either by direct sensory perception, or in the form of a thought or emotion, two things either simultaneously or in immediate succession...an Associative Link is formed between the two so that, in the future, experiencing one of the things will tend to evoke the other thing [and] *Rule 2: Direct, and Emotional Modeling*...an immediate kindling

of the same... emotion[s in others] an excellent example with which [all of us] are familiar [being] the cattle stampede.[4]

Such homophobes make us think of mass hysteria, ranging from that found in swooning mosh pits at rock concerts to the group bigotry of churches where the whole congregation collectively shouts "amen" when the pastor suggests that "the government introduced HIV to decimate a population it doesn't like as part of a genocidal conspiracy to destroy us."

Once again, I believe that such behavioral concepts fail as *sole* explanations for homophobia. This is because what does and does not become an associative linkage can, like cognitive errors, be determined by the emotional makeup of the individual and his or her emotional mindset of the moment. For example, those individuals who are already prone to homophobia show a readiness to form negative associative linkages, whereas those individuals who are not prone to homophobia do not do this. In addition, cultural factors facilitate or impede the formation of linkages. A culture that is prevailingly positive toward homosexuals will discourage negative associative linkage and encourage personal humanity, seeing to it that humanistic beliefs triumph over the simple reflex arc and so keep prejudicial associations from forming, thus preventing emotion from overtaking cognition—to become a serious case of mind over matter.

THE SYMBOLIC AND SOCIOCULTURAL PERSPECTIVE

Some homophobic men have never gotten over their adolescent struggle to develop and maintain a masculine identity, however simplistic the masculine ideal at the core of such an identity might be. These men emotionally or physically beat up on gay men, especially those who are easily identifiable, both because they do not fit their image of what a real grown-up man should be and as part of their own attempt to develop and affirm a macho self-image of which they can feel proud.

It is of course well known and not at all surprising that homophobic attitudes also originate in one's social network, either though passive identification with others in one's immediate environment or as the result of peer pressure to be homophobic. Many homophobes become homophobic after having introjected widespread social environmental homohatred to become individual internalized homophobia, with the homophobia arising, as Herek notes, not only out of "past [negative] interactions with lesbians and gay men" but also from experienced "religiosity, adherence to traditional ideologies of family and gender, [and] perception of friends' agreement with one's own attitudes."[5] As a consequence, also according to Herek, for heterosexuals "personal contact with lesbians and gay men represents the most promising strategy for reducing homophobia."[6]

However, some homophobes aver that their homophobic positions result from perceived social attitudes when, in fact, their homophobia mostly originates not externally but internally, in their individual psychopathology. Most of us, living in a society with mixed social attitudes, could easily avoid adopting the negative attitudes toward gays and lesbians that are rife in one segment of society by instead adopting the more positive attitudes toward gays and lesbians that exist and are always there for the taking in another. Most societies, like most religions, have conservative, moderate, and reformed/liberal arms, and individuals often choose which to buy into based on personal reasons. Too many homophobes claim peer pressure in order to deny their own individual proclivity. They blame others to escape their own inner guilt and the external criticism and opprobrium that might lead them to suffer the undoubted negative consequences that can occur as the result of being antigay in today's more liberal progay social climate.

To illustrate the possibility of resisting peer pressure and how peer pressure isn't a valid excuse, the woman in a straight couple in my neighborhood just recently said to me. "You know, my husband is in construction. Whenever he tells his buddies he lives where he does, all the guys snicker about how gay it is there. He, being of sound mind, replies not with a snigger of his own, but with a, 'Yup, and that's what makes it such a great, interesting place.'"

In conclusion, the interplay between cultural and individual factors is a complex one. What we call a cultural phenomenon can consist of a shared individual neurosis, or an individual neurosis can be thought of as culturally induced. The question is often asked, "If everyone is thinking unrealistically or anxious over the same thing, which is nothing, should the individual be considered to be personally ill or more likely be considered to be well, simply because everyone is doing it (as in 'Don't single me out, for all the guys hate queers')?" But what happened in Nazi Germany suggests that horrible societies are made up of horrific individuals, and the sheer numbers affected do not necessarily absolve all concerned from personal responsibility.

THE BIOLOGICAL PERSPECTIVE

Physical disorder in childhood can be one experiential factor behind the formation of adult homophobic attitudes. For example, in one of my patients an undescended testicle was partly responsible for setting the stage for a lifelong fear of femininity associated with an extreme sensitivity to the possibility of emasculation or humiliation, which regularly flared when gay men, all of whom he thought of as feminine, reminded him of his absent testicle and how it made him feel undesirably womanly. Additionally, the patient's mother had delayed his treatment for the undescended testicle, he thought because she "only wanted me to have one because she liked me the way I was, as only half a man who as such would not grow up and leave home and her." Because he felt like half a man, he had to try to make himself feel whole again. To do this he condemned other half-men, as he saw them, not only gays and lesbians, but also Jews, blacks, and Muslims, as equally defective so that he could, compared to them, have "bigger balls."

Those who write extensively about the biological origins of homophobia often view it from the perspective of the behavior of the animal within the breast of humankind. For example, they might agree that homophobes are homophobic because they compete with gays and lesbians in a way reminiscent of how other animals compete with each other for food, lodgings, or sex, as they jockey for position and move in for the kill. A patient who felt negatively about gay marriage said that, in his opinion, it was less the moral issue that most presumed it to be than a product of a competitive, size-counts quasi-morality, in which "I target you as immoral not because you actually abrade on my morality but so that I can put you down, have it all, and mine can be demonstratively bigger than yours."

PART III

Interventions

CHAPTER 13

Helping Homophobes Become Less Homophobic

Homophobes cause serious problems not only for gays and lesbians but also for themselves. I discuss the problems homophobes cause for gays and lesbians throughout. In this chapter I focus on the problems homophobes cause for themselves, in the process creating social havoc when their homophobia goes from being an individual to a local problem, then on to becoming a national crisis—with all concerned having to listen and respond to, as well as have their lives disrupted by, the homophobes' narcissistic rants, attention-seeking maneuvers, and highly misanthropic attitudes.

In the realm of causing serious problems for themselves, homophobia can and often does create personal havoc when it becomes sufficiently time-consuming and emotionally all-encompassing to divert the homophobe from more important matters, for always having to be resolutely moral and completely right takes time, effort, and energy away from potentially truly rewarding personal pursuits and professionally effective actions.

Furthermore, many homophobes fail to recognize that they hurt themselves when they avoid gays and lesbians even to the point that they deprive themselves of many of the potential pleasures of life. As spectators they do not attend certain performances, look at certain works of art, or read specific works of literature by, for, or about gays and lesbians. As bosses they refuse to hire, or harass or fire, some of the most talented workers, not only impoverishing their own lives, but also ruining their companies. As patients they avoid the gay doctor who could make the right diagnosis in favor of the straight doctor who has made the right family. As neighbors they shun the gays and lesbians who move in next door, although what they gain fighting sin and maintaining their smug morality they lose in the way of potential friends and helpers they could have otherwise had and enjoyed.

Although mostly they do not realize it, by being homophobic homophobes are actually damaging their own reputations, not merely with the gays and lesbians in their lives, but also with themselves and with the very straights—family and friends—they are trying to impress and win over. As for themselves, how can a truly moral religious individual preach compassion and love for all, then make exceptions based on sexual orientation without on some level feeling guiltily hypocritical? How can presumably logical people wear T-shirts that say, "How can a moral wrong be a civil right?" without wondering whether they are making the serious mistake of comparing apple wrongs to orange rights? And, as for hurting their relationships with their straight families and friends, all the world loves a lover, so that, at least in my experience, even some drinking buddies who approve of the homophobes' militant antigay stands at the bar the night before think twice the next morning and, finding the homophobes off-putting and sadistic, after complaining that they protest too much, ignore them as friends, do not vote for them as politicians, and make sure that their sisters marry someone else.

As an example of how widespread, shared homophobia can create social havoc, the family orientation of one town was partly to blame for the empty stores that silently testified not to any poor economic conditions that prevailed nationally at the time but to the local conflicts the town's inhabitants had about allowing gays and lesbians to live and work there. The town advertised itself as a family-oriented place (it even had a family tattoo parlor), in part to get the message across that it did not like gays and lesbians or, for that matter, anyone else too different from the white lower-middle-class people who populated the place—including (or especially) blacks, Jews, and Latinos. Once, when two gay men tried to open a microbrewery, which would have rehabilitated an abandoned eyesore near the center of town, the project was defeated using as an excuse its location a few blocks from an elementary school, such that it could corrupt the children. This decision was made not on practical grounds, since no children would have been involved in any way, let alone served any beer. As we might have expected, the two men who wanted to open the brewery were gay, and the town fathers were simply killing two birds by ridding themselves of one stone: salving their own consciences about both drink and sex by supposedly protecting the children from the demon homosexual.

This town is a parable for the self-defeating social aspects of homophobia, for by banishing gays and lesbians who paid taxes but did not use the schools (making their tax money mostly profit), fixed up their houses, and opened thriving, attractive businesses that encouraged tourism and attracted even more businesses, the town was acting like an enterprise that could have been profitable, except that it deliberately set out to discourage some if its best customers from ever entering it and patronizing its stores.

Perhaps the most egregious example of the negative social effects of homophobia, one that is very costly for and destructive to our country, is the high penalty paid for identifying and discharging gays and lesbians from the armed services and training their replacements. Sometimes the cost is not solely in money. Discharging Arabic military translators because they are gay has possibly cost American lives due to not having enough personnel available to translate the communications of Arabic-speaking terrorists.

Although symptomatic homophobia can, like other symptoms, be at least theoretically ameliorated through psychotherapy, unfortunately homophobic individuals rarely enter treatment for their homophobia. If they come for treatment at all, they come for other reasons and are only incidentally found to be homophobic and in need of assistance for their homophobia. For example, when I worked at the veterans' administration, I saw one homophobic patient after another, but not a single patient felt that his (more rarely, her) homophobia was a worthy symptom to be reckoned with, certainly nowhere near the importance of their other symptoms ranging from emotionally induced back pain to the flashbacks of posttraumatic stress disorder.

Homophobes mostly avoid getting help for their homophobia for at least three reasons. First, through a process of self-denial, they do not believe that they are homophobes. Or, second, they think that if they are homophobes, so what? As they readily remind us, their homophobic beliefs and attitudes find much support among civil and religious leaders, and so they believe that they are enhancing, rather than destroying, their reputations (and to an unfortunate extent they are right). And, third, if they do believe that they are homophobes, they deny that they are causing problems for gays and lesbians—beyond, that is, the problems they feel gays and lesbians deserve.

It is not surprising, then, that helping a homophobe therapeutically often requires approaching his or her problem not directly but indirectly. I was treating a homophobic man in psychotherapy for a generalized neuroticism. Like most homophobes he did not enter treatment with the chief complaint, "I am homophobic," nor with the expressed goal of curing his homophobia. If his homophobia came up at all during his sessions, he did not want to discuss it, and if he did discuss it, he resisted any suggestion that he change. As a result, I chose to handle his homophobia, when at all, in a roundabout way. This man abhorred and figuratively washed his hands of gays and lesbians because of a sense of moral superiority that was less a product of his conscious philosophy (as he thought it was) than a side product of his unconscious sexual guilt (as he failed to recognize). So I dealt with his homophobia by treating the sexual guilt behind it, without even mentioning the homophobia itself. In his case the outcome was favorable, for he became less homophobic in specific when he became less generally guilty about sex.

For those relatively few insightful homophobes that do exist, therapy *can* be directed to the homophobic symptom itself. It can help such homophobes distinguish what they do not like in others from what they do not like in themselves and stop them from projecting their own flaws onto others, thus condemning others outside of themselves for something inside them. They can learn that when homosexual practices take place between consenting adults and no one is getting hurt either physically or emotionally, their personal preoccupation with homosexual practices is nothing short of neurotic overinvolvement. They can learn to recognize that gay life holds no immediate importance for them, so that they can calm down and see it as neither a good nor a bad thing but as something that just is and that at any rate does not concern or involve them but is instead (as far as they are or should be concerned) a nonissue. They can then stop compulsively proselytizing against same-sex liaisons and marriage and instead start exploring why they are so involved with the topic, why they seem to be so threatened by homosexual possibilities, often to the point of hysteria, and why they waste so much time and energy creating and upholding laws when they do not work for a law enforcement agency. They might stop emulating my patient who received a flyer for a gay sexually oriented book in the mail and could not simply throw it away and forget all about it but began endlessly protesting to the authorities about the lax laws of today, until I had to question his true motives and point out that his obsession with cracking down on gays and lesbians clearly originated in his misguided obsessive attempts to crack down on himself.

Therapy helped one of my patients, a chief executive officer of a company, think rationally and judge gays and lesbians more fairly by helping him distinguish gay passion from gay profession, that is, gays' and lesbians' sexual orientation from gays' and lesbians' ability to do their jobs in his company. Therapy helped another one of my patients, a therapist, distinguish homosexuality from character pathology so that he stopped treating gays and lesbians for being homosexual when what he really ought to have been treating them for an actual personality problem or some other disorder more or less independent of the homosexuality itself. Therapy also helped another one of my patients, a politician, learn enough about homosexuality from me, a neutral third party, to stop confounding homosexuals with pedophiles, wife beaters, and murderers and see that most sex, gay or straight, when loving, is not an exploitative, hostile, or criminal act that needs to be quashed legislatively. As far as gay marriage was concerned, he learned that no one got hurt, quite unlike all those other things on his slippery slope, such as polygamy, which hurts partners and children, and bestiality, which hurts animals. Finally, therapy helped another patient, a pastor who was a religious homophobe, distinguish between true and anthropomorphic God and determine that he was not homophobic because God wanted him to be but that, instead, his God was homophobic because he wanted Him to be. Then he could stop proselytizing homophobically to his congregation and start urging them to create love in relationships where formerly there was only hate, to stop rejecting people who loved them, and to cease hurting people who were not doing them any harm and thwarting people who were actually trying to do them some good.

In especially favorable cases, with patients who are not only insightful but also motivated to change, therapists can help them see the wisdom of remedying the social problems their homophobia creates, so that they can not only stop sacrificing real gain for individual moral triumphs that closely resemble Pyrrhic victories but additionally transform their individual neuroses to become positive social activism through a process of healthy sublimation that represents not a cover-up but a sign of real internal change—from hating to loving, from wanting to hurt to hoping to help.

CHAPTER 14

Handling Homophobes

Gays and lesbians are in conflict among themselves as to the best way to handle homophobes. Clearly, no single method applies in all instances and works in every case.

What is certain is that many gays and lesbians, insightful or not, depressed or not, handle homophobes ineffectively—that is, they handle them in one of two counterproductive ways that can only make the homophobe's task easier, creating more, and more efficient, homophobia. First, they try to fix what is not broken in their own lives while letting what is actually broken stay that way. If they are criticized as poor workers because they are homosexual, even though their work is actually up to par, they repair their work, which does not need fixing, but not their ill-deserved bad reputation, which needs all their work. Second, they try solutions that actually make matters worse. They abdicate when they should fight back. They let others take advantage of them when they should call a halt to being abused. They appease when they should protest. They become like the man who left a high-paying 9–5 job with a short commute and excellent working conditions just because several of his coworkers were homophobic, deciding for that reason alone that "staying there just was not worth all the aggravation."

Gays and lesbians act this way for several reasons. They hope that if they cut off their noses to spite their faces, they will appeal to those homophobes who suffer gladly people who are scarred. They hope to catch a few crumbs that fall from the feasts of straights. They are afraid that standing up for themselves can only make matters worse—as they, in effect, model themselves on the lesbian who felt that suing the man who did not install her microwave oven correctly would ultimately encourage him to come back and write "dyke" all over her house and on the gay man who felt that if he reported a hate crime, he would be successfully sued for slander/libel. Also, already feeling guilty and morally outraged with themselves over being homosexual, they take steps to assure their own discomfort and failure. Moreover, as adults they tolerate abusive relationships with homophobes just because that reminds them of what home was like when they were children. In many ways, through self-abnegation they hope to convert homophobes into admirers or even into homophiles. They hope against hope, however, because, as they already do or should know, no one has yet succeeded in getting love from such particularly hateful stones.

As I believe I have amply illustrated throughout this book, serious homophobes, being disturbed emotionally, are likely to be terribly wrong about many things, especially about their homohating. Therefore, the core antithesis to homophobia involves gays and lesbians recognizing that all homophobia, and serious homophobia in particular goes beyond being simply an experiential or sociopolitical matter. It is not only something learned or just what all those healthy guys down at the sports bar are saying and doing. Nor is it strictly a political stance meant to seduce voters, and it certainly involves more than a fear of gays and lesbians based purely on ignorance and unfamiliarity with them and with their gay life. To a great extent, although the parallel is not exact and the equivalency is a rough one, homophobia is a symptom of an underlying emotional disorder, with prejudice an emotional state (disguised as an intellectual preoccupation) serving adaptive psychological functions, such as relieving anxiety and enhancing self-esteem, just like such symptoms as paranoid delusions or phobic avoidance. As such, homophobia can be best understood and most properly handled by developing insight into its psychological origins, causes, and manifestations. Victims of homophobia who understand homophobia through and through will almost certainly be less intimidated by it and so better able to cope adequately with the homophobia of today and to change the homophobia of tomorrow. Fortunately, laypersons can diagnose the emotional problems of homophobes even without formal psychological training and manage them by applying diagnosis-based therapeutic techniques worked out over the years by professionals that are easily adopted for use by nonscientists. To illustrate, those who understand that the banishment rituals of homophobia overlap conceptually, dynamically, and structurally with phobic avoidances and that thinking of gays and lesbians as disgusting buttheads readily reminds of the repetitive hand-washing compulsion of the obsessive-compulsive who fears germs and dirt and believes that you cannot be too careful of fecal contamination wherever you go will be in a position to handle the homophobe roughly in the same way a psychiatrist handles a phobic or an obsessive-compulsive patient.

Gays and lesbians can achieve mastery over homophobic myths that affect their lives by translating these myths into the unconscious fantasies of the mythmaker from whom the myths arise. In this manner, they can obtain broad insight into the homophobe's specific needs and intentions, then use this understanding to better tolerate and more effectively manipulate, that is, quash, the homophobia. Translating the bad names homophobes call gays and lesbians (names that are little more than minimyths), such as elitists, pansies, sickos, DINKS, flits, sissies, queers, fags, femmes, swishes, dykes, and butches, into the specific underlying fantasies behind the name-calling suggests countermeasures that can be taken based on an understanding of the homophobe's unconscious intent. For example, when one of my homophobic patients called gays and lesbians sick, that suggested that he had identified, to take a line from Leviticus, with the land that "vomited out her inhabitants"[1] and, after having fantasies of oral sex, was now in his fantasies visualizing taking the consequences and retching. Gays and lesbians tend to respond to being called sick by thinking that they indeed may be ill and just need to get better. But gays and lesbians who understand how projection of homosexual yearnings lurks behind the epithet sicko more easily tolerate hearing it and so more easily and quickly throw it off. They realize that the problem is not with their being sick and disgusting but with the homophobe who, speaking both figuratively and literally, has developed an abnormally constituted, overly sensitive gag reflex.

Of course, although there are distinct similarities between homophobia and emotional disorder, there are also crucial differences; the analogy breaks down at some point. For one thing, any homophobic person is to some extent an integral part of and a reflection of a society that represents the homophobic social norm. As Mautner notes, often our attitudes, which translate into behaviors, are learned by observing the people in our lives (teachers, parents, and friends) and through the media, which Albert Bandura famously refers to as our "vicarious world."[2] So it is not enough just to understand homophobia. Social antitheses such as proud activism are also needed, for they are integral to the remedy. In addition, the psychopathology in question may simply be the psychopathology of everyday life. That is, although the homophobia is structurally psychopathological, the psychopathology involved may not actually rise to the level of a full emotional disorder. That does not mean, however, that all homophobia is strictly a socially learned behavior that can be predictably socially unlearned via educating the individual and offering his or her social institutions greater enlightenment. Most homophobes are at least mildly mentally ill, which is why most prejudice and discrimination does not yield favorably simply to confrontation and arguments to the contrary.

In this chapter I first discuss specific antitheses to the different types of homophobia. Then I discuss general counterstrikes that have an overarching usefulness for many if not most forms of homophobia. The following rule applies throughout: targets should participate in the homophobe's disillusionment and resist all temptation to participate in the homophobe's therapy.

SPECIFIC ANTITHESES

In this section I first recap the main points about the different emotional disorders related to homophobia, then follow with specific antitheses for coping with and managing each.

Paranoid Homophobia

Most serious students of homophobia recognize the association between paranoid mechanisms and homophobia. Homophobes who use paranoid mechanisms condemn others' homosexuality in order to deny that they have homosexual feelings of their own. They also project their anger outwardly toward gays and lesbians. So they think, "I condemn you for being queer to prove to myself that I am not like you" and "I don't hate you and am not out to do you harm, but rather you hate me and are out to do me damage (e.g., dilute the sacred meaning of my heterosexual marriage or rape me)."

Antithesis

At least theoretically, managing paranoid homophobia involves cognitive restructuring—focusing on the homophobe's erroneous projective beliefs and conclusions to get homophobes to identify them in order to move toward dealing with and resolving their problems by methods other than attributing them to others. Therefore, and again at least theoretically, the proper reply to paranoid homophobes is the personal equivalent of "It takes one to know one," meaning that "queers wouldn't upset you so if they didn't push one of your very personal buttons," then adding, "Don't take it out on me, but, instead, bigot, heal thyself."

This said, paranoid ideation can only theoretically be dispelled through education, confrontation, and cognitive restructuring. In reality, these are not always effective interventions, for several reasons. First, it is difficult to cure mental illness by arguing with it, and, second, peer pressure and interpersonal connections, along with the advantages to be obtained from hidden and overt practical and sociopolitical agendas, fixate the homophobia, making it more entrenched. In the world today, most individual paranoid homophobes ultimately find their way to an intellectually clever and emotionally attuned group leader who, paranoid on his or her own, is in an especially good psychological position to stir up latent and give vent to overt individual paranoia. Third, confrontation can be dangerous, especially so with paranoid homophobes, who can even become violent when told in so many words that they only hate queers because on some level they are queer themselves. Therefore, Mautner suggests that with these homophobes, one should still take action but in ways that avoid direct confrontation that can put one in harm's way.[3] For instance, a sense of personal empowerment and catharsis can often be achieved simply by writing in a personal journal as a way to acknowledge the falsity involved, thus putting one in a better position to take the angry words and deeds less personally. Gays and lesbians should consider starting a journal with two columns on the page—on the left, the bigoted reality and, on the right, the comparative truth. That way, the irrationality will become clear, and what is said will begin to fade into unimportance. A sample journal entry might be, on the left, "If you are gay, you will make a bad soldier" and, on the right, "Lawrence of Arabia." A letter-writing campaign can also help, and writing an editorial for the local newspaper, even anonymously, is a good active choice that serves to educate as well as to ultimately increase one's self-efficacy.

Depressive Homophobia

Just as it is depressive to be excessively and unfairly critical of oneself, it is also depressive to be excessively and unfairly critical of others—and being homophobic, or otherwise bigoted, suits that highly judgmental purpose all too well. Depressive homophobes, in attempting to hurt not only themselves but also others along similar lines, know exactly how to go for the jugular and where to stick in the knife, so that they can render the gay individual's self-esteem very low, in the same way they lower their own. For judgmental depressive homophobes, small flaws and ineptitudes in themselves and others loom large and become unforgivable. In the next step the depressive homophobe comes to believe that unforgivably inept gays and lesbians, like the inept self, need to be brought up short or, even better, destroyed and sets out to do so in ways that range from devaluing gays and lesbians emotionally to hurting gays and lesbians physically.

Antithesis

Targets of depressed homophobes can at least theoretically manage them the same way that they can manage anyone else who is depressed, but very few would feel comfortable doing so. Few would want to take steps to alleviate a depressed homophobe's depression by giving him or her a pep talk along the lines of "none of us, you included, is as bad as you make me (and us all) out to be," and then, for the more charitably inclined, recommending new, more positive ways to think or actually making a referral to a good therapist. Therefore, a general self-supportive measure involves not taking the homophobes' criticisms quite so personally, after following what is perhaps the two most useful mantras not only for targets of depressed homophobes but also for targets of all homophobes, as well as bigots of all ilks: "Consider the source" and "Be assured that that source is not talking about you but is, like everyone else these days, mainly talking about himself."

Hypomanic Homophobia

Hypomanic homophobia involves malignant, narcissistic, sanctimonious grandiosity associated with feelings of superiority combined with easy irritability, leading to a tendency to irrationally devalue others, with very little provocation and on almost any grounds, based on the idea that "I'm way hot, and you're way not."

Antithesis

Theoretically at least, targets who spot hypomanic homophobes and understand that their problem is predominantly one of uncontrolled, speeding, high-pressure, irrational (but throwaway) devaluing anger will want to put their foot down and set limits—demanding that the homophobes control their words and actions. However, once again, these homophobes may be unstable, dangerous, or violent; therefore, instead of a vocal "stop it or else," a personal self-steeling mindset ("I prefer not to listen to this") may be the intervention of choice.

Dissociative Homophobia

Dissociative homophobia allows contrary ideas to exist comfortably side by side almost as if the individual espousing them has a multiple personality. For example, a homophobe says, "All lesbians hate men," then contradicts himself and says, "All lesbians want to be men," two postulates that are individually inherently incorrect and together entirely incompatible.

Anyone who creates, buys into, or propagates myths and stereotypes is effectively in a state of dissociation, because to stereotype it is necessary to ignore facts that do not fit. There is little substantive difference among the amnesiac who ignores true facts about his or her identity, the bigot who ignores the possibility that the Jewish Albert Einstein was not genetically inferior, and the homophobe who continues to suggest keeping gays and lesbians out of the armed forces after ignoring the famous fighters of yore who were known to be gay and who even, in some very unfavorable cases of personal hypocrisy, denies the fact that he or she himself is as queer as they come.

The oft-quoted expression "Love the sinner, hate the sin" uses the dissociative mechanism of separating the person from his or her actions. A more accurate (that is, nondissociative) formulation might be "Since I generally recommend judging people not by who they are but by how they behave and what they do, I must inform you that if you hate the sin, to some extent you must also deaffirm the sinner, so reconsider how you think and what you say."

Antithesis

Dissociative homophobes need to integrate contradictory beliefs and fantasies the same way patients with a multiple personality disorder, a fugue, or amnesia need to integrate the various parts of their personalities. Targets of dissociative homophobes need to be clear that all pictures that are distorted due to some of the important pixels being left out should be ignored as incomplete, so that they can continue to consider themselves whole persons in spite of the homophobes who view them as a sum of their lesser parts.

Obsessive-Compulsive Homophobia

Like all obsessionals, these homophobes not only figuratively but also literally treat gays and lesbians as if they are dirty spots who need to be washed off the homophobes' hands. They are also perfectionists who view gays and lesbians as a defined group collectively falling short of the homophobes' excessively high ideals and so properly condemned as imperfect. One result of this intense scrupulosity is that these homophobes define marriage narrowly as of necessity a holy union between a man and a woman, allowing that no other type will fit, because "either it's Webster's, or it's wrong."

Antithesis

Targets who are aware of these homophobes' obsessive perfectionism will save time and energy by not trying to talk them out of their narrow, ritualistic thinking and behavior. Instead, they will recognize that trying to talk such homophobes out of their homophobia is about as unproductive as trying to talk a compulsive hand-washer into stopping that process and getting on with life. Therefore, the remedy involves giving up and staying away. Fortunately, such homophobes tend to be private miniaturists who can be safely ignored and avoided, for generally they will go on to a new victim rather than attempt to elaborate and perfect an old victimization.

Narcissistic Homophobia

Narcissistic homophobes personalize, believing that everything their targets do is relevant to them, the homophobe, so that someone else's gay marriage must somehow be relevant to, interconnected with, and therefore properly compared to their own straight marriage. Not surprisingly, they are also controlling individuals who make their target's behavior their source of anxiety after making it their business, their personal concern, and their mission in life.

Such homophobes routinely feel superior to their targets. So they come to believe that they have both the ability and the right to abuse them. They also display a troublesome combination of being convinced that only they have the truth and that their way is the one and only right one. In addition, they have the self-deluding and self-congratulatory delusional idea that they are pure and others foul. Not surprisingly, they become fanatics who proselytize, demanding that the word that they (and only they) have be heard. Presuming themselves to be deep and brilliant thinkers, they accept no input and brook no argument from others. Instead, they respond to gays' and lesbians' legitimate protests about their homophobia by digging in and simply restating their cherished beliefs along the lines of "I know it to be so, and therefore it must be so, so listen to me." They demand an uneven playing field where they have rights and privileges that others should not be given. They are selfish as well, so that "Keep gays and lesbians out of the army" can often be translated to mean, "I and my ilk want to be the only one chosen to serve my country."

Antithesis

An important remedy involves being skeptical of all self-proclaimed experts and, instead of being cowed by them, simply dismissing their contentions as products of a self-appointed superior status that overlooks how they are, in fact, amateurs with little or no real training, who almost certainly know less than they think they do, who rarely have firsthand experience with and knowledge of the matters of which they speak, and who proclaim to be possessed of a universal wisdom that turns out to be little more than personal opinion. (They remind me of a reviewer of one of my psychiatric texts who, when challenged to give his credentials for writing the review, listed a lifelong interest in psychology and a degree in math.) It is important to question the expertise of such homophobes and to demand to see their credentials. Generally, doing so does not cause them to get unduly angry or become dangerous, for they take your wanting to see their credentials as a sign that you are interested in them, and they enjoy having become once again the center of attraction—for they thrive on any sort of attention.

The healing mantra against such homophobes is to remember that they are not only prejudiced but also often not as smart as they think they are and typically claim to be.

Phobic Homophobia

The often-heard argument that homophobia is not a true phobia is generally sustainable but not always, for some forms of homophobia do in fact follow the same structural and dynamic patterns that true phobias follow. In phobic homophobia, gay and lesbian targets are a symbol of what is truly feared and hated, that is, stand-ins for a specific conflict-laden issue for the homophobe who, after displacing his or her inner conflict onto the symbolic gay or lesbian, shuns the gay or lesbian as representing an internal fear, much as a true phobic shuns a plane because it has come to symbolize (sexual) freedom and penetration. For example, imagine a homophobe who, in conflict with forbidden sexual desires, condemns all sexuality in others because of his own personal experience of his parents' admonishing him for childhood budding sexuality. Next, he displaces this entire general conflict onto the homosexual in specific, so that instead of criticizing himself for his own unacceptable sexual longings the way his parents did, he shuns all homosexuals as symbolizing his unacceptable sexuality. He does this in order to avoid in any way being reminded of and to avoid condoning straight or gay sexuality and thus his own perceived perverse sexual desires Thus, his homophobia is less about "condemn and attack" than "fear and avoid." The bigot's familiar cry, "Don't let him be a pastor in your church, or be a scoutmaster, or get near your children," is then the approximate psychological equivalent of the dog phobic's cry, "Don't let that beast anywhere near me."

As with other phobias, the fear and avoidance are commonly rationalized secondarily. It becomes, "It makes sense to stay away from people who do frightening and disgusting things." So these homophobes do not view themselves as bigots. They think they are just being rational or even good citizens acting responsibly and doing their social duty. It is not much different with those who fear flying; they say they fear it appropriately because, after all, planes do crash. Then they get into their cars and drive off, feeling perfectly safe, even as they speed down the dangerous highway.

Antithesis

Coping with and managing phobic homophobia (true homophobia) involves refusing to be shunned, that is, meeting the avoider head on and not allowing oneself to be excluded but instead standing up for one's civil right to be there and resolutely backing that up with whatever affirmative action is necessary to ensure that one can stay. The correct response to the phobic homophobe is "I don't care if you fear or disdain me. You have to include me, and if you won't, I'll see you in court." Once again (and this always applies even when not stated explicitly), targets should not put themselves in any danger. Therefore, it is often best to accomplish one's ends impersonally, that is, by joining an organization with clout, rather than personally through direct confrontation.

Personality Disordered Homophobia

Homophobes express their bigotry in at least four different ways that are consistent with four different disordered personality styles: the psychopathic, the histrionic, the passive-aggressive, and the sadomasochistic. Therefore, managing such homophobes involves using methods derived from accepted therapeutic interventions geared to managing the relevant personality disorder.

The Psychopathic Style and Its Antithesis

We all know that bigotry can be a way to achieve some specific concrete end and accomplish a certain, often political, goal. For example, politicians count on homophobia to enhance their credentials so that they can win a certain vote or get a specific civil appointment.

The challenge becomes one of keeping bigots from achieving their ends as a reward for their unacceptable behavior. Social mechanisms, including the educative-behavioral methods Mautner describes below, are an effective way to avoid becoming pawns in the frontline of the homophobe's distractive antisocial (but personally rewarding and socially remunerative) game. Victims should never replace thinking for themselves with buying into a psychopath's persuasive but narrowly focused arguments—meant to stir the masses up to shared passions entirely for the benefit of the psychopathic striver who is eager for one thing only: to criticize gays and lesbians in order to complete his or her quest to realize selfish ambitions.

The Histrionic Style and Its Antithesis

Histrionic homophobes overdo their homohatred, for example, when they make invidious comparisons among homosexuality, incest, bigamy, and bestiality, then react with an intensity that is inappropriate given the relative unimportance of what they are concerned about and the unlikelihood that their fears will ever materialize. It is highly unlikely that gays and lesbians by getting married will debase straight marriage or cause the downfall of society as we know it, along the lines of "give them a finger and they will take an arm." As I see it, the belief that such things could happen comes close to the fear of one's own shadow characteristic of the histrionic *attaqué.*

One proper response to hysterical bigotry is "Calm down, take it easy, stop sounding the alarm, and just forget about it." Another involves calming down oneself and living one's own sweet life regardless and to the hilt, no matter what others say or do and how hysterical *they* get.

The Passive-Aggressive Style and Its Antithesis

As discussed in chapters 9 and 10, passive-aggressive homophobia is all the rage these days, for it allows the homophobe to both express and take back gay bashing at one and the same time and so make his or her homophobic point without being condemned for it and thus undermining his or her own cause by winding up cast out socially or politically for being a bigot. But homophobes who choose the passive-aggressive style are still homophobic, although they are nice homophobes who express their homophobia in more subtle ways than others. They do not actually come out and say that they hate homosexuals. Instead, they ask loaded questions that are in fact assertions, such as "Don't you think that you are ruining your life by moving in with a male lover?" Or they protest too much that they love homosexuals, at least certain ones, as in the familiar "Some of my best friends are gay." As parents they give a straight daughter and her husband one gift at Christmas and their gay son and his partner two separate ones. They introduce their son and his partner as "This is my son, and this is Bob." Often they precede their condemnation of gays and lesbians with a diversionary compliment in which the intent to cover-up is easily decipherable, for example, the much-overused and patently obvious "Though I love the sinner, I hate the sin."

As for the antithesis, passive-aggressives of all kinds, bigoted or not, need to be asked either to say what they mean openly and honestly, so that one can deal with it directly, or not to say anything at all, so that one does not have to think about such things. In addition, everything such homophobes say that ranges from neutral to complimentary should be overinterpreted, not accepted at face value. Victims should use their own responses as the key that deciphers the message. If you as a victim feel devalued, these individuals have probably actually devalued you; do not think "I am hypersensitive or paranoid" when you are actually reading a negative situation, however sugar-coated, quite correctly.

Since these homophobes are at their worst when they sense that gays and lesbians are getting too close and they express the most hostility when they feel threatened that way, it is often a good idea for gays and lesbians, whenever possible, to maintain distance without trying too hard to get passive-aggressive homophobes to warm up. Also, like all sadists, passive-aggressive homophobes are inspired by first blood. They either passively wait for it to appear on its own, or they actively draw the first drop. For this reason, passive-aggressive homophobes are best handled, if they must be handled at all, not by meek submission, with wounds seeping and pleading, but by taking strong, fully functional, put-up-with-nothing stances right from the start.

Victims should not save up their anger then blow up. Rather, they should deal directly as best they can with any friction when it first appears. They should right from the start counter those passive-aggressive homophobes they cannot regularly avoid, pleasantly but firmly and dispassionately. They should never masochistically put their tails between their legs and run. They can move from a small town to San Francisco if they like that city and want to be with their own kind, but they should not move as a retreat, going to a faraway place where they have no roots just to get away and lick their wounds.

So often passive-aggressive bigots are lonely people who feel bitter as part of the misery that comes from leading solo lives. Therefore, fighting fire with love usually works. However, it is a technique that few gays and lesbians can or would even want to muster the strength and courage to use.

The Sadomasochistic Style and Its Antithesis

Sadomasochistic homophobes set out to hurt the target of their hatred, but they always seem to hurt themselves in the process. They have a need for self-destruction, which they live out, for example, in the form of a Freudian slip that gets them fired as they momentarily forget themselves and condemn someone powerful for his or her sexual orientation. It is not uncommon for them to throw away caution and criticize gays and lesbians to someone who has a family member who is gay, only to find themselves criticized and excluded in turn.

Avoidance is best, since limit setting just increases their sadism as they, feeling threatened, angrily protest, sometimes even to the point of becoming dangerously physical.

GENERIC COUNTERSTRIKES

Generic counterstrikes are those that are generally viable and often indicated to supplement or replace the above-mentioned specific antitheses to the different forms of homophobia.

Overview

Mostly prejudice and discrimination is a transference reaction that involves projecting one's personal agenda onto the blank screen of the target, thus making that target into what one needs and wants it to be for one's own transcendent emotional reasons and practical purposes. As such, the words bigots speak about others actually speak volumes about them. For, as Levinson in essence suggests, if bigots say the same thing about blacks and Jews as about all victims, and the same thing about all their targets from the same class even though they are a heterogeneous group, then what they say has to come from within, not from without, so that what they say "depends... upon their own psychology."[4] It follows that the operative action for targets of most forms of homophobia is to recognize that as targets they function as impersonal inkblots. Because what homophobes say is not about *you* but about *them*, projected onto you, targets should not take what is said personally but instead continue to view themselves as individuals in their own right. Because any response must not be one that evokes violence, it is a good idea to respond in an assertive way but without being aggressive. One way to do that is to not be demeaning or hostile by saying the equivalent of "shut up" but instead saying something firm but not contentious, like "This is what works best for me."

Consensual Validation

It is always wise for gays and lesbians, as much as possible, to stick with supportive people who, if they do not accept them entirely, at least make their homosexuality the nonissue that it in fact is. Thus, a calming e-mail reached the man who had to endure the homophobic "I hate all c**ksuckers" tirade: "it is so upsetting to hear something like that; I know how it ruins your night."

Gays and lesbians can often improve their self-esteem and sense of well-being by joining support groups. These include mutual admiration societies, such as therapeutic groups that help gays and lesbians explore why they reply to others knocking them down by bringing themselves down in response (making it much easier for homophobes to devastate them further) or activist groups that fight homophobic negativity directly by helping counter gays' and lesbians' tendency to believe the bad things homophobes say about them and by discouraging gays and lesbians from reacting to abuse by prostrating themselves in the hope of gaining some advantage or a little friendship of sorts (although any advantage that might accrue will be temporary, and any friendship they might garner little more than condescending and ultimately counterproductive).

Passive Acceptance

Some gays and lesbians decide to live with a bad situation. Since they recognize that they cannot change the world, they feel that they might as well live with the world as it is. So they accept the inevitable and focus not on changing other people but either on changing themselves or just going about their lives, business as usual.

These gays and lesbians decide to just accept abuse as background noise and refuse to become dysfunctional, depressed, or personally ghettoized in response. They instead decide to ignore, avoid, or otherwise silently come to terms with homophobia. There is what Loraine O'Connell calls a process of "agreement" whereby the target handles judgmental bigots by deciding that "some things just aren't worth getting upset about."[5]

Of course, everyone knows that there are dangers in being too passive with homophobes and that it is possible to carry the moderation that may be the order of the day too far. Targets can be beaten down until they become too weak to care anymore. Then they let homophobes get away with their homophobia, only inspiring the more sadistic homophobes to even higher transports of homohatred, as they go from hating a person or defined group for all the usual reasons to hating the person or group even more in the belief that the group can be hated, devalued, and emasculated with impunity. Furthermore, passive acceptance risks inner cognitive dissonance that can ultimately further lower self-esteem, thus keeping victims from strengthening personal boundaries that give clarity and weight to their own values.[6]

A summary of the positive aspects of remaining passive in the face of homophobia and deciding it is the better part of valor to retain one's perspective or sense of humor and let things pass include being spared further punishment, feeling less guilt about speaking up aggressively, and avoiding wasting one's time and effort in those situations where protesting prejudice is as ineffective as protesting mental illness. Passive, accepting gays and lesbians often eventually come to find that bigotry bounces off them and so, although they are still bigotry's targets, they are no longer truly bigotry's victims.

Activity

Some gays and lesbians decide to handle homophobia by being active, even becoming activists. Feeling that they can make a bad situation better to the point that they will no longer have to live with it, they protest loud and long, often to some avail.

Boycotting is one such activist approach. I asked Mautner how she would handle the case of the foul-mouthed homohating restaurateur. I suggested the gays and lesbians in town consider boycotting his restaurant. She replied as follows, "Boycotting is good, but not enough. The problem with an incident like that is that it is hearsay that one can always subsequently deny." She recommend "a letter campaign, writing directly, asking for an apology (and raising his awareness), perhaps pointing out how large the gay population is that frequents (or might have frequented) his restaurant. I believe that even one letter pointing out the stereotype, although it does not seem like much, makes the person think twice about the prejudice. But the letter must be respectful and factual. Another good choice involves joining a relevant action group of one's own where there is strength in numbers, political influence, and funding in place to effect real world change."[7]

However, Mautner qualifies her recommendations to fight back as follows:

What I am learning is that it is not easy to fight group defamation and discrimination through legal means. The courts have made it difficult in order to avoid the likelihood of frivolous cases, and also because it is hard to award any kind of damages to a large group, e.g. Italian Americans, blacks, or gays and lesbians. So to combat negative stereotyping (which is really at the root of all bigotry—because as Albert Bandura found in his famous observational learning theory experiments in the 1960s, the media has a causal effect on behavior), one should always be one's own ambassador by not turning the other way when individuals or the media portray a particular group in a defamatory way. Our job as members of a negatively stereotyped group is to raise awareness, sensitize, and educate. As individuals, we can do a lot to start changing societal attitudes by enlightening and informing those around us.

Therefore we must do the following:

1. Be attentive to false generalizations that reduce a certain group in the eyes of society. Do NOT let derisive humor get past you without informing the joke-teller that it is offensive (if they want to know why, explain, if not, let it stand at that).
2. Write letters to media personnel if they have portrayed a particular group in a negative stereotypical way. Contemporaneously send a copy to the organization that best represents the defamed group.
3. Educate wherever you can. If you are blessed with a brain, you have to use it. Write to newspapers and magazines. Talk to local schools, libraries, etc. There are many organizations and institutions who love a free speaker. Put this in your calendar to do at least twice a year. It is the best type of pro-bono work there is.
4. Once armed with information and facts, make sure you use them whenever the opportunity presents itself in social circles, in the home, and in the workplace.[8]

I might add: Although targets cannot always convince or cow individual homophobes into no longer hating them, they can almost always help pass laws that keep homophobes from acting on that hatred. Education and psychoanalysis are among the best ways to change a homophobe's mind. But legislation is probably the best and fastest way to change a homophobe's behavior.

Activism is not only a good way to alert certain homophobes that their negative views are unjustified, it is also a good way for the targets of homophobia to improve self-esteem via the pride that comes from successfully defending oneself and the pleasure that comes from knowing one has actually had a hand in reducing the amount of homophobia in the world—by speaking up against its soul instead of cowering in its face.

However, there are also some negative aspects of activism. As previously mentioned, activism can present a personal danger to targets. Many homophobes are quick on the trigger and armed, especially the paranoid ones who keep guns in case of, dynamically speaking, what they consider an attack from the rear. Targets sometimes get hurt or killed when they supposedly assault such people. Especially with homophobes who bash gays and lesbians to cope with their own unacceptable homosexual feelings, the wrong countermeasures can easily inflame their deepest negative desires and touch on their worst fears. Because of the potential for emotional, physical, and professional harm, Mautner advises activists to

weigh the situation carefully and judge for yourself before choosing a course of action. Then be prepared for the consequences. One Italian American woman, for example, worked for an international company where her co-workers referred to their Italian clients as "dagos." When she protested, she was fired for not getting along with her co-workers. Therefore, two important distinctions must be made. The first is the one between impersonal and personal assertion, for example, letters to the editor versus direct confrontation. The second is the one between assertion and aggression ("That upsets me, so I would appreciate it if you would stop, please," versus, "I am going to talk to my lawyer and see what I can do to get you fired for that."). In many situations it is best to act with silent strength and without cloying passivity, discouraging abuse, while avoiding passive submission on the one hand and dangerous confrontation on the other: in effect, saying "please" and "thank you" but "I mean what I just said."[9]

Compromise

Compromise, which often entails setting one's sights lower, is the least risky but probably also the least satisfying and least effective approach of them all. Yet it is worth considering when faced with opposition from homophobes that is so overwhelming that the ideal may not be achievable, leading to the inevitable conclusion that, so to speak, half a loaf is better than none. Does it make sense to consider accepting civil unions rather than full marriage? Should one draw the line at compromising when it comes to being allowed to be a scoutmaster, or should one thwart one's ambition and not climb up too far on the corporate ladder because one is better off where one already is? What is clear is that compromise should not involve masochistically abdicating without at least trying to work things out first; for example, one should not avoid a promotion due to on-the-job prejudice just to avoid conflict. One must always remain strong enough to remove the pleasure of the kill for those sadists who are absolutely inspired by masochistic screams of pain and so attack even more when they see the red eyes of those of their victims who have been weeping.

SELECTING THE RIGHT COUNTERSTRIKE

The *passive-aggressive* counterstrike stands in contrast to the *aggressive* counterstrike. It is what Mautner refers to as the "broken record technique," contrasting it with the "door in the face and foot in the door" techniques. It is a semiaggressive technique that involves strong persuasion toward the desired end, attacking with one's wits, not with one's fists, while avoiding the need to have, as Mautner puts it, "an arsenal at home."[10] It is particularly relevant when countering intellectual homophobes and attempting to win a debate. It avoids open aggressiveness, which is safe only with a bigot-wimp, and you cannot always differentiate types of bigots in advance. Aggression is cathartic and effective, but with the macho-bigot you might be putting yourself in danger.

The *hypomanic* counterstrike involves living well as the best revenge. In this approach, targets respond to homophobia by ignoring the putdowns and glass ceilings and by thriving and prospering regardless or being defiantly generative, deliberately, out of spite. Direct offense as the best defense may be indicated with those homophobes who get worse when no one takes them firmly in hand and sets limits.

The *narcissistic* counterstrike involves what O'Connell calls the "fogging technique"[11] and what I call the "gay-pride counterstrike." Here the individual counters that what he or she is being criticized for is "one of the things I like best about myself."[12] Using this technique, targets can counter prejudice by citing the advantages of being exactly who they are and what they are being condemned for.

AVOIDING CERTAIN PITFALLS

The following list of caveats, that is, pitfalls to be generally avoided, pertains to all counterstrikes. Some of these pitfalls have already been mentioned.

1. A counterstrike should never be a first strike. That is not protection against but rather provocation of homophobia.
2. The aim of counterstriking is actual accomplishment, not mere emotional satisfaction. When dealing with homophobes, gays' and lesbians' primary goal should not be to be liked but to be left alone.
3. Direct counterstrikes are dangerous with homophobes who are unstable. In this case, roundabout confrontation is often the best idea.
4. The timing must be right. Targets should try to avoid having to think on their feet, which often involves thinking reactively and emotionally. They can respond most effectively after they have thought out their approach carefully and given consideration to the best time and place for their counterresponse.

Specific pitfalls include the following.

Trying to Win Homophobes Over

Too many gays and lesbians develop a Stockholm syndrome in which they grow to love those they hate. Alternatively, they forgive unforgivable homophobia. A restaurateur who was told of the homohating words of the above-mentioned restaurateur swore to me he would never eat in that man's restaurant again. Then a few days later I spied him eating there anyway with a large group of gay friends who, instead of enjoying a hot meal, should have been joining a cool boycott.

Imagining Homophobia in Its Absence

Gays and lesbians should not respond to criticism that is constructive as if it were per se a sign of prejudice or homophobia. "A reader" who criticized my book *Treating Emotional Disorder in Gay Men* was wrong to decide I must be a homophobe ("Friend or 'Phobe"?) just because I raised the possibility that some gay men had the same emotional problems as straight men.[13] As a supervisor of psychiatric residents I once had to discipline a gay resident because he was having sex with patients in the clinic. The resident called me a homophobe, but my actions had nothing to do with the specific acts involved and everything to do with the exact place and time where, and the person with whom, he was performing them. Targets of homophobia should never fight homophobic irrationality by themselves becoming equally irrational, especially if that means becoming irrationally heterophobic or socially disruptive.

Being Self-Homophobic

The bigoted seed grows best in fertile ground, particularly ground that is well fertilized by low self-esteem and extreme self-doubt. Gays and lesbians who are ashamed of themselves and are already convinced that they are somehow defective or sinners are at special risk for buying into what the homophobe has to offer them and doing penance by treating themselves in much the same shabby and even bigoted way that homophobes have just treated them. Therefore, managing others' homophobia also involves managing one's own self-homophobia, which means developing a positive self-view that does not let another's negative assessment in.

CONCLUSION

This chapter presents a stepwise guide to helping gay and lesbian individuals cope with prejudice and discrimination. It emphasizes three main approaches:

- Coping through self-defense via understanding where the homophobe is coming from, thus making it easier to discount his or her contentions by appreciating the flaws in his or her logic and the emotional, hence irrational, underpinnings of his or her behavior.
- Personal growth through self-exploration and self-improvement.
- Community action through enlisting the community's help to influence the bigot directly and quash the bigotry sociopolitically.

There are generic countermeasures geared to dealing with most or all types of homophobia regardless of their origin. But because there are different types of homophobia depending on the personality and the profession of the homophobe, with typology depending on what emotional problem(s) prevails and generates the homophobic ideation, there are also specific antitheses available to deal with the different homophobias, in particular with the unique underlying psychopathology that spins off each form of prejudice and the accompanying discriminatory behavior.

TOOLBOX FOR CHANGE

For the Individual

Existing images of homosexuals lead to perceptions and behaviors that need to and can be changed. These are often rooted in emotional disorders such as paranoia with projection or depression with low self-esteem, leading to pathological, often emotional thinking and other homophobic distortions notable for being derived from egregious cognitive error.

Strategies for change consist of:

- Viewing bigotry as a product of mental illness and therefore not to be taken at face value.
- Understanding bigots' illogic and confronting their irrationality.
- Setting up internal firewalls (becoming inured to bigotry).
- Developing personal pride.
- Joining groups for strength in numbers.
- Living well as the best revenge.

For the Community

The community suffers when it becomes a mediocre place due to inhibition or destruction of some of its finest, highest-functioning, and most creative members leading to loss of power, multidimensionality, and range of talent in the community as well as to divisiveness and infighting between pros and antis (homophiles and homophobes).

Strategies for change consist of:

- Educating leaders.
- Raising popular awareness of the distortive nature of bigotry in the media.
- Countering and correcting stereotypes with facts.
- Passing antibigotry laws.
- Encouraging activism by targeted members of the community.
- Educating members of the stigmatized groups so that they stay informed about bigotry and can correct misinformation when they hear it—be it in the home, at social clubs, in churches, or in schools.
- Raising awareness of people in the stigmatized groups by having certain of its members write editorials, give public workshops, and conduct research.
- Hitting bigotry where it hurts the most—in the pocketbook. That is, members of the community should not buy products from advertisers who sell by portraying false negative stereotypes, or frequent businesses owned and run by bigots.

For Practitioners and Educators

Patients and students suffer because of prophetic, self-fulfilling negativity toward defined groups that leads to treating and educating them differently based on preconceived notions. These preconceived notions can even lead people to behave in the very way that is expected of them, thus creating the very problems that were initially wrongly identified as intrinsic.

Strategies for change consist of:

- Educating educators.
- Passing laws that assure equal treatment for all patients and students.
- Affirming all patients and students, making certain in a practical way that across-the-board fairness will exist, regardless of sexual orientation, age, and race.

Notes

INTRODUCTION

1. Jacobs, A. 2007. "A City Where Gay Life Hangs by a Thread." *New York Times,* December 2, 2007, 39, 44.

2. "Zimbabwe Leader Condemns Homosexuality." 1995. *New York Times,* August 2, 1995, A7.

3. Reader 2008. 2008. "The Most Comprehensive Book on AvPD." Amazon.com, February, 2. Retrieved August 18, 2008, from http://www.amazon.com/review/product/027597829X/ref=cm_cr_dp_all_helpful?%5Fenc.

4. Bowman, B. 2007. "Ocean Grove Suit Tossed." *Asbury Park Press,* November 9, 2005. Retrieved November 14, 2007, from http://www.app.com/apps/pbcs.dll/article?AID=2007711090356.

5. Ibid.

6. Ibid.

7. Jacobs, "City Where Gay Life Hangs by a Thread," 39, 44.

8. Robertson, P. 1992. *The New World Order.* Boston: G. K. Hall, 329.

9. Carter, Michael. 2008. Personal communication.

10. Fone, B. 2000. *Homophobia: A History.* New York: Picador USA.

11. Laycock, B. "Labradorman." 2000. "An Interesting, Absorbing, but Seriously Flawed Study!" Review of *Homophobia: A History,* by Byrne Fone. Retrieved January 28, 2008, from http://www.amazon.com/Homophobia-History-Byrne-Fone/dp/0312420307/ref=sr_1_1?ie.

CHAPTER 1

1. Fone, B. 2000. *Homophobia: A History.* New York: Picador USA.

2. McGurn, W. 1996. "The Iconoclast Who Found God." *Wall Street Journal,* April 17, 1996, A18.

CHAPTER 2

1. Fenichel, O. 1945. *The Psychoanalytic Theory of Neurosis.* New York: W. W. Norton, 427–28.

2. Kort, J. 2008. *Gay Affirmative Therapy for the Straight Clinician: The Essential Guide.* New York: W. W. Norton, 47.

3. Kantor, M. 1999. *Treating Emotional Disorder in Gay Men.* Westport, CT: Praeger.

4. The Holy Scriptures according to the Masoretic Text: A New Translation with the Aid of Previous Versions and with Constant Consultation of Jewish Authorities. 1917. Philadelphia: The Jewish Publication Society of America. Leviticus 18, 29.

5. Tatchell, P. 2005. "RATZINGER—FUNDAMENTALIST POPE. Disaster for Women, Gays and Liberals." April, 1–3. Retrieved November 16, 2007, from http://www.petertatchell.net/religion/ratzinger.htm.

6. "Letter to the Bishops of the Catholic Church on the Pastoral Care of Homosexual Persons. Congregation for the Doctrine of the Faith," 3, 4. Retrieved January 2008 from http://www.vatican.va/romancuria/congregations/cfaith/documents/rc_con_cfaith_doc_19.

7. The Free Library by Farlex. 2005. "Some Considerations Concerning the Catholic Response to Legislative Proposals on the Non-Discrimination of Homosexual Persons." February 1, 2005. Retrieved August 15, 2008, from http://www.thefreelibrary.com/Some+considerations+concerning+the+Catholic+response+...

8. Hyde, M. O. 1994. *Know about Gays and Lesbians.* Brookfield, CT: Millbrook Press, 52–53.

9. Cooperman, A. 2006. "Conservative Rabbis Allow Ordained Gays, Same-Sex Unions." *Washington Post,* December 1, 2006. Retrieved August 1, 2008, from http://www. washingtonpost.com/wp-dyn/content/article/2006/12/06 AR2006 120601247_pf.

10. Berndt, E. 2005. "Debriefing Scalia." *The Nation,* April, 1–2. Retrieved August 1, 2008, from http://www.thenation.com/doc/20050502/berndt.

CHAPTER 3

1. Froias, S. 2008. "Don't @!%$ with Me, Fellas!" *triCityNews,* March, 12.

2. Fenichel, O. 1945. *The Psychoanalytic Theory of Neurosis.* New York: W. W. Norton, 433.

CHAPTER 5

1. Laycock, B. "Labradorman." 2000. "An Interesting, Absorbing, but Seriously Flawed Study!" review of *Homophobia: A History,* by Byrne Fone. Retrieved January 28, 2008, from http://www.amazon.com/Homophobia-History-Byrne-Fone/dp/0312420307/ref=sr_1_1?ie.

2. Kantor, M. 1999. *Treating Emotional Disorder in Gay Men.* Westport, CT: Praeger.

3. A customer. 2002. "Gay Psychotherapy Book...from Friend or 'Phobe????" Review of *Treating Emotional Disorder in Gay Men,* by Martin Kantor. Retrieved

March 7, 2008, from http://www.amazon.com/Treating-Emotional-Disorder-Gay-Men/dp/0275963330/ref=sr_1_.

4. Ibid.
5. Ibid.
6. Ibid.
7. Ibid.
8. Ibid.
9. Ibid.
10. Ibid.
11. Kantor, M. 1999. *Treating Emotional Disorder in Gay Men.* Westport, CT: Praeger, 73.
12. "Gay Psychotherapy Book... from Friend or 'Phobe????"
13. Ibid.
14. Ibid.
15. Kantor, *Treating Emotional Disorder in Gay Men,* 158.

CHAPTER 6

1. Couser, T. 1996. "Marked Car." *Brown University Alumni Magazine,* March, 56.

CHAPTER 7

1. Jones, E. 1953–1957. *The Life and Works of Sigmund Freud.* 3 vols. New York: Basic Books, 284.
2. Herek, G. M. 1986. "On Heterosexual Masculinity: Some Psychical Consequences of the Social Construction of Gender and Sexuality." *American Behavioral Scientist* 29 (5), 563–77. Excerpt, 1–2. Retrieved November 16, 2007, from http://psychology.ucdavis.edu/rainbow/html/bibabs.html.

CHAPTER 8

1. Herek, G. M. 1984. "Beyond 'Homophobia': A Social Psychological Perspective on Attitudes toward Lesbians and Gay Men." *Journal of Homosexuality* 10 (1–2), 1–21. Excerpt, 1. Retrieved November 16, 2007, from http://psychology.ucdavis.edu/rainbow/html/bibabs.html.
2. Herek, G. M. N.d. "Psychological Functions of Sexual Prejudice. Sexual Prejudice: Motivations." pp. 1–2. Retrieved August 1, 2008, from http://psychology.ucdavis.edu/rainbow/HTML/prej_func.html; Herek, "Beyond 'homophobia,'" 1.
3. Herek, "Psychological Functions of Sexual Prejudice," pp. 1–2.
4. Herek, "Beyond 'Homophobia,'" 1.
5. Stein, T. S. 1996. "Homosexuality and Homophobia in Men." *Psychiatric Annals* 26 (1), 37–40, 39.
6. Herek, "Beyond 'Homophobia,'" 1.
7. Sanford, R. N., Adorno, T., Frenkel-Brunswik, E., and Levinson D. J. 1982. "Measurement of Antidemocratic Trends." In *The Authoritarian Personality (Abridged Edition),* ed. T. W. Adorno, E. Frenkel-Brunswik, D. J. Levinson, and R. Nevitt Sanford. New York: W. W. Norton, 170.
8. Ibid., 169.

9. Adorno, Frenkel-Brunswik, Levinson, and Sanford, *The Authoritarian Personality (Abridged Edition)*, 304–5.

10. "House Votes to Bar Gay Marriages under Federal Law. 1996. *U.S. News Story Page*. July 12. Retrieved August 1, 2008, from http://www.cnn.com/US/9607/12/gay.marriage/.

11. Sanford, Adorno, Frenkel-Brunswik, and Levinson, "Measurement of Antidemocratic Trends," 169.

12. Freud, S. 1957. "Psycho-Analytic Notes upon an Autobiographical Account of a Case of Paranoia (Dementia Paranoides)." In *Collected Papers*, vol. 3. Translated by Alix Strachey and James Strachey. London: Hogarth Press.

13. Fenichel, O. 1945. *The Psychoanalytic Theory of Neurosis*. New York: W. W. Norton, 428.

14. Ibid., 433–34.

15. Freud, "Psycho-Analytic Notes."

CHAPTER 9

1. Foust, Michael. 2008. "MARRIAGE DIGEST: New Jersey Governor Would Sign 'Gay Marriage' Bill, after Election." February, 2. Retrieved August 14, 2008, from http://www.bpnews.net/bpnews.asp?id=27481.

CHAPTER 10

1. Fone, Byrne. 2000. *Homophobia: A History*. New York: Picador USA, 334.

2. Gibbon, E. 1776–1788. *The Decline and Fall of the Roman Empire*. Reprint, London: Viking Press, 1980, 287–90.

3. Kort, J. 2008. *Gay Affirmative Therapy for the Straight Clinician: The Essential Guide*. New York: W. W. Norton, 27.

4. Freud, S. 1957. "A Phobia in a Five-Year-Old Boy." In *Collected Papers*, vol. 3. Translated by Alix Strachey and James Strachey. London: Hogarth Press.

5. Feder, S. 1992. *Charles Ives: My Father's Song*. New Haven, CT: Yale University Press, 337.

6. Wharton, T. 1998. "Robertson Says Gays Bring about Earthquakes, Tornadoes, Bombs." *Norfolk Virginian-Pilot*, June 10. Retrieved August 2, 2008, from http://www.skeptictank.org/hs/patrob3.htm.

7. "FAIR's Bob Grant Success." 1996. *Fairness and Accuracy in Reporting (FAIR)*, Extra! Update, June. Retrieved February 5, 2008, from http://www.fair.org/index.php?page=1343.

8. "Bob Grant Retires from Radio." 2006. NewsMax.com, January, 16. Retrieved February 5, 2008, from http://archive.newsmax.com/archives/ic/2006/1/16/114430.shtml.

9. Purnick, J. 1996. "Recalling a Gay Rights Non-Crisis." *New York Times*, March 21, B3.

10. Fone, *Homophobia*, 379.

11. Melville, H. 1851. *Moby Dick*. Reprint, New York: Bantam Books, 1981, 232.

12. Hugo, V. 1862. *Les Miserables*. Reprint, London: Penguin, 1982, 995.

13. Hernandez, R. 1995. "Youths on Racial Slurs: They're Only Words." *New York Times*, June 26, B2.

CHAPTER 11

1. Webster, M. 2002. *Webster's Third New International Dictionary of the English Language Unabridged.* Springfield, MA: Merriam-Webster, 2174.

2. The Holy Scriptures according to the Masoretic Text: A New Translation with the Aid of Previous Versions and with Constant Consultation of Jewish Authorities. 1917. Philadelphia: The Jewish Publication Society of America. Leviticus 26:1.

3. Leviticus 18:22.

4. Leviticus 19:16.

5. Leviticus 19:19.

6. Ursano, R. J., and Silberman, E. K. 1988. "Individual Psychotherapies; Other Individual Psychotherapies: Cognitive Therapy." In *The American Psychiatric Press Textbook of Psychiatry,* ed. J. A. Talbot, R. E. Hales, and S. C. Yudofsky. Washington, DC: American Psychiatric Press, 870.

7. Lacey, M. 2008. "Attacks Show Easygoing Jamaica Is Dire Place for Gays." *New York Times,* February 24, 2008, 4.

8. Leverich, L. 1995. *Tom.* New York: Crown, 554.

9. Froias, S. 2008. "Not a Shining Moment for Long Branch." *triCityNews,* April, 12.

10. Beck, A. T. 1985. "Cognitive Therapy." In *Comprehensive Textbook of Psychiatry/IV,* ed. Harold I. Kaplan and Benjamin J. Sadock. Baltimore: Williams and Wilkins, 1437.

11. Bemporad, Jules R., and Pinsker, H. 1974. "Schizophrenia: The Manifest Symptomatology." In *American Handbook of Psychiatry,* 2nd ed., ed. Silvano Arieti and Eugene B. Brody. New York: Basic Books, 532.

12. Lacey, "Attacks Show Easygoing Jamaica Is Dire Place for Gays," 4.

CHAPTER 12

1. Herek, G. M. 1984. "Beyond 'Homophobia': A Social Psychological Perspective on Attitudes toward Lesbians and Gay Men." *Journal of Homosexuality* 10 (1–2), 1–21. Excerpt, 1. Retrieved November 16, 2007, from http://psychology.ucdavis.edu/rainbow/html/bibabs.html.

2. Herek, G. M. 1990. "The Context of Anti-Gay Violence: Notes on Cultural and Psychological Heterosexism." *Journal of Interpersonal Violence* 5 (3), 316–33. Excerpt, 6. Retrieved November 16, 2007, from http://psychology.ucdavis.edu/rainbow/html/bibabs.html.

3. Herek, "Beyond 'Homophobia,'" 1.

4. Kirk, M., and H. Madsen. 1989. *After the Ball: How America Will Conquer Its Fear and Hatred of Gays in the 90s.* New York: Doubleday, 120–24.

5. Herek, G. M. 1988. "Heterosexual's Attitudes toward Lesbians and Gay Men: Correlates and Gender Differences." *Journal of Sex Research* 25 (4), 451–77. Excerpt, 5. Retrieved November 16, 2007, from http://psychology.ucdavis.edu/rainbow/html/bibabs.html.

6. Herek G. M. 1986. "The Social Psychology of Homophobia: Toward a Practical Theory." *Review of Law and Social Change* 14 (4), 923–34. Excerpt, 2–3. Retrieved November 16, 2007, from http://psychology.ucdavid.edu/rainbow/html/bibabs.html.

CHAPTER 14

1. The Holy Scriptures according to the Masoretic Text: A New Translation with the Aid of Previous Versions and with Constant Consultation of Jewish Authorities. 1917. Philadelphia: The Jewish Publication Society of America. Leviticus 18:25.
2. Mautner, R. 2008. Personal communication.
3. Ibid.
4. Levinson, D. J. 1982. "The Study of Anti-Semitic Ideology." In *The Authoritarian Personality (Abridged Edition)*, ed. T. W. Adorno, E. Frenkel-Brunswik, D. J. Levinson, and R. Nevitt Sanford. New York: W. W. Norton, 57.
5. O'Connell, L. 1993. "Sitting in Judgment." *Asbury Park Press*, August 12, E1.
6. Mautner, R. 2008. Personal communication.
7. Ibid.
8. Ibid.
9. Ibid.
10. Ibid.
11. O'Connell, L. 1993. "Sitting in Judgment." *Asbury Park Press*, August 12, E1.
12. Ibid.
13. A customer. 2002. "Gay Psychotherapy Book...from Friend or 'Phobe????" Review of *Treating Emotional Disorder in Gay Men*, by Martin Kantor. Retrieved March 7, 2008, from http://www.amazon.com/Treating-Emotional-Disorder-Gay-Men/dp/0275963330/ref=sr_1_.

Index

About the Author

MARTIN KANTOR, M.D. is retired Staff Psychiatrist for the Department of Veterans Affairs Medical Center in East Orange, New Jersey. Kantor has written thirteen other books for Praeger including *Uncle Sam's Shame* (2008), *Lifting the Weight* (2007), *The Psychopathy of Everyday Life* (2006), and *Understanding Paranoia* (2004).